Black
Men and
Divorce

Understanding Families

Series Editors: *Bert N. Adams, University of Wisconsin*
                   David M. Klein, University of Notre Dame

This book series examines a wide range of subjects relevant to studying families. Topics include, but are not limited to, theory and conceptual design, research methods on the family, racial/ethnic families, mate selection, marriage, family power dynamics, parenthood, divorce and remarriage, custody issues, and aging families.

The series is aimed primarily at scholars working in family studies, sociology, psychology, social work, ethnic studies, gender studies, cultural studies, and related fields as they focus on the family. Volumes will also be useful for graduate and undergraduate courses in sociology of the family, family relations, family and consumer sciences, social work and the family, family psychology, family history, cultural perspectives on the family, and others.

Books appearing in **Understanding Families** are either single- or multiple-authored volumes or concisely edited books of original chapters on focused topics within the broad interdisciplinary field of marriage and family.

The books are reports of significant research, innovations in methodology, treatises on family theory, syntheses of current knowledge in a family subfield, or advanced textbooks. Each volume meets the highest academic standards and makes a substantial contribution to our understanding of marriages and families.

Erma Jean Lawson
Aaron Thompson

Black
Men and
Divorce

UNDERSTANDING
FAMILIES

 SAGE Publications
International Educational and Professional Publisher
Thousand Oaks   London   New Delhi

For information address:

SAGE Publications, Inc.
2455 Teller Road
Thousand Oaks, California 91320
E-mail: order@sagepub.com

SAGE Publications Ltd.
6 Bonhill Street
London EC2A 4PU
United Kingdom

SAGE Publications India Pvt. Ltd.
M-32 Market
Greater Kailash I
New Delhi 110 048 India

Printed in the United States of America

Library of Congress Cataloging-in-Publication Data

Lawson, Erma Jean.
   Black men and divorce / by Erma Jean Lawson and Aaron Thompson.
      p.   cm. — (Understanding families; v. 15)
   Includes bibliographical references and index.
   ISBN 0-8039-5954-0 (cloth: acid-free paper) —
   ISBN 0-8039-5955-9 (pbk.: acid-free paper)
   1. Divorce—United States.   2. Afro-American men—Family relationships.
   3. Afro-American men—Psychology.   4. Afro-American families.
   I. Title.   II. Series.
   HQ834.L38   2000
   306.89′081′0973—dc21   98-40251

This book is printed on acid-free paper.

99 00 01 02 03 04 05 7 6 5 4 3 2 1

Acquiring Editor:	Jim Nageotte
Editorial Assistant:	Heidi Van Middlesworth
Production Editor:	Wendy Westgate
Production Assistant:	Nevair Kabakian
Typesetter:	Lynn Miyata
Indexer:	Jean Casalegno

Contents

Acknowledgments

I am grateful to many people for their support and assistance with this project. Special thanks go to Vidella White for reading portions of the preliminary draft of the manuscript, to David Klein and Bert Adams for their close review of the manuscript, and to Robert Staples for sustaining my interest in the project and for sparking my interest in divorce and providing questions for the questionnaire. Thanks go to Tanya Tyler, who proofread and copyedited the manuscript and provided a number of suggestions on sentence clarification.

Acknowledgments go to Glaydes Hayes-Moore and Donald Moore for affirming my assumptions and discussing many of the ideas incorporated in this book. Words cannot express my appreciation. I also acknowledge Janice Anderson Elliott and Danny Pigman, as my conversations with them confirmed my reality and assumptions. Special thanks go to Karen Kennedy, who helped with the editing, and to Toni Warren for her beautiful poem. For their timely inspiration, I thank Susan Eve, Carolyn Rollins, and Tyson Gibbs at the University of North Texas.

I am grateful, more than words can say, to my brother, Carl Barefoot; my aunt, Dollie Savage; and my cousin, James Hines, Jr., who encouraged this work with caring and interest and provided valuable insights into the conceptualization of the fatherhood chapter. Special thanks go to La Francis Rodgers-Rose for being an excellent role model during my graduate school and professional career. My thanks, most of all, go to the 50 men whose voices give life and meaning to this book.

—Erma Jean Lawson, Ph.D.

Acknowledgments

There are many people who I would like to thank for their assistance and encouragement with this book. First, I thank the men who participated in this study. The patience and time they took to share their stories and experiences with us created the richness in this book and clearly assisted me in becoming a better researcher. Second, my move to the Department of Human Development and Family Studies at the University of Missouri played an integral part in having the assistance and time to devote to finishing this project. Third, I thank several people for their editorial assistance, especially the series editors, Bert Adams and Dave Klein, and Beverly Peterson, who has provided me with unending editorial suggestions over the years. Finally, I thank my daughter, Sara, for helping me to understand what it means to be a father and for the strength and courage she has displayed in being the daughter of a Black divorced man.

—Aaron Thompson, Ph.D.

1

Introduction

We loved each other and were married for 10 years. It was exciting beginning life. Our marriage started out beautiful, and we were there for each other. My home life was solid; we had two sons. I finally got control over my finances by working two and sometimes three jobs. My older son was in junior high school and looking forward to college. My youngest son was given a scholarship to a school for gifted children. We celebrated our 10th wedding anniversary with family and friends. Then my wife said she wanted a divorce and that she could not continue to live like this. In the midst of this, my mother developed breast cancer, my father died a year before, and my brother was arrested on drug charges. I moved out, then back in, and finally I moved out for good. Boom—my whole world was gone. My whole life changed. I was unaware that I wasn't being sensitive. I thought I was doing it the way it should have been done. A lot of people think that divorce is painless, especially for Black men. There are no painless divorces; divorce is a hurting thing. I was hurt so bad that I would catch myself crying. My nerves fell apart, and it seemed like my life would never be the same. I couldn't come to the realization that my marriage was really over. I have been through some upsetting times. When I separated from my wife, I desperately wanted to read anything I could get my hands on about the divorce experience of Black men because society has glorified divorce. I'm telling you my story to help others understand what Black divorced men experience. Maybe my story will help the public understand that Black men hurt, that Black men cry, and that all Black men aren't deadbeat dads.

—a 42-year-old Black divorced man

In the past 30 years, divorce has increased among Black families (Cherlin, 1992; Farley & Allen, 1987). For example, in 1970, 69% of Black families had both husband and wife present, compared to 50% by 1990 (Pinkney, 1993). By 1997, 59% of the total White population over 18 years of age were married with spouse present, compared to 34% of the comparable Black population (U.S. Bureau of the Census, 1997). The same year, 26% of the Black population over 18 years of age were either divorced or separated, compared to 15% of the comparable White population (U.S. Bureau of the Census, 1997). The divorce rate among African American families is especially problematic because Black marriages also are declining (Cherlin, 1992). For example, 76% of Black men in their 20s had never married, compared to 63% of comparable White men (Glick, 1997). Thus, more than one half of Black marriages end in divorce (higher than the national average), and two of three Black children in a two-parent household will experience the dissolution of their parents' marriage by 16 years of age (U.S. Bureau of the Census, 1995). The separation rate also is higher for Blacks. In 1993, approximately 16% of Black women between 18 and 44 years of age were separated, compared to 4% of comparable White women (U.S. Bureau of the Census, 1983). In 1997, 15% of the Black population were separated, compared to 5% of the White population (U.S. Bureau of the Census, 1997). Racial differences in divorce persist independently of education, residence, and parental marital stability (U.S. Bureau of the Census, 1996). There is an absence of research on Black divorced men. Interviews with Black women have provided information about Black divorced men, even though their divorce experiences differ (Kitson, 1992; Reissman, 1990). Discrepancies have been documented between divorced men's and women's reports of child support payments (Wright & Price, 1986), fathers' involvement postdivorce (Seltzer & Bianchi, 1988), and postdivorce marital relationships (Goldsmith, 1981). It is essential, therefore, to examine the divorce experience of Black men to understand the high Black divorce rate.

The Purpose of the Book

This book explores Black men's experiences of divorce in the context of postmodern social marginality and economic disenfranchisement. We argue that the social construction of race has important implications for Black marriages. For example, we use social discrediting and social marginality interchangeably, indicating that Black men are stigmatized and socially marginalized. Those who label them as debased individuals develop a belief system to explain their discredited or socially marginalized position (Wilkinson, 1977). It is this belief system and its influence on Black marital stability that are of concern here.

Why Did We Explore This Research Topic and Write This Book?

THE FEMALE PERSPECTIVE

My graduate school experience provided the impetus to write this book. Standard textbooks and journal articles often failed to describe Black men who experienced remorse, guilt, and failure following the dissolution of their marriages. Although Black men often were stereotyped as inferior, nonproductive, and dysfunctional, positive family male role models contradicted my educational experience. Unfortunately, the image that identifies joblessness, poverty, and marital instability as internal characteristics of Black men has remained largely unchanged.

Questions from students and their need to understand the experience of Black divorced men also contributed to writing the book. Students voiced concern with institutional aspects of racism and its influence on Black male and female relationships. An examination of social marginality and its effects on marital stability would assist students in understanding divorce.

The selection of this topic also related to an increased distrust between Black men and women. For example, I have heard women state, "What's a Black woman to do because most Black men are uncommitted to relationships?" I also have listened to male bashing from Black women. In Zimbabwe, Africa, women also recited a list of Black men's negative characteristics including their being unreliable, self-centered, unfaithful, and immature.

The prevention of shattered marriages is critical for the Black community. The culture of violence pervading a large number of Black communities with many Black youths placing less value on family life suggests that it is crucial to examine Black family formation and dissolution. In fact, this is the first time since the breakup of slave families that external and internal factors have had a profound effect on Black family structure.

THE MALE PERSPECTIVE

I began this research because there was a dearth of research on Black divorced men and, more specifically, on Black divorced fathers. I was unsure what to expect because this was a qualitative approach. Because I had been a quantitative researcher with theoretical models to guide me, I was somewhat apprehensive about using the qualitative approach without theory. However, I knew that the only way in which to develop a solid, valid description of the lives of Black men was not to succumb to past theoretical approaches. Thus, the idea for a study of Black divorced men arose from my academic interest in discovering the unique contribution of qualitative research.

During the research, I discussed it with a number of personal friends and professional colleagues. On all occasions where it was mentioned, people showed a profound interest. Even married couples and never-married singles were eager to learn about the subject. It was a topic of immense interest. People called and asked me to speak on the issue, and seminars were organized to discuss it. Given the interest in Black divorced men, concern about divorced father-child relationships, and the implications of these problems for society, I believe that a book dealing with Black divorced men is long overdue.

Why This Book Is Needed

Although several books have explored various experiences of Black men, few books have focused solely on Black divorced men. For example, Gibbs's (1988) *Young, Black and Male in America* explores the thesis that young Black males have been alienated from social progress. Bowser's (1991) *Black Male Adolescents* critically assesses the experiences of Black males and social organization. Kunjufu's (1995) *Countering the Conspiracy to Destroy Black Boys,* Majors and Billson's (1992)

Cool Pose, and Staples' (1982) *Black Masculinity* contribute to an understanding of how contemporary society limits the functioning of Black men.

A number of books on divorce have been published and have produced valuable insights on the divorce experience. However, most of these studies have failed to use Black samples, with the notable exception of Kitson's (1992) *Portrait of Divorce.* Reissman's (1990) *Divorce Talk* suggests that divorce is different for White men and women. Wymard's (1994) *Men on Divorce* explores the turmoil of divorce among White men, and Arendell's (1995) *Fathers and Divorce* analyzes 64 White, 3 Black, 4 Hispanic, and 2 Asian American divorced fathers.

Theoretical Considerations

PATHOLOGICAL TREATMENT: THE DEFICIT MODEL

Black families have been investigated from several theoretical perspectives. However, previous research often has used a pathological deficit model to explore Black families. For example, the 1965 Moynihan report, "The Negro Family: A Case for National Action" (see Rainwater & Yancey, 1967), describes low-income Black families as "a tangle of pathology." Although external factors, including racism and recession, contributed to the functioning of Black families, the Moynihan report concluded that the "matriarchal" structure of Black families contributed to their deterioration (Staples, 1991). Research, however, has not supported the Moynihan report. For example, Tenhouten (1970) and Heiss (1972) fail to substantiate the dominant family role of Black mothers suggested in the Moynihan report.

CULTURAL DEVIANT AND CULTURAL EQUIVALENT APPROACHES

The cultural deviant and cultural equivalent theories often have explained Black family structure. The cultural deviant theory attributes Black family functioning to internal rather than external factors and is popularly known as "blaming the victim" (Billingsley, 1968). The cultural equivalent framework suggests that social class accounts for racial differences in family structure. Thus, given similar economic conditions, Black and White families are equivalent (Johnson, 1997).

Frazier's (1932, 1939/1966) views parallel the cultural equivalent perspective. He concludes that as Blacks conform to White middle class norms, the disorganization of Black families disappears. However, in *Black Bourgeoisie,* Frazier (1939/1966) observes that middle class Blacks often escape into a fantasy world with a feeling of emptiness and futility.

The cultural deviant and cultural equivalent perspectives suggest that America is culturally homogeneous and that groups should conform to universal family norms. Both models view Black families as negative because they deviate from White middle class norms. As a result, Black families are portrayed as unstable and disorganized (Rubin, 1978). In a critique of the cultural deviant and cultural equivalent theories, Billingsley (1968) argues that Black families are examined without consideration of social and environmental factors. Researchers also have argued that, given the historical experiences of Blacks in America, White and Black families are not equivalent (Aldrige, 1989; Johnson, 1997; Rodgers-Rose, 1980; Stewart, 1993).

Counterarguments to Deficit Models

Cultural variant and cultural relativity perspectives, as well as comprehensive approaches (holistic and ecological models), have countered Black family deficit theories.

CULTURAL VARIANT AND
CULTURAL RELATIVITY MODELS

Cultural variant theorists assert that Black family life is distinctive due to its particular historical context and that the distinctive features of Black family life are not pathological (Allen, 1978). The cultural relativity school argues that culture and historical experiences account for the family structure of Blacks. As a result, Black family patterns are neither related to nor modeled on White middle class norms. Cultural relativity theorists emphasize the strengths of Black families rather than their weaknesses. They also suggest that social scientists must not use their own cultural framework to explain Black family functioning and structure (Johnson, 1997).

HOLISTIC PERSPECTIVE

In a holistic approach, consideration is given to external and internal factors that affect family functioning by emphasizing their diversity and strengths. DuBois (1899), a proponent of the holistic framework, contends that it is important to assess historical, cultural, social, economic, and political forces on Black family functioning. According to DuBois, the social marginality of Black families necessitates a description of their linkages to various subsystems (Stewart, 1993). Although this approach is important and significant, few researchers have analyzed Black families using a holistic perspective (Hill, 1989).

COMPREHENSIVE FRAMEWORK

Consistent with DuBois (1899), Billingsley (1968) characterizes Black families as a social system mutually interacting with subsystems in the Black community and in the wider society. Three significant patterns are identified:

1. external subsystems in the wider society including social forces and institutional policies associated with economics, politics, education, health welfare, law culture, religion, and the media;
2. interactions with external subsystems in the Black community including schools, churches, peer groups, social clubs, Black businesses, and neighborhood associations; and
3. interaction within internal subsystems in families such as intrahousehold interactions involving husbands and wives, parents and children, siblings, other relatives, and nonrelatives (Billingsley, 1968).

Billingsley (1968) also presents a typology of Black family types that includes 32 variants of nuclear, extended, and augmented households. This theoretical model addresses a weakness of DuBois's (1899) formulation by focusing on the internal dynamics of Black families (Stewart, 1993). Allen (1978) extends Billingsley's (1968) approach by incorporating developmental concepts into the analysis. Thus, Black families devise coping strategies in response to limited economic opportunities during various developmental stages (Allen, 1978).

The family ecology approach focuses on human and environmental linkages (Bronfenbrenner, 1979). Irrespective of structure, race, ethnicity, life stage, and social class, families adapt to certain conditions to survive (Ingoldsby & Smith, 1995). This framework accepts diverse family definitions and clarifies the relationship between Black families and the external environment. Comprehensive theoretical frameworks, such as holistic and social ecology approaches, have improved the quality of research on Black families (Stewart, 1990).

Theoretical Framework

This book considers Black divorced men from a reciprocal relationship with mainstream culture. In other words, we employ a culturally relevant model emphasizing that Black men's varied cultural backgrounds influence their divorce experiences. Consequently, we believe that it is senseless to discuss divorce without concomitant explorations of the ways in which Black men have waged, and continue to wage, a relentless struggle against economic exploitation, social marginality, and personal dehumanization. For example, imagine how a Black father feels as he watches creativity and intellectual motivation sapped out of his children by schools that assume that Blacks are intellectually inferior. For a moment, envision yourself as a Black husband who is denied a promotion and earns lower wages for no other reason than he is Black. For a moment, pretend to be any Black man and feel his hopelessness when he discovers that to live near a Black man jeopardizes the status of a White individual. Coupled with these societal stressors, feel the anguish of a Black man when his own father fails to establish an ongoing relationship and neglects to bridge the gap. This book, therefore, addresses divorce in the context of being a Black man in America so that we can comprehend the family life of Black men who live in a postmodern racist society.

Black Family Disruption in History

Research has linked the disruption of Black families to several historical periods (Blassingame, 1972; Stampp, 1956; White, 1985). Slavery sabotaged Black relationships in that slave owners often viewed Black men as virile and promiscuous. The liberal statesman, Thomas Jefferson, crystallized the perceptions of Whites about Black men's inability to sustain relationships. He suggested that Black men possess a profound sexual desire rather than a "tender mixture of sentiment and sensation" (Jordon, 1977). Although slaves were forbidden by law to enter into contractual marriages, the pervasive racist ideology that viewed Blacks as innately inferior for familial roles undermined emotional bonds between slave men and women. Historians disagree as to how many slave families were separated by their owners. Slave relationships, however, were disrupted by the selling and trading of slaves, the awarding of slaves as prizes in lotteries, and the wagering of slaves at gambling tables (Stampp, 1956). Although slaves confronted insurmountable odds against building enduring relationships, extensive ties to loved ones were pervasive (Blassingame, 1972). In fact, slave courtship was a practice that slave owners could not eliminate (White, 1985). Male slaves often waited until dark before cutting from trees girlfriends who had been beaten. Slaves often were whipped after protecting bondswomen, and free Black men frequently purchased their partners and children from slavery (White, 1985).

Research also indicates that the post-Civil War plantation economy and the disorganization of the South affected the stability of Black families (Jones, 1985). For example, to support their families, Black husbands established residences in various geographical regions. While some former slaves migrated to Louisiana to work on sugar plantations, others found employment in Tennessee coal mines and lumbering camps along the Florida and Alabama coasts (Jones, 1985). Consequently, a large percentage of Black families were disrupted by Black men's search for employment (Jones, 1985).

The most notable change in Black family life occurred when southern Black men and women migrated north and west (Blassingame, 1972; Frazier, 1939/1966). Between 1916 and 1921, an estimated half million Blacks, or approximately 5% of the southern Black population, migrated north and west (Jones, 1985). The movement of Blacks from the South to urban northern cities resulted in increased desertion and marital instability. Black men often worked in distant cities and were absent from their homes for extended periods. They resided in boarding houses close to jobs while their families lived elsewhere.

The northern urban environment had a profound influence on the functioning of Black families. Compared to those in small southern towns, urban Black men adjusted to a vastly different culture in which alcohol, pool halls, and an underground economy were accessible. According to Frazier (1939/1966), the Black family structure was difficult to maintain in an urban setting without substantial economic and cultural resources. Thus, the instability of Black families emerged not as a legacy of slavery but rather as a result of the destructive conditions of northern urban life. Although formal slavery ended in a costly war, a system developed that relegated the descendants of slaves to a subordinate position in society. Therefore, we contend that race has an impact on Black family structure and functioning independent of, and interacting with, class.

Methods

A total of 50 Black men who had been divorced for no more than 3 years, the period most salient in making sense of their past marriages, were interviewed (Reissman, 1990). The men were located through referrals from individuals contacted through Black organizations such as the Urban League, Black churches, and the National Association for the Advancement of Colored People. Recruitment was restricted to (a) men who were currently divorced and had not remarried, (b) men who were currently in the labor force, (c) men who had experienced only one divorce, and (d) men who had been married for at least 2 years. The men were apprised of the study through phone calls, and appointments were made for interviews. None of the men contacted refused to be interviewed. The purpose of selecting men in the labor force was to eliminate the psychological distress associated with unemployment.

The research was described as a study of Black divorced men. All respondents who were asked agreed to participate, stating, "It is time that the voices of Black divorced men are heard." The men interviewed referred other Black divorced men. The men interviewed were considerably accessible and cooperative, and they demonstrated honesty in their answers. For example, many of the interviews were quite painful for the men. They complained of being unloved and belittled by their former wives as well as by an oppressive social system. Several men cried as they discussed relationships with their fathers and children and as they explained events preceding their divorces. As they reviewed their courtships and the evolution of their family structures, we were struck by the magnitude of turbulence that divorce created in Black families. For example, divorce disrupted extended family members' activities and birthday parties for children, and in some instances it severed father-child relationships. The men overwhelmingly accepted our presence. All were willing to talk, and some even called a year later to report on their progress. A series of incidents during the course of the study convinced us that the men viewed the research as "therapy." The first clue was that many of the interviews lasted much longer than expected, some as long as 6 hours. The men talked about a number of incidents that occurred during their marriages, separations, and divorces. They also formulated perspectives and philosophies about relationships in general and about Black relationships in particular. On occasion, they took issue with the perception of how Black men are portrayed in the popular media and scientific literature. They were particularly impressed that a female would conduct research to understand the lives of "everyday" Black men without the common male-bashing approach. In one of the earliest interviews with a security guard who had been separated for less than a year, the man talked endlessly about the plight of Black men in the United States. He cried because a stable family seemed too difficult to establish in the context of social discrediting and economic marginality. He said that too much negative information was being circulated about Black men and that the general public needs to know that there are Black men who care for their families.

Indeed, the men desperately wanted the public to know what the everyday, hard-working, Black divorced man experienced. However, in many instances, they were the worst critics of Black men. For example, several men said, "There are some Black men who mistreat Black women, try to control them, and are unfaithful, but there are a lot who treat Black women with kindness and respect." Another unexpected issue was getting through the information needed for the study. Most of the men said that the interviews felt like therapy. They were surprised that they had so much to say. As the study progressed, most of the men said, "I've been holding this in for so long. Now I feel better. I guess I was like a lot of Black men who believe that talking would not help very much." It was not uncommon for men to cry during the interviews as they recalled the effect of divorce on their biological children as well as on the stepchildren. A few men wanted specific counseling referrals to provide assistance for the overwhelming emotional pain. All of the men agreed to participate in the study due to a desire to help other Black men who were experiencing divorces. They believed that few people appreciate what it means for men to experience marital failure. Individuals construct accounts, giving "histories of marital failure, stories of what their spouses did and what happened." These accounts serve important psychological functions by imposing order on an otherwise disordered phenomenon. Whereas psychologists suggest that these accounts represent attribution theory in an effort to reestablish a sense of control during termination of a relationship, Black family theorists suggest that storytelling represents the resilience of Blacks.

SAMPLE CHARACTERISTICS

Approximately 34% of the respondents were between 40 and 44 years of age, 80% had 1 to 2 years of college education, 45% reported annual incomes between $30,000 and $50,000, 30% were raised by two parents, and 32% married women who had children prior to their marriages. All of the respondents were parents, and large percentages had been married for 10 to 15 years (42%) and had been divorced for 1 to 3 years (56%). With the exception of one man, all of the men indicated that the mothers gained custody of the children, and 32% of the men had children born before marriage. Table 1.1 shows that the sample consisted of middle-aged, working/middle class Black men who were recently divorced for the first time and were parents.

The sample is not representative of Black divorced men in America or even of Black divorced men in the northeastern area of the United States. There were men in prison or who lived in rural areas who were not contacted. Divorced men from various classes, regions, and occupational statuses, as well as those who have experienced multiple divorces, must be the focus of future research.

INTERVIEWS

The data were collected through face-to-face interviews and were conducted in the settings of the men's choice, most often their homes or places of employment. The interviews were tape-recorded and tran-

TABLE 1.1 Demographic Characteristics of the Sample ($N = 50$)

Demographic Characteristic	Percentage
Age	
20-34 years	18.0
35-39 years	20.0
40-45 years	34.0
46-50 years	18.0
Over 50 years	10.0
Education	
0-12 years	15.0
1-2 years of college	70.0
4 or more years of college	15.0
Income	
$20,000-$29,999	20.0
$30,000-$39,999	20.0
$40,000-$49,999	45.0
$50,000 or more	15.0
Length of divorce	
1-3 years	56.0
4-9 years	42.0
10 or more years	2.0
Length of marriage	
1-5 years	6.0
6-9 years	24.0
10-15 years	42.0
16-20 years	28.0
Number of biological children	
1 or 2	82.0
3 or more	18.0
Family of origin	
Two-parent family	20.0
Mother only	50.0
Extended family only	30.0
Married women with children	
Wife had no children	66.0
Wife had 1 or 2 children	32.0
Wife had 3 or more children	2.0
Children before marriage	
No children	68.0
1 or 2 children	32.0

scribed. The tapes were transcribed verbatim, with the average length of each transcript ranging between 30 and 40 single-spaced pages.

We began by exploring general research questions rather than by deducing hypotheses from a preexisting body of theory. The respondents were asked to be informal and spontaneous in telling a story that included the quality of marital life preceding separation and postdivorce, experiences during divorce and postdivorce, the quality of their parents' marriages, relationships with children pre- and postdivorce, and support and coping strategies postdivorce. A list of probes were addressed to respondents if they failed to discuss a topic of interest (see Appendix).

There are several advantages of an open-ended interview format. First, it illuminates aspects of divorce that could not be ascertained in a programmed format (Strauss, 1987). Second, it allows discussion of issues that investigators fail to consider. Third, interviews enable linkages of personal marital distress to broader social contexts (Ely et al., 1991).

The coding process involved several steps. First, we coded the data for the respondents' assumptions, meanings, feelings, actions, and beliefs. Second, analytical categories were developed and refined (Strauss, 1987). Throughout the analysis, we wrote memos to examine ideas and behaviors that were revealed in the data to determine patterns (Strauss, 1987). Third, observations of behaviors were noted and coded when respondents cried (e.g., tears) or laughed during the interviews.

PARTICIPANT OBSERVATION

Participant observation of the respondents' social worlds was conducted for 2 years. Participant observation methodology is defined as observation of behavior within natural settings (Bogden, 1972; Denzen, 1970). The men provided lists of their social activities and places that they frequently visited. We visited those places, which included church activities, Black lodges, fraternity meetings, community meetings, and social events.

Participant observations validated information gathered from the interviews. For example, men complained about long waits in court for child support reevaluation. With interview statements alone, one might wonder whether these complaints were exaggerations and reflected the respondents' frustration with the legal system.

Research Questions

This book builds on divorce research and studies on the Black family. We focus on several basic questions:

1. What social, historical, and personal factors influence mate selection?
2. What factors do Black men perceive as causing marital distress and divorce?
3. What strategies do Black men use to cope with marital distress and divorce?
4. How do Black men acquire a fatherhood identity that shapes father-child relationships pre- and postdivorce?
5. What stressors do Black men perceive as causing significant postdivorce distress?
6. What types of relationships exist between Black divorced men and women?

To preserve the anonymity of those interviewed, all names and identifying information have been changed. Each person interviewed has a different name and appropriately disguised life circumstances. Because of the sample's characteristics, occupational status is the primary axis of social diversity. Some men worked in blue-collar jobs, whereas others were employed in professional or managerial positions. Some men grew up in middle class families, whereas others were raised in poverty. The issue of race is especially important because research has been criticized for assuming that Black men are monolithic and homogeneous. This book tries to avoid stereotypes of Black men and argues instead for complex variation in what divorce means to the individuals involved despite the commonalities of race they might share. Although there are statistics on marriage and divorce, they fail to capture the fullness of the divorce experience. For example, when the study began, we did not realize the extreme degree to which men would emphasize their distress over going to court for periodic child support increases. The open-ended interviews revealed that respondents regarded periodic court appearances as distressful as the divorces themselves. We have tried to do justice to the informants by quoting their eloquent statements and by presenting many vignettes from their lives. Thus, our examination of divorce by various strategies contributes to an understanding of how Black men make sense of their former marriages and current emotions as well as how they perceive the effects of marital termination on their former wives. Charles said,

> When I was served divorce papers, I felt so much pain, but I couldn't find anything to read from a Black male perspective. I wanted to know if other men felt this way. Most divorce experiences are written from a woman's perspective. But the pain of divorce should be dealt with from the male point of view. The divorce experience is not only a female thing.

As he described how the experience profoundly affected his life, Charles began to cry. The surprise at his outburst made us realize that the paradigm of divorce is rigidly focused on the problems of women and children and that the sight of a tearful Black professional man appeared to be a radical distortion. By recalling the divorce experience, Charles drew us into his vulnerability. The more we listened to Black divorced men, the more we realized how few of us had ever had an honest conversation with a Black divorced man about the meaning of his experience. This is especially critical in the "waiting to exhale" era of male bashing from Black women. The need for information on marriage dissolution among Blacks is particularly urgent for the following reasons. First, one of every three Black couples will not remain married longer than 10 years, and for Black males under 25 years of age, marriage is practically nonexistent. Second, there is evidence that divorce affects the level of educational attainment of Black children. Third, changes in the Black family structure often are a barometer of future trends in the larger society; thus, a study of Black men and divorce has implications for the direction of trends in American family life. Fourth, research indicates that Black custodial parents often are overburdened and unable to attend to children's economic and psychological needs. Consequently, divorce often compromises the well-being of Black children. Yet, few studies have examined the postdivorce father-child relationship, reasons for marital failure, and the postdivorce adjustment of Black men. Chapter 2 discusses reasons why the men married, presents the process of marital deterioration, identifies factors that may influence divorce in Black marriages, examines major reasons for forming marital bonds, explains personal attraction, and presents views of marriage. We explore mate selection in the context structural conditions and describe beliefs that motivated coupling.

Chapter 3 reviews the literature on the causes of divorce including socioeconomic status, changes in divorce laws, cultural value shifts, the sex ratio, the criminal justice system, substance abuse, and incompatibility issues. Delineating the causes of divorce, explanations are offered that often are neglected in the scholarly literature. This chapter also examines the complexity of marital deterioration as characterized by frequent separations and reconciliations.

Chapter 4 articulates the experience of divorce and points to the importance of social environmental factors that influence marital disruption. This chapter also provides an extensive discussion of the role of periodic unemployment, wives' unemployment, consumer and personality incompatibility, and marital violence as creating profound marital instability.

Chapter 5 addresses divorce-related stressors including financial strain, child support stressors, racial biases in child support determinations, noncustodial parenting, and noncustodial stepfathers. Varied responses to separation and divorce also are presented in this chapter.

Chapter 6 examines attachment to former spouses, explores postmarital relationships, and considers reconciliation. This chapter also analyzes postdivorce in-law and grandparent roles and describes the difficulty of informing family members of divorce. Explanations are given for retained postdivorce in-law relations.

Chapter 7 reviews strategies for coping with divorce. Among the issues discussed in this chapter are family support, involvement in church-related activities, increased social participation, and the unique stress-reducing cultural cognitive style. The role of postdivorce friends, both of the same and opposite sex, is discussed in this chapter. Finally, consideration is given to characteristics desired in future marital partners.

Chapter 8 describes the respondents' constructions of fatherhood and provides a discussion of fathers, stepfathers, play fathers, and mothers as models in the development of a fatherhood identity. We identify positive, absent, aloof, and alcoholic fathers to delineate the types of fathers.

Chapter 9 explores the tensions inherent in noncustodial parenting and the responses of children to divorce. The concerns of noncustodial stepfathers and fathers of biracial children are clarified, as are perspectives on the future of Black fatherhood.

Chapter 10 provides a synopsis of the study, discusses approaches to strengthen Black families, and suggests future family policies to enhance Black families. Finally, this chapter presents a brief 1-year follow-up of some men and a discussion of the interviewing process.

2

Forming Marital Bonds

*[She] loved me and I loved her. I thought she would support anything
I wanted to do. I thought the love she had for me would make her
supportive regardless of what I did. I didn't think she would hassle
me. I thought that was a sign that she was happy. I thought I could
do no wrong and there would be no conflicts or arguments. Now I
know that belief is silly, but I believed it at the time of my marriage.*

—Sam

Relationship formation has changed drastically (Goode, 1959;
Staples, 1985). Previously, marriages were arranged as a result of
negotiations between families or groups. In the 1920s, dating was used
to assess potential spouses (Goode, 1959). It involved an exclusive
relationship and developed into marriage through a series of stages—
going steady, informal engagement, and formal engagement (Lamanna
& Riedmann, 1994).

Dating, however, rarely has been a structured process for Blacks
(Ladner, 1972; Staples, 1981). Black mate selection often has been a
catch-as-catch-can matter (Ladner, 1972; Staples, 1981). This chapter
explores marriage selection and describes the social circumstances that
influence marriages. Emphasis is placed on articulating various definitions of love in presenting the complexity of pair bonding.

Finding a Mate

Blacks meet their future mates in school, in the neighborhood, in churches, or at house parties (Staples, 1981). Those meeting places often no longer are available due to the increasing mobility of Blacks. The lack of membership in a stable community has a profound impact on mate selection and subsequent Black marital stability. First, couples have little knowledge of a dating partner's character in settings that are new to both individuals. Second, relatives' and friends' assessments of a potential mate are absent, which often results in a lack of attention to signs of marital incompatibility (Staples, 1981).

Because Blacks often do not use dating to assess potential mates, the question remains as to how they do select potential mates. Personality characteristics and marital expectations are reasons why Black women select marriage partners (Staples, 1981). Moreover, Black men and women often marry people who approach them first (Staples, 1981). As a result, mate selection may be a subjective readiness to marry and available opportunities. Although such problems are not unique to Blacks, they are heightened by an ideology of stigmatization that reduces Black males to a physical entity and depicts Black women as assertive, super-strong matriarchs.

Marital Commitment Versus Freedom

Black men view marriage as a constraint (Anderson, 1989). Because Black men often are prevented from economically providing for family members, they reject marriage. Cazenave (1984) labels this situation as the "double-bind" in which society expects Black men to assume traditional roles yet denies them financial resources.

The racist ethos of American culture also shapes gender socialization for marital roles. During the postslavery period, Black mothers overprotected their sons, which made them less aggressive to racist attacks (Randolph, 1995). This also was an adaptive child-rearing strategy during the pre-civil rights era. However, the ideology to protect Black men from the harsh reality of racism continues to plague a large number of Black relationships (Chapman, 1997). Consequently, Black women often tolerate Black men's undesirable marital behaviors because they require protection in a hostile environment (Collins, 1991).

In addition, Black men are exposed to different forces that make commitment problematic. The glamorized image of Black playboys and super-studs reinforces the idea that Black men are uncommitted to relationships. Some men also adopt dysfunctional patterns, such as participation in the underground economy, which is antithetical to marital commitment. Moreover, similar to White men, timing may be crucial in Black men's commitment to relationships. They may pursue professional careers in the early stages of their lives and make career versus mate decisions.

Past relationships with the opposite sex also may influence Black men's attitudes toward commitment (Staples, 1982). For example, when Black men's relationships have resulted in rejection, they ponder whether the risk of commitment is worth the possible reward. Relationship rejection may be more problematic for Black men than for White men because Black men often feel rejected on the societal level (Staples, 1982).

Few decisions in life are as important as selecting a mate. Age, residential propinquity, class, religion, race/ethnicity, and sociocultural factors influence mate selection (Lamanna & Riedmann, 1994). However, more recently, forming strong emotional bonds have become particularly difficult because few people in modern society share the same social backgrounds, interests, and lifestyles. The following discussion explores interpersonal attraction and examines the process of choosing a mate.

Why They Married

Jim was a 40-year-old auto mechanic. He was drawn to Coleen immediately. Jim said he had been wounded deeply in a previous relationship 2 months before meeting Coleen, which explained his difficulties with commitment and intimacy. Jim said,

> The best thing that happened to me at work was meeting Coleen. I had some problems in a previous relationship and was determined not to make the same mistakes. Like, I would drop by, and my last girlfriend com-

plained how little I gave. If I'm really honest with myself, all I wanted to do was to get laid with no demands and then go home. I was really uninterested in having a relationship with her. On the other hand, when I saw Coleen, there was an emotional connection. She brought her car in for repair. She walked up and asked if we could discuss the car problems over dinner.

I said, "Of course." I looked at her and noticed her fine shape. She said, "What about this evening?"

"Sure, where?"

"At my place?"

Coleen was the only child, and I'd seen her in high school. But we hung in different crowds; we had never talked until that incident. She lived with her mother, and she had already begun to make a name for herself locally singing, although she taught school. Coleen's father was retired from the marines. Coleen and I got together on weekends; we would listen to music, talk late into the night, and attend the movies. We went to parties and had picnics on the beach. Sometimes we just sat and talked and listened to jazz. She made me want to be around her all the time. I guess my nose was opened; I fell in love. She had a great sense of humor, and I loved to make her laugh. She was outspoken and had a temper, but her anger did not last very long. Like, she would get mad at something, and the next day she forgot about it. That was one quality I liked. I viewed her as a challenge, as someone who had class, beauty, intelligence, and talent. She was intrigued by my knowledge of cars and my experience with the street life. I told her my dream of opening a car repair shop. She seemed to understand my drive and ambition. Coleen was able to touch emotions that I thought I didn't have. Like, one time we went to Arkansas and went fishing. That was the first time in my life I went fishing. We walked along the beach at sunrise and ate breakfast at a little restaurant on the pier. Afterward, we went to the dog races, and I felt like I was missing sharing my life with someone. I fell hard for Coleen, which was very strange for me. She inspired me to say I loved her and to feel good about saying it. And she said it to me. It was unlike anything I had ever experienced because I knew when Coleen said she loved me, she really meant it.

Jim and Coleen enthusiastically planned a wedding, recalled Jim as he leaned back, crossed his arms, and continued.

We were married in 1992. I was 38 years old and was eager to take the vows with Coleen. I called friends and told them the news. They congratulated me, but few expressed joy. Some of my friends asked me if Coleen was really the right person for me and encouraged me to reconsider the marriage. I was angry because they couldn't see Coleen's inner beauty and strength. At the wedding, I felt people searching my eyes, looking for signs of fear and doubt. I stood there and repeated the vows as the minister told me to do. I felt that I would love her til death do us part. I thought maybe I would find peace and happiness because I thought love would conquer all the problems we would encounter.

Despite the belief that love conquers all, Black men, like other men, make marital choices in socially patterned ways. Thus, an understanding of the respondents' reasons for marriage illuminates why some of their marriages were fragile and resulted in divorce.

Married for Love

A majority of men reported love as the reason for marriage. A representative remark was "I was in love." A variation of this theme included "I married for love because when I love, I love very hard. I mean that I will be there for her." Most marriages began with two people believing that they loved each other and viewed love as an essential prerequisite to marriage. Of interest is that, unlike Staples' (1981) sample of Black middle class singles, men in this study mentioned love as the most important factor in choosing a mate, which defies the folk belief that women are more socialized to fall in love than are men.

However, critics of romantic love argue that marriage might result from an obsessive passion when, in fact, it should be based on a passionate choice. Falling in love suggests an unconscious decision and eliminates the idea of personal responsibility in relations (Lederer & Jackson, 1968; Melive, 1983), suggesting that the feeling of love might lead to marital instability.

What Is Love?

LOVE IS TRUST AND RESPECT

Research has shown that trust is an essential component of love (Ehrenreich, 1983; Fromm, 1956; Rubin, 1976). The respondents defined trust as a belief that wives would not disrespect them either in private or in public. This is illustrated by the comments of Leon, a 40-year-old city employee: "I loved my ex-wife, Carol, because I believed she would never make an idiot or a fool out of me at home or in public. I thought she would respect me and never hurt me because I would be there for her."

Trust developed from sharing inner thoughts and feelings. For example, Leon said that he felt an emotional connection to Carol: "I trusted her with my deepest feelings—feelings that I had not told one single soul. It was like this chemistry that happened when I first met her." Leon further explained,

> Carol and I would talk about Richard Wright's [1940] *Native Son.* I told Carol I identified with Bigger Thomas, whose racial fears led him to accidentally suffocate a White woman. Bigger Thomas felt the same things I felt, like restlessness, anger, and hopelessness. I'd open up to Carol my innermost thoughts and feelings. Most of the books that Carol and I were given in school were about the lives, feelings, and experiences of Whites. So, it seemed like our reality did not exist. We started reading books by Black authors and discussing them. We read books that took us places we would never have dreamed, and we developed a sense of trust and love that I've only seen in the movies.

Other men talked about trust as former wives complementing their sense of personhood. A frequent comment was of the following variety: "When I looked at my ex-wife, I saw the part of myself that was missing."

LOVE IS GIVING MATERIAL POSSESSIONS

A majority of the men equated love with material possessions. For example, some men purchased cars, clothing, microwaves, and stereos and remodeled houses to please former spouses, whereas others purchased expensive jewelry, compact disc players, and large-screen television sets. They often believed that such items represented a stable marriage. A representative comment was, "I gave my ex-wife everything she wanted. She did not have to want for nothing." As a result, they poorly understood their spouses' need for companionship.

Moreover, some men displayed a "martyr complex," believing that love was giving their wives more than they should receive in return. For example, Todd, a 38-year-old auditor for the Internal Revenue Service, said, "I married my wife because she wanted me to. I just said, yeah, we'll get married." Another example was Ivan, who bought his wife a house, even though he preferred to live in an apartment. Finally, Bernie, a 26-year-old truck driver, said, "Even though I did not want any more children because we already had two, I gave in because Shelia wanted another child and I wanted to please her."

Although martyrs sound noble, they often are aware that they are not receiving as much as they are giving in their marriages (Walster, Bersheid, & Walster, 1974). Subsequently, martyrs often become angry and frustrated in their marriages. Couples in loving relationships are balanced in terms of what they are giving and receiving from the relationships (Szasz, 1976).

LOVE IS NO HASSLES

Men also equated love as nonconfrontational and submissive behavioral traits. The combination of "no hassles and no confrontations" was generally an indication of marital stability. Therefore, disagreements were viewed as a sign of marital distress. As Sam, a 32-year-old graphic artist, said,

> Because my ex-wife, Velma, loved me and I loved her, I thought she would support anything I wanted to do. I thought the love she had for me would make her supportive regardless of what I did. I didn't think she would hassle me. I thought that was a sign that she was happy. I thought I could do no wrong and there would be no conflicts or arguments. Now I know that belief is silly, but I believed it at the time of my marriage.

Marital conflict is necessary, and disagreements should be confronted rather than avoided. However, whereas most men were reluctant to disagree, their wives often refused to accepted a nonconfrontational style. The couples' dissimilarity in problem-solving strategies often had destructive effects on the relationships. Crohan (1992) examined the communication patterns of 133 Black and 149 White newly married couples. Couples who believed in avoiding marital conflict were less happy than others 2 years later.

A Knight in Shining Armor

Some men married to rescue women from self-doubt and inadequacy. This resulted in a large number of respondents marrying women whom they could "save." This was a representative comment: "She needed me, and I wanted to help her." A variation on this theme was the following:

> I fell head over heels because she needed me. My ex-wife was going through some hard times and heartaches. I felt like I could rescue her. Her first husband treated her so badly; he stole her money and sold her things to get money for drugs. I wanted to help her deal with the pain. I felt sorry for her because she had been through some troubling times.

Some men thrived on their ex-wives' dependency, and they felt comfortable when they were in the position of the knight in shining armor. The rescuer model of a husband, however, cannot be understood without an examination of the social context of Black men's lives. The stereotypes of Black males involves several themes. First, they are perceived to be emasculated by White society. Second, the emasculation process suggests that Black men often fail to reach emotional maturity. Consequently, Black males tend to be poor husbands and fathers.

One mode of adapting to a maligned identity by the dominant sector is through the adoption of rescuing behaviors. Some men were shoulders on which their wives depended; other husbands were actively involved in household decisions. As a result, they were extremely influential in their households. Moreover, according to rescuers, their former wives developed new skills including appreciation for books, sports, and traveling as well as completion of college degrees. Studies have shown that White men tend to marry women who are slightly inferior. This tendency, the marriage gradient, occurs on the dimensions of education, social status, and even height (Surra, 1990). However, the marriage gradient may be changing and may operate differently for Black and White men. Mare (1991) found a weakening of the traditional marriage gradient with respect to education because some White men desire to marry women with prospects of great earning power. The men's comments indicate that the marriage gradient for some Black men might be strengthening. In a culture where manhood is defined largely in terms of economic resources and occupational status, and where few Black men have status or power, they may seek women who are slightly inferior.

An interesting implication of the marriage gradient is that Black women at the highest educational levels have a smaller selection of potential mates because most high-status Black men marry down. In Staples' (1981) sample of Black middle class singles, professional Black women complained that they often are excluded as eligible mates because of their educational status.

A Great Mother, a Good Marriage Partner

Approximately 65% of respondents reported that maternal potential was an important characteristic for selecting a mate. According to Cowan and Cowan (1992), men pay attention to a woman's maternal potential and often become cautious if they fail to observe this characteristic in potential marital mates. Stanley, a 33-year-old elementary school teacher, indicated that he was attracted to a woman who could care for children because he could nurture children better than a woman. He remarked, "I wanted a woman who could be a good mother because I can care for children just as good as a woman can. I can love them and meet their needs just as good as a woman."

Although Stanley married a woman who loved children, this characteristic eventually created marital distress that caused him to feel "second in the relationship." In response to this paradoxical position, Stanley said,

> I told Paula we needed to allocate time for each other, but she was so consumed with the kids. She didn't trust babysitters to care for young children. Paula was so happy with the kids and often paid little attention to me.

The most attractive quality Stanley desired in a mate became a marital liability. Research has shown that children produce marital strain (White, Booth, & Edwards, 1986). Spouses who are parents not only are busier but also spend less time with each other and share fewer decisions (White et al., 1986). Child-free marriages are consistently happier than those with children (Glenn & McLanahan, 1982; Houseknect, 1987). It is ironic, therefore, that most men in this study desired children and evaluated potential mates on mothering skills.

Something to Do

Some men reported that they married because "it was something to do—similar to going to a baseball game." They often had difficulty understanding why they married. Edward, a 34-year-old factory worker, explained,

> I married thinking it was just something to do. I didn't give much thought to it. I had seen my parents do it, and they seemed okay with it. No one told me that this was a very serious thing. I thought, well, if it doesn't work out, I'll just leave it alone. I had no idea of what to expect or what marriage was all about. I looked at marriage like I paid the bills. As long as I paid the bills, I could do what I wanted to do.

Willy also married because it was "something to do" and did not consider marriage as a serious decision; thus, he continued a single lifestyle. He explained,

> I liked being married, but I wanted to be single at the same time, I wanted to go out every other weekend and just flirt—just to see if there was anybody better. I wanted a little section of my life for myself. It was just like a little escape, but I wanted to be married. Donna was not doing anything wrong. I wanted an outing every now and then, even though I wasn't sexually involved with anyone outside of my marriage. I just wanted to know if other women found me attractive, although I really loved Donna and there was nothing I would not do for her.

Although Willy was satisfied with married life and believed he had much to gain from marriage, he maintained a certain amount of freedom to continue his "outings." These excursions allowed him to maintain a degree of autonomy and increased his self-worth when women were attracted to him. However, over time, Willy's outings led to marital distress and subsequent divorce.

Clyde, a 41-year-old electrician, also talked about the benefits of marriage but felt he was unable to devote his full attention to a marriage and family. He also said that marriage was "analogous to taking a trip" and further explained,

> For a short while, married life seemed to agree with me. Then I struggled with just enjoying the family life, but my heart wasn't in it. When I married, I thought it was something to do. I didn't think very hard about it. I tried visiting relatives and friends with Betty, my ex-wife, and being around people that she enjoyed. God knows I tried. After a while, I got back into checking out the happy hours and began hanging out. For me, the marriage was a compromise, such as the joys of being with my daughters, but the strain of trying to make a marriage work eventually got the best of me. It made me feel out of sorts and depressed. I was caught in the Peter Pan complex; I didn't want to grow up and thought of marriage as fun, you know, like taking a trip.

There are several reasons why these marriages were doomed to fail. First, given that these men married because it was something to do, they often failed to consider whether former spouses would be suitable mates or whether they had matured for marriage. As a result, Clyde said that he advised his daughters not to marry until they are at least 35 years old, when they have matured, established a sense of identity, and settled in careers.

Second, people who married because it was something to do divorced more readily if their marriages destabilized rather than remain unhappily married. For example, Clyde spent little time with his family. On occasion, this realization led him to invest more energy into his family— at least for a time. However, it often produced profound emotional distress. Rather than remain in an unhappy marriage, he filed for a divorce.

The Right Time to Marry

Time was an important factor in the decision to marry. Specifically, most respondents believed that at a certain age, a man should assume family responsibilities, usually when he is 25 years old. This belief was analogous to women feeling the pressure of a "biological clock." A frequent representative comment was, "I'd been running long enough, so I thought it was time to settle down." There also was a sense of urgency about an appropriate marital time. As Bronson, a 43-year-old car salesman, said,

> I believed it was time for me to have a family. I wanted an exclusive relationship, but I had a tendency to overlook positive qualities in women. I thought, "How long will I keep doing this—until I am 60 years old?" I wanted to have children before I got too old, so I married.

Thus, some men married because it was what they were supposed to do at a certain life stage in that it symbolized a rite of passage to an adult status.

Parents and peers pressure singles to marry (Cate & Lloyd, 1992). According to some men, family members frequently inquired about their marital plans. However, the respondents often ignored family pressure to marry and based their marital decisions on a subjective readiness to settle down.

Pregnancy and the Need to Marry

Ten men married because of premarital pregnancies. A representative comment was the following: "My ex-wife was pregnant. We knew each other for a couple of years, and I felt like I should marry." Ben, a 46-year-old accountant, said,

> My marriage happened like it did to a lot of Black men who grew up in the Sixties. When I was in junior college, my ex-wife got pregnant, and my son was born when I was a senior. Back then, it was unthinkable not to marry. In my hometown, it was a stigma *not* to marry if the girl was pregnant.

Eric, a 37-year-old junior high school teacher, reported that although he married his wife due to a pregnancy, he felt that the pregnancy was intentional:

> My ex-wife, Bonnie, was pregnant. I was confused because she told me that she was on "the pill." Bonnie said, "If I don't have this child, I may

never be able to have children." I wondered, had this woman become pregnant intentionally? I felt like something was happening to me that was untimely, improbable, and crazy. I knew it couldn't be true, and I suspected that Bonnie's negligence was intentional. Bonnie threatened to leave the city, and I would be separated from my son. I did not want to be a stranger to my kid like my father was to me. As I stood at the wedding, I felt nothing that people call joy or happiness, but I paid my dues to my child whom I would bring into the world.

Other men shared the belief that a premarital pregnancy was the woman's fault and felt emotionally betrayed, which influenced the stability of their marriages.

One factor that reduced the damaging effects of pregnancy-inspired marriages included controlling subsequent fertility. With the exception of one respondent, each of these men had another child a year later. None of the men considered an abortion, generally because it never occurred to them. The premarital births occurred when the respondents were young. Age at first marriage has been associated with marital instability (Cherlin, 1992). Those who marry at a young age often are more emotionally immature, educationally deficient, and economically unstable than those who marry at a later age (Cherlin, 1992; Furstenberg, Bennet, Bloom, & Craig, 1989). However, marriage has virtually disappeared among Black youths (U.S. Bureau of the Census, 1992). Thus, an interesting question is what factors contribute to a large number of Blacks separating marriage from child rearing.

The Military and Marriage

The military played a role in several respondents' decision to marry, especially the war in Vietnam. For example, Truman, a 49-year-old store manager, said,

I was in the military when I married my ex-wife, Barbara. I was in Japan and felt miserable. I wanted to have someone to receive a letter from or to call when I was in a foreign country. Men in the military often cling to women to ease the loneliness. I was comforted knowing that my ex-wife and kids were waiting for my return.

Similar to men who married due to premarital pregnancies, military men often failed to consider whether their ex-wives were compatible mates prior to marriage. According to these men, their former wives were delighted to marry men who were gainfully employed. A Black military man might be especially attractive to a large number of Black women, resulting in contemporary structural conditions influencing Black mate selection.

The Gulf War highlighted marital disruption among Black men in the military. Black soldiers are three times more likely than their White counterparts to be separated from their spouses while serving in the U.S. military. Consequently, Black married soldiers often place their lives and marriages in jeopardy (Staples & Johnson, 1993). Moreover, once their period of enlistment ends, Black veterans experience a higher rate of unemployment, compared to Black civilian males with no military service (Staples, 1994). Although there are approximately 415,000 Blacks in the miliary, representing 20% of all military personnel (U.S. Bureau of the Census, 1983), few studies have investigated Black military families.

Summary

The reasons for marriage were complex and included the following: (a) being in love, (b) rescuing a former spouse from feelings of inadequacy, (c) changing a problematic behavioral trait, (d) feeling an appropriate time to marry, (e) desiring to be morally responsible to an unborn child, (f) needing someone while in the military, (g) desiring to parent based on assessment of the future spouse's mothering potential, and (h) perceiving that there was nothing better to do at the time.

The belief that love conquers all problems prevented prudent marital decisions. Indeed, in movies and through popular music, one's ideal mate is revealed by a bolt of romantic lightning, thus eliminating incompatibility issues. Moreover, despite its importance, the meaning of love often was misunderstood and was different for each partner, for example, adopting a martyrdom role, providing material possessions as a demonstration of love, being a rescuer, or ignoring marital disagreements interfaced to increase marital instability.

Timing also influenced marital decisions. Thus, to remain single during one's 20s was unacceptable. In addition, being in the military often encouraged marriage, suggesting that military bases should offer extensive premarital counseling and education programs. Although marriage during a transient military lifestyle provided emotional security, it also destabilized marriages.

There were several problematic reasons for marriages. First, pregnancy-inspired marriages increased marital instability. Some men believed that it was solely the fault of the women, resulting in a sense of betrayal permeating the marriages at the beginning. Second, marrying because there was nothing better to do made divorce probable. This view of marriage has particular significance for middle and working class Black men, who often work and live in isolation from familiar social networks. The throw-away approach to relationships fragments a segment of society most in need of permanence, support, and stability.

The assessment of future mates' nurturing abilities reveals the importance of Black mothers. According to Christian (1985), a great deal of sanctification surrounds Black motherhood (Christian, 1985). However, this characteristic often became a liability in some marriages. Such a paradox can be understood in the context of Black family life. The priorities of Black parents include finding quality education for children (because local school boards are less responsible to Black parents than to White parents), locating affordable housing, securing stable employment to elevate the families' economic positions, controlling their children's exposure to illicit drugs and crime, and integrating their families into a White social environment. The strain of coping with these problems in the context of restricted opportunities might leave little time for Black parents to keep a marriage satisfying.

3

Correlates of Marital Separation
and Divorce

*Black men need more jobs with better salaries. That's why the under-
ground economy is so appealing to many Black men; they can earn
as much as $1,000 a day. They want to live out the American
dream—nice houses and cars. But even with money, marital distress
occurs over spending decisions, the value one spouse places on
money, debt accumulation, periodic unemployment, working in jobs
that erode their self-esteem, and being denied promotions and salary
increases based on race. It's a complex situation.*

—Vincent

In Chapter 2, we identified reasons for marriage that subsequently
influenced marital termination. In this chapter, we turn to causes that
respondents perceived as disrupting their marriages and compare their
views to the scholarly literature. We discuss structural conditions, followed by an examination of internal factors that prompt marital failure.
We also explore marital distress, frequent separations, communication
failure, and perceived postmarital personality changes. The high number
of separations followed by reconciliations, as well as separations extend-
ing for years, indicates a confusing mixture of events in severing marital
bonds.

External Factors Related to Divorce

SOCIOECONOMIC

Extensive research has investigated the relationship between socio-economic status and marital dissolution (Litcher, LeClere, & McLaughlin, 1991; Norton & Glick, 1979; South & Lloyd, 1992; Taylor, Chatters, Tucker, & Lewis, 1990). Studies consistently have found an inverse relationship between income and divorce, suggesting that economic contraints increase the probability of divorce. Indeed, the divorce rate is higher among unemployed Black males (Broman, 1991; South & Lloyd, 1992; Staples, 1985). Moreover, according to Kunjufu (1995), for every 1.0% increase in male unemployment, there is a 4.3% increase in wife abuse.

Research consistently has shown that, compared to White families, Black families are economically disadvantaged (Staples, 1994). For example, when stocks, bonds, and property are converted to cash, the median wealth of White families is 12 times that of Black families (Staples, 1987). Black males also are more likely than their White counterparts to work in jobs that are susceptible to layoffs (Billingsley, 1988). In fact, 32% of Black working men have incomes below the poverty level (Dickson, 1993). Moreover, 53% of new jobs in the private sector are given to White women, 26% to White men, and 12% to Hispanics, whereas Blacks and Asians obtain 5% of new jobs (Hill, 1993).

The household income in the top 20% income distribution demonstrates the discrepancy between Black and White wealth. In 1988, Blacks in the top 20% had a median income of $47,160 compared to similar White households' median income of $419,057 annually (Hill, 1989). In addition, the median income of college-educated Blacks ($46,980 annually) is only 86% of that of White college-educated Americans ($54,680) (Hill, 1989).

In addition to being employed in the lowest status positions in government and private industry, Blacks are more likely than Whites to be unemployed and to experience layoffs. In fact, the rate of unemployment for Blacks has not dropped below 6.4% since 1954 (Hill, 1989; Pinkney, 1993). In 1990, Blacks constituted 11% of the labor force but accounted for 22% of the unemployment (Pinkney, 1993).

There is an absence of research that investigates reasons for the inverse relationship between income and marital dissolution. Thus, Coombs and Zumeta (1970) conclude that the amount of income might be irrelevant and that, instead, the attitude of the couple toward its economic situation might lead to divorce. As a result, debt accumulation and dissimilar consumption patterns have been implicated in divorce (Coombs & Zumeta, 1970; Mott & Moore, 1979).

OCCUPATIONAL STRESSORS

In a number of Black marriages, one or both spouses work shifts. Shift work is defined as work before 8 a.m. or after 4 p.m. In one quarter of all dual-earner couples, one spouse works shifts (Pressor, 1987). In approximately 15% of dual-earner couples, the husband works shifts; in 6%, the wife does shift work (Pressor, 1987). Blacks are more likely to work shifts (White & Keith, 1990). Shift work disrupts home life, reduces marital satisfaction, and increases the probability of divorce (Levinger, 1966).

Furthermore, Black employed wives and husbands might work a "second shift" that may affect marital stability. Second shift is unpaid family work that amounts to an extra month of work each year (Hochschild, 1989). Ferree (1991) found that, among 382 mostly White dual-earner couples, husbands and wives averaged 60 hours per week of employment and housework. Because Black men tend to engage in household chores to a greater extent than do White men, Black men may be caught between the demands of their occupations and working the second shift. Performance of second shift work may deplete their psychological resources for marital communication, conjugal cooperation, and conflict management.

CULTURAL VALUES

Cultural values also influence marital stability and subsequent divorce. Cultural value shifts, including a greater emphasis on self-realization and fulfillment, have been implicated in the increased divorce rate. These developments reflect an individualistic ethos, which emphasizes self-fulfillment in personal relationships and deemphasizes spousal and partner obligations. Cultural value trends make marriage more difficult because of combined expectations of personal happiness and fulfillment. A marriage is evaluated by its ability to foster individual growth rather than by responding to the needs of a partner. A marital relationship also often is viewed as deficient when one partner does not meet the other's needs of affection, companionship, and understanding.

The postmodern capitalistic society, based on purchasing power, has influenced relationships in general and Black relationships in particular. Consequently, Black couples often fall in love when they feel that they have found the best partners available on the market. The attitude that "I give you as much as you give me in a marriage" often is the prevalent ethical maxim in a postmodern capitalistic society. However, the market perspective of relationships appears to be more exaggerated and devastating in Black marriages than in White marriages.

SEX RATIO

There are 1.4 million more Black women than Black men in the United States. In part, this is a function of the higher mortality rate of Black men, particularly those between 15 and 35 years of age. The low ratio of eligible Black males in the marriage pool also has been attributed to Black males' violent and accidental deaths, substance abuse, and incarceration (Staples, 1994). Since the end of World War II, Black women have had a diminishing pool of eligible Black men to marry (Gibbs, 1993).

The male shortage in the Black population also has been related to adultery, out-of-wedlock births, divorce, and less marital commitment (Guttentag & Secord, 1983). The imbalanced sex ratio suggests that Black women compete against each other for the low supply of Black men. According to Scott (1986), the male shortage has resulted in a modified Black polygynous climate that undermines the stability of Black marriages. In examining the polygynous tendencies of Blacks, McAdoo (1997) cautions Blacks to avoid the belief that plural marriages will eradicate problems that confront Black American families because support of one Black family in America is difficult.

CRIMINAL JUSTICE SYSTEM

The incarceration of Blacks also has disrupted a number of Black families. For example, 609,000 Black males who are in the marriageable group between 20 and 29 years of age are in jail, on probation, or on parole (Staples, 1994). This represents 23% of the 20- to 29-year-old Black male population, a greater proportion than are enrolled in colleges and universities. Although Black males account for approximately 61% of robbery arrests and 55% of homicide arrests, they represent only 6% of the general population (Brown & Gary, 1987; Staples, 1978a). Blacks are arrested for 45% of all serious violent crimes and 34% of all arrests for serious property crimes including burglary, larceny/theft, motor vehicle theft, and arson. Within inner cities, the arrest rate for Blacks exceeds that in the suburbs and rural areas.

A large proportion of Black fathers are in prison. An estimated 144,263 (or 36%) of inmates in local jails have children younger than 15 years of age. These inmates have a total of 326,903 children (Kemper & Rivara, 1993). There are 10 times as many imprisoned fathers as imprisoned mothers (Kemper & Rivara, 1993). A father in prison may be a risk factor for marital instability for a subsequent generation of Blacks.

Internal Factors Related to Divorce

SUBSTANCE ABUSE

Substance abuse also has been associated with the disruption of Black marriages (Staples, 1982). For example, alcohol-related illnesses and deaths have contributed to the instability of Black marriages. Black males die from cirrhosis of the liver at twice the rate of Black females, and the death rate of cirrhosis for Black men also is twice that of White men (U.S. Department of Health and Human Services, 1992).

Urban Blacks have been especially affected by the prevalence of illicit drugs. A higher proportion of Blacks (3%) use crack than do Latinos (2%) or Whites (1%) (Pinkney, 1993). Crack/cocaine use has been most acute among males of marriage age. Approximately 82% of all reported addicts are males between 21 and 30 years of age. Of the nearly 500,000 reported regular crack users, more than 200,000 are men (Pinkney, 1993). The crack euphoria creates feelings of power and aggression, and the users and dealers frequently intimidate family members and communities.

The strong craving produced by this drug propels users to spend thousands of dollars weekly. For many crack users, the source of such income is theft, even from family members. Unfortunately, a large proportion of men and women report that crack often provides an illusion of power to block the pain of social discrediting, economic marginality, and dysfunctional families. Without the lack of successful role models, drug dealers and users have become heroes to a number of inner-city Black men (Gibbs, 1988).

INCOMPATIBILITY ISSUES

Incompatibility has been related to divorce including failure to compromise, lack of respect, and inability to communicate. Although educational and class dissimilarity have been implicated in divorce for Whites, it is unknown whether such factors exert similar influences on Black marriages. An explanation of divorce based on individual pathology also has been associated with the dissolution of marriages. According to this view, divorced individuals bring neurotic interactions into marriages and are less likely to maintain the marriages than are persons without preexisting psychological disabilities. Thus, "healthy" people stay married, and less healthy people divorce.

The previous discussion has highlighted external and internal factors of divorce in the scholarly literature. In the following sections, the respondents express their views on socioeconomic status, occupational stressors, cultural values, the sex ratio, and the criminal justice system as influencing the termination of Black marriages. We also explore the respondents' assessments of internal factors as being particularly destructive in the Black marriages.

External Factors Related to Divorce

SOCIOECONOMIC STATUS AND DIVORCE

The respondents were asked whether economics played a role in the disruption of Black marriages. Most men agreed that for Blacks who are in lower socioeconomic classes, lack of financial resources prohibit adequate marital role performance, which increases the probability of divorce. However, Vincent reported that the correlation between men's economic situations and marital stability was too simplistic:

> Black men need more jobs with better salaries. That's why the underground economy is so appealing to many Black men; they can earn as much as $1,000 a day. They want to live out the American dream—nice houses and cars. But even with money, marital distress occurs over spending decisions, the value one spouse places on money, debt accumulation, periodic unemployment, working in jobs that erode their self-esteem, and being denied promotions and salary increases based on race. It's a complex situation.

Although socioeconomic status has been consistently documented in the dissolution of Black marriages, without exception, the men believed that the types of jobs held also contributed to their marital distress. For example, some men worked in the horse business, others in construction, and others as long-distance truck drivers, which required being absent from home for extended periods. Although these jobs often paid decent salaries, the multiple separations created extreme marital distress. Thus, the men believed that the limited occupational options available to Black men contributed to the high Black divorce rate.

OCCUPATIONAL STRESS

More important, the men perceived occupational stress as a risk factor for divorce. For example, they viewed occupational stressors such as racial discrimination in promotions and lack of social acceptance in the work environment as inextricably related to marital instability. Leon said that race-based employment discrimination made it difficult for him to invest energy in developing a collaborative marriage:

> The greatest stress that carried over to my marriage was fighting racial stereotypes. I was not promoted on my job, even though I was more qualified than most of the Whites I worked with. I had to train young, inexperienced White men who eventually became my bosses. I argued with my wife a number of times because I just didn't have the energy to work out a solution. I just said, "No, I don't want to hear it." I was feeling so drained from being humiliated on my job and knowing if I wanted to keep a job, I had to keep my mouth shut.

Shift work precipitated marital distress. For example, Kenneth, a 37-year-old policeman, worked from midnight til 7 a.m., whereas his ex-wife worked the evening shift from 3 p.m. to 11 p.m. He complained that he hardly slept with his wife and that it contributed to the breakup of his marriage.

CULTURAL VALUES

Approximately 60% of the men indicated that cultural values with an emphasis on individualism influenced their marriages. A frequent comment was "It's all about money," translated to mean that marriages often are focused solely on acquiring money. As Fromm (1956) observes, American capitalism has promoted a hedonistic culture that promises materialism and luxury sustained by the business marketing system. Consequently, respondents often believed that marriages were self-centered, with one partner neglecting the needs of the other.

THE SEX RATIO

Most men believed that the sex ratio has had an adverse effect on Black marriages. Several respondents reported that some Black men often have viewed the dating scene as a candy store with many desirable choices. Allen, a 45-year-old college instructor, said,

> A lot of single Black professional women are hard-pressed to find [men] to marry on their level. If you subtract Black men who are in jail, gay, on drugs, unemployed, or just plain crazy by being in the mainstream system, Black women have very few men to select for suitable marriage partners.

According to some respondents, men exploit their endangered species status, which often leads to frustration in relationships. As Jim explained,

> A lot of Black men think they have made it since they are in great demand. Their relationships with women are superficial, and they often crave the attention they get from many women. Plus, the only asset many Black men think they have is their appearance because their other qualities are largely ignored by mainstream society.

On the other hand, Todd remarked,

> I take my special status as a moral obligation to show respect to women.
> It is time for a man to speak up for sisters who often have been humiliated
> and disappointed by men. My sister's husband had a baby by another
> woman while he was married to my sister. Can you imagine how that
> made my sister feel? My niece's boyfriend is in prison for selling drugs
> while she is raising her son alone. Many brothers are down and out,
> hurting sisters, and wasting away while the world is passing them by.

Carl and Curtis also discussed the consequences of the sex ratio for
Black relationships, stating that it has resulted in utilitarian and
tentative associations.

THE CRIMINAL JUSTICE SYSTEM

Several men reported that their children's marriages often were
disrupted by the criminal justice system. Arthur, a 55-year-old horse
trainer who had been separated 5 years before his wife filed for a divorce,
recalled the effects of the criminal justice system on his daughter's
family:

> My oldest daughter is 30 years old, and her husband is in jail for selling
> cocaine. Although she is a good mother—she takes care of her kids—her
> 17-year-old son is having trouble. He sees what his father is doing and
> wants quick and fast money. My daughter visits her husband in jail
> and tells me [that] in some prisons there are whole families in prison—
> brothers, uncles, and cousins. At one time, her husband and son were both
> in jail at the same time. I felt so sorry for her visiting a husband and son
> in jail. She hired the same lawyer to help both of them, and he made money
> off her. I thought to myself that White criminal lawyers have created a
> cottage industry supported mostly by young Blacks on drug charges.

Ben also recalled the effects of the criminal justice system on Black
families:

> Of the seven houses on my block where I grew up that had young men in
> their households, six have one or two young men serving time. I hurt for
> a couple who lived next door to my family. They have two sons in jail.
> They live with the agony of having one son who will probably spend the

rest of his life in prison and another son who has taken a life. This was a solid, hard working class family. Their sons' charges were drug related.

Most men expressed intense frustration associated with the destructive consequences of the criminal justice system.

SOCIAL DISCREDITING AND MARITAL STABILITY

The men made distinctions among economic marginality, social marginality, and racism. Although most respondents did not believe that all Whites were racists, they reported that stereotypes are diffused in American racial mythology based on White supremacy. Inherent in the ideology of White supremacy are meanings assigned to physical distinction and biological difference that take on a political character. Graham made the point when he stated,

> When I watch pro sports, I see people in the stands cheering for Blacks like they loved them to death. Black pro sports players play so well because the football field and the basketball court are the only places where White Americans let them know they believe in them; those are the only places where they don't battle racial stereotypes of inferiority. Can you imagine the accomplishments of Blacks if that attitude prevailed in every facet of American society?

The respondents reported that American society has made it difficult for them to conform to an ideal middle class Eurocentric family structure because the atmosphere of American society is infused with the idea of a White racial privilege. As Gerald pointed out,

> Our culture believes strong individuals can transcend their circumstances in a powerful White world. Even though I owned two houses, I felt at times I did not have a chance. I kept feeling that somehow the deck is stacked unfairly against Black men. Every aspect of my life as a Black man is affected by how society mistreats me. When I dealt with racial stereotypes day in and day out and being degraded and humiliated, my relationship with my ex-wife suffered. And nowadays, when I discuss racism, people tell me I have a victim complex.

Gerald also said that he was drained after he had stood in line for 30 minutes and then a White clerk helped him only after she had waited on several other Whites. Todd reported being frustrated when a bank teller refused to cash his check for $1,000 at a bank he frequently used. After spending 30 minutes verifying his identification, he said, "I guess the tellers thought that a Black man could not have a check for $1,000." Later, he argued with his ex-wife over an insignificant matter. Edsel said that he was turned down by several banks for a home loan, even though he had great credit and earned $50,000 a year. This increased marital frustration because his ex-wife wanted to move into a better neighborhood.

Dwayne reported that he argued with his wife after a waitress refused to serve them at a local restaurant. He confronted the manager about the treatment they received, whereas his ex-wife, Claire, wanted to passively accept the discrimination. Finally, Solomon, a trained trauma nurse, gave his ex-wife the silent treatment after a 78-year-old White woman preferred to die rather than to permit him to insert an oxygen tube. He was emotionally drained, and this carried over into his marital relationship. He said,

> I am a qualified nurse. I was completely shaken when a White woman would rather die than permit a Black man to save her life. I just couldn't believe that, and I had trouble talking with Kaye. Somehow, society retains certain illusions. They can blame Black men for their own faults, and yet society makes it so difficult for them to have stable marriages. That is the tragic flaw of American society. If I could tell White people anything, I would tell them that there is no need to fear Black men because the destiny of Whites [is] directly tied to Blacks.

Because marriages are embedded with a social cultural context, the respondents believed that for White America to understand Black marital instability, White America must recognize that even though much time has passed since slavery, the Black male social image has changed very little. Although respondents agreed with a majority of the findings in the divorce literature, they repeatedly stated that social scientists should investigate the Black family from an ecological perspective including the criminal justice system as well as occupational and institutional racism. They also recommended studies on the effects of social discrediting on Black family life as well as research on the effects of social marginality on Black youths. They also were clear that poverty and the lack of income were major factors that disrupt Black families.

Internal Factors Related to Divorce

SUBSTANCE ABUSE

Although substance abuse has been related to divorce, only one respondent, Derek, a 51-year-old horse trainer, said that the alcoholism of his ex-wife, Joan, contributed to marital distress and frequent arguments:

> My father drank and worked. I decided that I wouldn't drink because all of his brothers drank. My father abused my mother when he drank. He drank on the weekends, even though he worked everyday. My mother stabbed him with a knife, and he almost died, but he recovered. Then my mother filed for a divorce. Joan, my ex-wife, would go to bars and drink. We had numerous fights about her need for a daily drink.

Derek also said that Joan had drinking binges in which she initiated arguments. Although he avoided alcohol because of his father's drinking patterns, he married a woman who abused alcohol, suggesting that he was strongly influenced by his father's drinking patterns. Consequently, he recommended premarital programs especially designed for Black children of alcoholics and for those who lived with chemically dependent parents.

Most important, the respondents stressed that the impact of crack/cocaine on Black families has been neglected in family studies. They believed that a dearth of information and interventions that focus on illicit drugs reflects a lack of understanding of the way in which drugs destroy a large number of Black families. For example, Bert, a 52-year-old construction supervisor, cried as he talked about his daughter, who started using crack:

> I believe that crack has taken drugs to another level. My 22-year-old daughter was a secretary for an attorney. She had a good job until she started using snow. She sold everything to get the stuff. She lost her job, her children, and her marriage. She told me, "That stuff got the best of

me, and I couldn't figure out how to get away from it." She was a drug
zombie for about 5 years. I felt helpless and didn't know what to do. She
was in and out of drug rehab programs while her daughters stayed in a
foster home. I took care of her children for a while, but it added so much
stress and strain on our household that they were placed in foster care.

Repeatedly, the respondents talked about men hustling for drug
money and emphasized that crack/cocaine not only was destroying
marriages of a younger generation of Blacks but also was destroying
the Black race. Indeed, the prevalence of drugs with Black communities has reduced the quantity and quality of Black life (Nobles &
Goddard, 1986).

INCOMPATIBILITY ISSUES

Incompatibility has been correlated with divorce. For example, Levinger (1966) and Burns (1984) found that sexual incompatibility is the
most significant issue contributing to marital dissatisfaction among
Whites. However, in this study, personality incompatibility was reported
as a greater problem than sexual incompatibility. Personality incompatibility was mentioned as displaying erratic or "mean" behavioral characteristics. For example, Graham explained,

> When I married Tina, I did not know she was schizophrenic. She would
> snap, and I didn't know what was wrong. She would watch television and
> say, "What'd you say about me?" She had different personalities and a
> previous hospitalization in a state mental institution. Tina's mind would
> come and go, and I tried to deal with her sickness. She was so paranoid,
> and we made each other miserable.

Although Graham remained married for 15 years, he reported that
Tina's condition became unbearable. He had married a woman who
was paranoid, unpredictable, and often dangerous. He expressed
extreme frustration about the lack of knowledge that prevented an
accurate assessment of Tina's personality. He suggested that premarital education should include information on mate selection as well as
on the emotional costs of educational, class, and background incompatibility.

To understand Black divorce, however, it is important to explore marital separation. The following discussion explores the withdrawal of emotional and physical accessibility that underlie marital separation. We consider the gradual failure to communicate and former spouses' personality transformation following their marriages and the extent to which these factors contributed to divorce.

MARITAL DETERIORATION

Jim and Coleen experienced the first signs of tension when Coleen's father died. Their schedules conflicted. Coleen spent most of the time with her mother, while Jim was consumed with his car repair business. They spent few weekends together and gradually led independent lives. Jim viewed another pregnancy, the death of his father-in-law, and little shared time as increasing marital strain:

> I can understand why old folks advised young people to take time and get to know a woman's affairs. A week after Coleen buried her father, she told me she was pregnant. I thought we had decided to wait until I opened up the business before starting a family. I was in an emotional fog, and my life became more complicated than ever. Here I was, sinking all my money in a business with a child on the way. After Coleen and I lived together for 6 months, it became clear to me that my love for her was truly blind. She quit working and stayed with her mother for days and forgot about my dreams of owning my business. We needed money, and there was no reason for her to sit around and comfort her mother. Coleen said I was selfish, and she couldn't understand why I didn't sympathize with her mother's situation.
>
> She'd say, "Why can't you be happy wanting a child like I want."
>
> I'd say, "You knew how important it was for me to own a repair shop. I want what you want, just not now. Plus, I should come first, not your mother's needs. It just doesn't work that way, you can't always have what you want."
>
> Three months after Coleen's father died, her mother came to live with us. My mother-in-law was warm, but she had some personality quirks, which increased the tension in the house. Arguments increased over time and involved fights around [Coleen's] mother, our son—you name it, and we argued about it. She kept telling me how she felt, and I kept telling her how I felt. The tension in the house increased. I moved out and found an apartment. I felt miserable, even though I began going to

singles' bars. I felt guilty about leaving Coleen. I wondered if I should try harder to get along with Coleen's mother.

I started spending more time with Coleen, to see if we could save what was left of the marriage. I still loved her deeply, and she was the mother of my son. One year after I moved out, I returned. Two months later, Coleen told me she was pregnant again. In the meanwhile, my mother-in-law had a heart attack and almost died. This was too much.

"How," I asked, "could a pregnancy happen again?" After my second son was born, I was determined to hang in the marriage for the children's well-being. I wanted a chance to impress my ideas and values on their lives. Coleen and I were unhappy. We lived in the same house but lived separately. After a heated argument, I decided to move out again. As I moved my clothing and personal items, it was a sad picture. I felt ashamed and disgusted, looking at a woman who was once the love of my life and who I once loved more than life itself and wondered, "How did it come to this?"

Jim's marriage had been deteriorating for months. Following four separations, he moved to his own apartment permanently.

In contrast to studies on White males (e.g., Arendell, 1995; Weiss, 1975), the deterioration of Jim's marriage was shaped by race-specific factors. First, the core value of Black families involves a willingness to provide instrumental support (Billingsley, 1992). Thus, Jim's lack of eagerness for housing his mother-in-law created intense marital strain within the context of the Black family value system.

Second, Jim perceived that another child would threaten his goal of owning a business. His perceptions of financial security were heightened by the large number of failed Black businesses. He reasoned that high fertility rates often prevented Black economic upward mobility. For Jim, the paradox of adopting financial strategies, which included lower fertility patterns, and conforming to the wishes of his former spouse was at the center of marital discord.

FAILURE TO COMMUNICATE

The respondents reported a breakdown in marital communication during the deterioration of their marriages. Some men diminished their wives' self-esteem by calling them immature, silly, and crazy. The couples bombarded each other with criticism, often voicing hurts that had occurred before the marriages. As Gerald said, "Molly called me 'no good' because I asked her best friend out 10 years ago. At the time, I didn't even know Molly well."

The couples' morale often was bruised and damaged by various assaults. Therefore, husbands had trouble trusting their own judgment. Furthermore, some respondents thought that they were mentally ill for remaining married. Ben said, "I thought I had a brain problem because I stayed in the marriage for 12 years and tolerated so much craziness and hostility [that] something must be wrong with me."

"SHE TURNED ON ME"

The men often believed that their wives changed drastically following the marriages and, hence, "turned on them." This belief was particularly prominent among the men who married for love. The perception that wives voiced ownership of husbands' economic resources also was pronounced postmarriage. The following was a representative remark: "What was mine was hers, and what was hers was hers. My ex-wife believed in managing her own money and believed I should manage my own money, but she spent mine and saved hers."

Black women's tendency to save their money can be explained in the context in the labor market exploitation of Black women. Black women earn less than White men, White women, and Black men, considering full-time work (Billingsley, 1988). One presumable consequence of Black women's earning discrimination may be a tendency for them to save their earnings.

SEPARATIONS

Similar to the case with White men, the deterioration of the respondents' marriages often involved frequent separations. Some men reported leaving for motels or friends' apartments before finally divorcing. In several cases, the wife often packed up the children and stayed with relatives. Jean, Allen's ex-wife, moved out of the house when he was on a weekend fishing trip. In three of the marriages, one member of the couple planned the separation. Vincent secretly rented an apartment and then selected a time to tell his wife. Sam told his mother-in-law that he was leaving, and his mother in-law broke the news to her daughter.

In some instances, couples lived separately in the same households. Douglas went places alone and became inaccessible to his wife. He said, "I lived in the basement for 2 months before I finally separated. It gradually seemed realistic to divorce rather than to continue in the present marriage." The men reported gradually leading independent lives and returned home when their wives were asleep. Others stayed at relatives' homes, returning weekly to pick up personal items. Other men spent more time with friends and at work, whereas wives often became more involved with children, family, and church activities.

Unlike the premarital period when the respondents desired to share themselves with their mates, in the deterioration phase, they pretended that their wives did not exist. Other times, they returned home rationalizing that their ex-wives were nice persons and still attractive. Thus, they tried harder to make their marriages work but eventually moved out of their homes.

Separations, reconciliations, and eventual divorce was a frequent pattern. In several cases, separations remained for years. In most marriages, one partner impulsively moved out, feeling hurt by the other, both verbally and physically. For example, Ernell was escorted out of his house by the army police following a fight, and Dee filed for a divorce 1 week later. In most cases, the husband departed, leaving the wife and children. In five cases, the wives left the homes. Bert's ex-wife told him that she wanted a divorce and left the following day. However, most divorces occurred following extended periods of mutual alienation.

PROLONGED PERIODS OF ANGUISH

According to Wymard (1994), death and divorce share similarities because both involve coping with loss, confusion, abandonment, and sadness. Because there is nobody to mourn in divorce, it often is labeled "disenfranchised grief" (Wymard, 1994). Jim explained,

> There is little that can match the damage to a husband's self-esteem when a marriage ends. I often ask myself, "Who am I now?" Before I was Coleen's husband. It was hard for me to express my grief. Most people don't know what to do when they see a Black man cry.

Therefore, Jim and others emphasized a need to change the popular assumption that Black men suffer few ill effects following divorces.

Summary

Marital distress is complicated by a number of structural conditions, as indicated in the research literature. Although socioeconomic factors limit the functioning of Black men's performance of family roles, the men believed that occupational stressors including (a) shift work, (b) working in jobs that require being away from home, and (c) work-related racial discrimination assume a prominent role in the failure of Black marriages.

The respondents agreed with the scientific literature on the external and internal correlates of divorce. However, they rated the following as greater problems that result in the failure of Black marriages than usually are reported in the scholarly literature:

1. incarceration of Black men;
2. substance abuse (especially crack/cocaine);
3. personality incompatibility;
4. economic marginality and social discrediting; and
5. the effects of parents' alcoholism and chemical dependency on mate selection and marital stability.

They also suggested that research and programs should focus on Black children of alcoholic and crack/cocaine-addicted parents and the ways in which parents encourage Black children to compete in White America. Moreover, they argued that scholars need a better understanding of strategies that Black families use to cope with social discrediting and economic marginality.

Assessing perspectives on the imbalance of the sex ratio, respondents believed that it will continue to deny large numbers of Black women mates and that some Black men will continue to exploit their endangered species status. Thus, they recommended public discussions on the consequences of the imbalanced sex ratio.

Postmodern racism, such as denial of a home mortgage or the requirement of extensive identification when cashing a check at a bank, was inextricably connected to marital conflict. These daily race-related inconveniences created profound distress. According to the men, a number of Blacks and Whites are in denial about the effects of social marginality on Black family life. Thus, they suggested that the public

discourse of race should be centered on the social and personal consequences of racism rather than on Black victimization and White guilt.

Divorce followed prolonged periods of anguish and involved frequent separations and reconciliations. In most cases, men left the
households. Separations occurred due to communication failure and
from a perception that marriage negatively changed a partner. Nevertheless, the decision to separate often prompted questions about one's
identity, producing feelings of confusion, abandonment, and sadness.

4

The Divorce Experience

I was a provider and prided myself on being able to function in a hostile world. I was laid off twice in different cities when Whites refused to buy cars from me. During my marriage, I worked hard to have enough money to make it through periods of unemployment. . . . I spent more time working than focusing on home.

—Maurice

As shown in Chapter 2, some men married with a fairy tale quality of marital expectations. As a result, marital distress and subsequent divorce were most likely to occur. A combination of personal and social factors motivated the men to enter into marriages in which dissimilar views about ideology of romantic love increased the probability of marital instability. In Chapter 3, we described the causes of divorce and discussed the deterioration of marriages. In this chapter, we focus on how the divorce experience may be both similar to and different from that of non-Black populations. We present reasons for divorces as respondents recall and reinterpret the factors that created marital distress. Illuminating factors that have received little attention in the empirical literature, we explore the unemployment of wives, the men's perception of being overwhelmed by family demands, and value incompatibility issues. Discussion of the conceptualization of violence with a reflective analysis of the role of spousal abuse provides an in-depth analysis of the respondents' experience of marital dissolution. We begin with a review and critique of the literature on the process of divorce and marital dissatisfaction, followed by the men's accounts of their divorces.

Marital Happiness

Most divorces occur relatively early in marriage. In 1988, approximately 9% of couples married for 3 years divorced, compared to 1% of couples married for 25 years who divorced (National Center for Health Statistics, 1996). Approximately one third of divorces in 1988 occurred among couples married less than 5 years, and two thirds were among couples married for less than 10 years (National Center for Health Statistics, 1996). Thus, long marriages are less likely to end in divorce, although marital happiness declines over time (Lamanna & Riedmann, 1994).

Research has found a strong association between marital happiness and divorce. For example, Booth, Johnson, and White (1984) report that individuals with low marital happiness are four to five times more likely to divorce over a 3-year period than are those with high marital happiness. Moreover, those who initiated their divorces and those who were not initiators do not differ in marital happiness (Black, Eastwood, Sprenkle, & Smith, 1991).

Nevertheless, the high divorce rate has been attributed to Americans' high expectations of marital happiness. Although marital dissolution occurs in part because of marital unhappiness, others may dissolve marital relationships because of unrealistic expectations for marital happiness. Couples whose expectations for marital happiness are realistic tend to be more satisfied with their marriages than do those who expect marriage to fulfill all of their needs (Troll, Miller, & Atchley, 1979).

Marital happiness has been associated with shared time together and associated with lower divorce rates (Booth et al., 1984; Hill, 1988). The literature on spouses' shared activities has shown a positive relationship between spousal interaction and marital happiness (Hill, 1988). For example, Snyder (1979) found that spouses' common interests and the amount of shared leisure time predict overall marital happiness. Because divorce has been linked to working two jobs and overtime hours, the amount of time that Black couples share deserves more research attention as a factor of marital instability.

Recently, thinking about divorce during the predivorce process has received substantial attention. This research implies that divorce reflects consideration of alternatives and barriers rather than a simple process of marital unhappiness. For example, Levinger (1966) argues that spouses weigh their marital happiness against alternatives to marriage and barriers to divorce. Kitson, Holmes, and Sussman (1983) investigated separation and divorce petitions to determine factors that lead to divorce. Their findings indicate that reconciliations are more likely when the costs of divorce are high such as the presence of children. When alternatives are low such as husbands' lower incomes and wives' unemployment, divorce is more likely to occur.

Black men may perceive that divorce results in few advantages. For example, the cost of lawyers, time required to negotiate child support, conflict with former spouses, and children may prohibit Black men from filing for divorce. Nevertheless, as Black men consider divorce, they balance anticipated, moral, social, economic, and familial consequences as they experience periods of agonizing, indecision, ambivalence, and vacillation before gradually defining themselves as single.

Marital Dissatisfaction

The sources of marital dissatisfaction have been documented extensively. For example, Levinger (1966) sampled 600 couples filing for divorce and explored sources of marital dissatisfaction. He found that wives of lower income status were dissatisfied with finances and husbands' physical abuse and alcoholism. By contrast, husbands' lack of love and expressive demands made by husbands were dissatisfactions reported by middle class White women.

Thurnher, Fenn, Melichar, and Chiriboga (1983) also considered socioeconomic status in marital dissatisfaction and found that less educated men and women are more likely than those with higher levels of education to mention husbands' infidelity as a cause of marital dissatisfaction.

The literature reports that marital dissatisfaction differs on the basis of gender. Men often are dissatisfied with relatives and in-laws, change of jobs, and deaths of relatives, whereas women typically are dissatisfied with money, sexual problems, and spouses' personalities (Hill, 1988). Moreover, parents are more likely than nonparents to be dissatisfied with marital communication patterns, verbal abuse, and infidelity. However, a paradox exists regarding the role of children in marriage. The presence of children decreases marital happiness but increases marital stability. Although children may serve as barriers to marital breakups, they also may reduce spousal interaction, which decreases marital happiness and increases marital instability (Hill, 1988).

Several studies have examined gender differences regarding the sources of marital dissatisfaction. For example, Burns (1984) found that both White men and women ranked sexual incompatibility and lack of communication as the first and second most significant sources of marital dissatisfaction. Similarly, Cleek and Pearson (1985) reported that both men and women rated communication problems, basic unhappiness, and incompatibility as the first, second, and third most significant causes of marital dissatisfaction.

Kitson et al. (1983) investigated a sample (73% Whites, 26% Blacks, 1% Asians) regarding reasons for divorce. The findings indicate that individuals from lower socioeconomic backgrounds tend to be dissatisfied with the instrumental aspects of marital life such as the division of household chores and child-rearing duties. By contrast, those from higher socioeconomic backgrounds tend to be dissatisfied with the quality of communication and incompatibility of interests between spouses.

The Process of Divorce

Divorce has been identified as a process in which the family system transforms in a manner that involves a series of stages. The phases of divorce evolve over a period of time in which former spouses regain personal autonomy and develop the capacity to make new attachments. Bohannan (1985) describes the divorce process in six interrelated stages and emphasizes the processes that occur subsequent to legal divorce: emotional divorce, legal divorce, economic divorce, coparental divorce, community divorce, and finally psychic divorce. The psychic divorce includes a healing process that individuals must complete before they can enter new intimate relationships.

According to Bohannan (1985), emotional divorce is the first and most important stage. In this period, the partners are aware of their dissatisfaction and sense that their relationship is deteriorating. As one partner becomes disillusioned, the negative features of the marriage surface, which ultimately leads to psychological divorce. Ponzetti and Cate (1986) describe a developmental course of conflict in the failure of marriages and identify the following stages of divorce: recognition, discussion, action, and postdissolution.

Despite basic similarities in the conceptualization of marital termination, there has been a lack of attention to the initial separation as a stage in the divorce process. Furthermore, there has been an absence of studies that explicate individual experiences within each stage. Perhaps the most significant blind spot in this area of research is the failure to consider the larger contexts in which divorce takes place. For example, people in lower socioeconomic classes might experience difficulty in the economic divorce. Lawyer fees and child support payments might be problematic for those with few economic resources. Poverty also limits social involvement because a lack of money for transportation and recreational activities might prohibit the emotional divorce. Moreover, the day-to-day struggle of coping with occupational racism and with Black stereotypes might deplete mental and physical energies necessary for the psychic divorce.

The reviewed literature emphasizes that divorce is conceptualized as a process rather than as a single life event. The passage of time that occurs as an individual progresses through the phases of the divorce process appears to be an important factor in resolving conflicts inherent in separation and divorce.

Much of the literature on the marital dissatisfaction with the divorce process makes several assumptions that are problematic:

1. Despite the basic similarities of these studies, there appears to be a lack of attention to the personal and therapeutic importance of the larger macro issues in shaping marital dissatisfaction and the divorce process. An understanding of marriage and divorce must be articulated into larger concerns on the macro level as well as an examination of human behavior on the micro level (White, 1990). For example, how does capitalism, as a social system, help to generate individualism, social mobility, and competitiveness that make marital satisfaction and coping with the process of divorce more difficult?

TABLE 4.1 Frequency of Causes of Divorce ($N = 50$)

Factor Contributing to Divorce	Number of Respondents
Financial strain	50
Consumerism incompatibility	40
Personality incompatibility	35
Failure to negotiate conflict	30
Religious behavior incompatibility	25

NOTE: Child-rearing issues, in-law problems, and sexual incompatibility were mentioned by fewer than 20 respondents.

2. Despite much attention to the delineation of stages within the divorce process, there is little elaboration regarding whether stages differ based on race, geographic region, or socioeconomic status. Findings do suggest, however, that the initial separation is the most stressful, particularly for White women, suggesting that Black women and men show little emotional stress following separation and divorce.

3. Marital dissatisfaction should not be treated as a stable, constant factor. Levels of marital dissatisfaction do not necessarily remain the same over time.

The following section explores both macro and micro factors that resulted in marital dissatisfaction and subsequent divorce.

Too Much Work and Too Little Time

Table 4.1 shows the rank order of factors that the respondents attributed to divorce including working too much, consumerism incompatibility, incompatible personality characteristics, failure to negotiate conflict, and differences in religious behavior.

The family was an important source of satisfaction for men in our study. The following example of Carl and Rita illustrates the absence of shared time as an important factor that influenced the stability of their marriage.

Carl was an independent toddler, fond of exploring the world by taking walks to the grocery store alone. Neighbors often returned him home. His father did not consider himself unkind, but he used a stern approach and frequent beatings to change Carl's behavior. It worked. Carl had trouble exploring the world as an adult and learned to operate within the confines of his neighborhood. He married a young woman who lived next door. Although he could have attended college in another city due to his musical talents, Carl decided to go to the local college, to study political science, and to live at home. In recalling the motivation for these decisions, Carl stated, "I did what was expected of me."

Mr. and Mrs. Harris, Carl's parents, were not educated past the eighth grade and were convinced that Carl was headed for great things, which meant a good steady job, even in the post office, and a good marriage to a Christian girl. The parents scraped together enough money to help Carl and his seven siblings obtain college educations. At home, Mrs. Harris taught Carl to pray every night, to say thank you, and not to play in the alley with "street kids" or to think that "White people are better just because they own everything." His father admonished Carl to "work hard, get a college education because White people can't take what is in your head away from you, and never let Whites know what you are thinking."

There always were tensions between Mr. and Mrs. Harris that Carl could not understand. Remembering his parents' relationship, Carl said,

My father believed that a man should be the head of the house. So, he did what he wanted to do in the relationship and used Bible scriptures to justify his behavior such as the verse that says, "Wives submit yourselves to your husbands." He also believed that my mother was too soft in raising a Black man to cope in a racist society, so they argued about this.

At times, Carl felt as if he were in the middle, but he could not grasp the cause. When he looked at his father, he saw sadness and disappointment resulting from "having a son who was not a football jock, but instead he had a son who liked classical music and reading poetry." When he looked at his mother, he saw a woman who had cleaned houses for White people and had little time for her own family and for herself. However, Carl believed that he had more reason to be happy than most of the kids in his neighborhood. He was well fed, clothed, and safe.

During the interview, Carl remembered these years and realized with astonishment that he had, by 15 years of age, decided on most of the assumptions that he would have for the rest of his life—that couples should not remain married if they are unhappy, that love is essential for a good relationship, that a husband must support his family, and that with a good education he would not be in the same position as his father.

After earning a college degree in political science, Carl married his "high school sweetheart." His wife, Rita, seemed perfect for Carl. Whereas he was artistic, she dealt with facts, money, and obtaining status. Carl was sure he loved Rita and trusted her. In elaborating on the reasons he married Rita, Carl explained, "We grew up together and had the same values. We just came together and did a lot of things together." Carl eventually left his parents' tense home. He and Rita rented a small one-room apartment two blocks from where they grew up. Carl worked in a factory in addition to working as a part-time general equivalency diploma (GED) instructor, while Rita finished a 2-year course in office management. Carl would go to law school after saving for a year, while Rita would work to support the family. Once Carl had a law degree, their future would be secure. They had worked it all out. Explaining his future plans, Carl remarked,

> I wanted to make something of myself because all around me were people who were not given opportunities to do something with their lives. Like Bobby, who never finished high school but was smart in business. He could have ran any major corporation in America. The world outside his neighborhood never opened its doors to see what Bobby could really do. He died in a prison cell 2 years ago.

Although Carl and Rita could drive, they did not own a car. They rode buses and begged Mrs. Harris to drive them around. Carl found employment in a factory, while Rita worked as a clerk-typist. Carl worked part-time, spending much of his time commuting. Nevertheless, he described the first years of marriage as "the happiest time of my life because we were both working toward a goal and we wanted the same things out of life, although my jobs were dull and I was tired after the long bus rides."

Carl and Rita's lives became routine. They occasionally entertained family and friends. Carl always shared domestic chores including the laundry, grocery shopping, and housecleaning. After 8 months of marriage, Rita missed her period. She looked squarely at Carl and said, "I'm pregnant."

"Pregnant?" Carl said. "I thought you were taking birth control pills."

"How could this have happened? This wasn't supposed to happen," Carl thought. According to the script that Carl had written for himself, he was supposed to attend law school and to live the rest of his life trouble free. He somehow felt that the baby was Rita's fault, although he was aware that rationally this idea was ridiculous.

The company for which Rita worked did not like a Black pregnant woman in its office and fired her when she was 3 months pregnant. It was then, Carl reported, that the pregnancy symbolized the ending of his personal goals. His life from then on was owned by another person. He explained,

> I gave up my dreams of becoming a lawyer. I would have been a great public defense attorney, but all I could think of for years was putting food on the table. I do not believe in abortion, and Rita equated abortion with murder.

Carl received a raise and moved his family to a one-bedroom apartment, a place with a bedroom, living room, and kitchen. Rita became pregnant again with twins, and Carl worried constantly about money. Rita resumed working 6 weeks postpartum, and life seemed a little better because material circumstances had improved. Carl purchased a home with three bedrooms, a living room, and a separate dining room in a neighborhood designed to isolate Blacks. When Blacks moved in, Whites moved out, leaving a stable Black working class.

With a factory job, working part-time, and Rita working, Carl's life was a little easier. Carl painted, wallpapered, refinished furniture, and washed and waxed the floors of his house; it was his pride and joy. In talking about this period in his life, he stated,

> Owning the house seemed surreal, like an out-of-body experience, like maybe I was daydreaming and might be awakened any moment because I had achieved more than my parents. At least I owned a home and my kids would not grow up in the projects. I grew up in the projects, where I saw people who had no goals but to get a fix or to wait until the next

party. On the building walls where I walked everyday [was] old graffiti
with slang and curse words. I could smell the stink of urine in the hallways
of the building. I shared a room with my two brothers as long as I
remember and heard daily fights from the people who lived upstairs.

With little warning, Carl was laid off. Rita worked two full-time
jobs, while Carl remained at home. He checked the employment
agencies daily to no avail. Recalling this period in his life, Carl
explained,

> I felt like a failure, especially since I had a college degree. The kids were
> growing so fast and needed so many things I could not give them. The
> lack of money was hard with three children, but the lack of self-respect
> caused by unemployment was worse. I hated for my kids to see me
> unemployed, sitting around the house and feeling miserable.

Following 3 years of unemployment, Carl decided to leave the city
and look for work in a midwestern city. He explained, "My family
would be better off without me, and I promised to send for them after
finding work." Carl felt guilty for failing to maintain a home for his
children and, therefore, perceived unemployment as lessening his
ability to command respect from his children. Elaborating on his
move, Carl said,

> When a White worker migrates, it is often because he had a job offer or
> a transfer. When a Black man migrates, it is most often because he is
> currently unemployed or working irregularly, which has been the experi-
> ence of Blacks since slavery.

Carl moved to Detroit, found work, and lived with seven relatives
in a one-bedroom apartment. Two years later, he sent for Rita and the
kids. One year after the move, Rita filed for a divorce. In explaining
the cause of the divorce, Carl stated, "I was consumed with work. I
was never home. I worked a full-time job, a part-time job, and played
in jazz clubs at night. I directed a church choir on Sundays and spent
virtually no time at home." Remembering the marriage, Carl remarked,

> I strove to make ends meet, and I wanted to have enough money saved
> for hard times. Plus, I wanted to have enough money saved so I could help
> my older daughter go to graduate school. I wanted to help my kids more

than my parents were able to help me. The more I worked, the less I thought of Rita's needs, but I had to work because we lost everything before and were starting all over.

At the time of the interview, Carl lived with his 78-year-old mother in the same apartment and neighborhood in which he grew up. In commenting on his divorce, Carl said,

> What's a Black man to do? I've tried to do all the right things, like get an education and work hard—and look where it has gotten me. I wanted to save my marriage, but there were so many things influencing it, like having to work so hard to support my family. Society is about keeping the Black man down.

Carl repeatedly returned to the events of his marriage, trying to identify what went wrong and speculating about how he could have worked differently to pay bills and give Rita the attention she needed. He also recalled the humiliation of working two and sometimes three jobs, only to have the marriage end. He reported feeling persecuted by his inability to earn $40,000 annually without several jobs. He also left the area for 2 months, hoping that by doing so, he also could leave the memories. However, his mind was fixed on Rita's excruciating words: "I want a divorce. This is not the marriage I want because you are never home; all you do is work. I need more out of marriage than this."

Although an inverse relationship between income and the likelihood of divorce has been documented extensively, in this study the level of wages per se was not as centrally related to marital dissolution as were the respondents' efforts to prevent the devastating effects of intermittent and sporadic unemployment. Among Black males employed in the labor force, one out of three will experience unemployment in a given year (Staples, 1985).

John's experience also illustrates the efforts required to prevent downward social mobility and its effects on marital stability. John, a 42-year-old factory worker whose marriage of 10 years had ended 2 years earlier, grew up with five older sisters. John's father worked in a factory, and his mother was employed as a domestic servant. John's comments demonstrate the quality of his parents' marriage, which he described as supportive and emotionally close: "My parents were married for 40 years. They were poor but loved each other. We had a lot of love in our family, and that kept us close. My father and mother were very supportive of their children." Although his father had a sixth-grade education, John emphasized the importance of a college education. John graduated with a bachelor's degree in sociology from a historically Black college, where he met his ex-wife, who had one child born outside of the marriage. In recalling the decision to marry, John reported,

> We got married because we wanted to; she was not pregnant. I thought we could make it because she handled money wisely and worked hard. She earned an accounting degree, and I considered her daughter my own biological daughter. And at age 36, we owned two houses.

John described the period of cohabitation and the early years of marriage as a period of contentment and stability.

Similar to Carl, the reality that a college education did not guarantee economic security contributed to John's divorce. Although John had a college degree, he also experienced a layoff resulting from his company's downsizing. During his unemployment, he was a househusband while his wife supported the family. The frustration he endured in this situation was revealed by the comment "I hated to see my wife work like a man to support a family." Subsequently, he moved the family to another city, where he found better employment opportunities and worked constantly to decrease the debts they had accumulated over the years. He attributed the divorce to the layoff, which caused considerable marital tension. His comments revealed the marital tension that was due to the company layoff. He explained,

> Before the company closed, we took vacations and entertained friends. I was making good money when the company just closed. During that time, my son was born and we had purchased a home, and we also had a 2-year-old daughter. When our lifestyle changed, our marriage fell apart. I worked three jobs to get financially stable, but we could not get our marriage on track after the layoff. I promised myself to have enough money saved for future layoffs.

John and Carl both believed that their marriages were off track because they worked too much to counteract the negative effects of sporadic and recurrent unemployment. John's comments were typical of the Black divorced men we interviewed:

> I worked too much and spent little time at home. I wasn't with other women but [rather was] working for my family. She was always complaining because I was not at home. Yet, we needed more material things. I left home at 7 a.m. and did not return until 10 p.m. I had to work because we had child care costs over $1,000 a month and monthly bills of $2,000.

In response to this paradoxical position, John stated,

> It is ironic that my efforts to provide for my family made me vulnerable to charges of being distant and uncaring. I told my wife that you can't have all these material things and have quality marital time.

John admitted that during his marriage, he suffered from ulcers and often had nightmares about being unemployed and having his family homeless, even though he had a college education.

Maurice, a 40-year-old car salesman divorced for 5 years, also explained,

> I was a provider and prided myself on being able to function in a hostile world. I was laid off twice in different cities when Whites refused to buy cars from me. During my marriage, I worked hard to have enough money to make it through periods of unemployment. . . . I spent more time working than focusing on home.

Maurice concluded,

> Since I did not inherit wealth, nor do I have knowledge of the stock market, the only way I know to make it to a middle class status is to work. So, I worked to save money for hard times. I even went to various cities to work, thinking that the material rewards would satisfy my ex-wife, Elaine. Apparently, it did not because she had an affair with a retired neighbor who gave her the attention she needed.

Other men reported that working too much interfered with the quality of their marriages and contributed to marital distress. For example, Alvin, a 36-year-old auto mechanic, revealed his schedule during his marriage. He reported, "I worked from 9 a.m. to 5 p.m. Monday through Friday. From 6 p.m. to 10 p.m., I painted houses and took care of neighbors' yards for extra money. On Saturdays I managed a club, and on Sundays I went to church." According to Alvin, he spent too much time working rather than focusing on his marriage to counteract the negative effects of unemployment. He assumed that his marriage would maintain itself because he was a good provider.

Periodic unemployment can profoundly threaten the functioning of Black families. Because education alone has failed to stabilize employment for Blacks, the relative unemployment gap between Blacks and Whites increases with a college degree. Consequently, the men represent the "working worried" who work several jobs to cushion the adverse effects of periodic unemployment and have little time to devote to the maintenance of a satisfying marriage. Insufficient shared time between spouses has been associated with higher rates of divorce. The strategies the men used to cope with economic marginality represent the tensions they faced in establishing economic security and their effect on marital stability in a society where a marriage often is viewed as deficient when one partner does not meet the need for companionship.

Education never has offered a profound solution to the Black man's dilemma in America, although Blacks view education as a pragmatic function to train people for work. For example, an education was one of the few attainable accomplishments for Blacks within a system of Jim Crow. Education also had special significance for Black men because of the pervasive notion that Blacks were ignorant and intellectually deficient.

Although Black men may acquire college educations, racism sustains and reinforces the privileges of White Americans. For example, Hacker (1992) reports that Black male college graduates end up just a few dollars ahead of White men who only attended high school. Hacker notes that the advice offered to Blacks to stay in school only assists them to move ahead of others of their own race. There is little evidence that spending more years in school will improve their position in relation to Whites.

Entrepreneurship and Family Instability

The disruption of the men's marriages also involved the struggle to obtain economic security through entrepreneurship. For example, Robert, a 48-year-old, was an employee counselor in the city government, where he met his spouse, Anne. He recalled the reason for his marriage: "I met Anne, this beautiful, intelligent woman, and 2 months later married her. We talked about wanting to start our own photography business."

Following the marriage, they moved from Washington, D.C., to Anne's hometown, a small southern town, to open up a photography studio. Robert was disappointed when the business failed, and he claimed that the financial loss caused the divorce. He explained,

> I had to market and promote the business in addition to being the guy in the darkroom. We closed the business 1 year after the move and lost about $60,000. Afterward, the marriage deteriorated and we grew apart.

Robert further explained that disagreements resulted from Anne's lack of interest in, and refusal to help with, the photography business.

> I was the photographer, the guy in the darkroom, and the promoter. I had little help from my wife, so the business failed. Anne basically said that she would be there for 8 hours [a day], but don't ask [her] to go out and market and meet people and politic and do what was necessary to keep the business going.

Thus, Robert described a generalized frustration in which the business loss caused dissatisfaction with himself, his life, and his marriage.

Similarly, James was a 35-year-old accountant who established his own consulting firm 5 years after his marriage. He attributed his divorce to the loss of a business and the additional burden of children. "We had never thought it all through in terms of the reality of the demands that we would have to face to make it all work," James explained. Marital strain first appeared when he invested so much energy into being successful. He said, "We were constantly angry, in bad moods, and emotionally drained since we were sinking so much money in a business and saw little profits." When the business failed and James lost $40,000 due to mismanagement, he became increasingly dissatisfied with the marriage:

> My ex-wife, Ellen, wasn't supportive of me, and we realized that what each needed from the other, the other was not in a position to give. We were still in love with each other, but we couldn't work things out. It got to the point [where] Ellen didn't want to fix dinner for me or she didn't want to be bothered with anything that was about taking care of me, her husband.

In addition, there were times when James felt that his wife was particularly lonesome and wanted him to spend the day at home because he had been working evenings and rarely saw her during the week. He refused, explaining that he was in the middle of important projects and was needed at work. He reasoned that Black entrepreneurs must work harder to be more successful than Black wage earners to amass wealth in America. Ellen, however, felt troubled because his job seemed to be more of a priority than the marriage. In assessing the cause of divorce, James remarked,

> I told Ellen that what we want should come last because we got two kids to raise. That meant I had to work to become economically stable. I did not have time to be attentive working 16 to 18 hours per day. Ellen's thing was that she should come first because she was the wife.

Approximately 90% of small businesses initiated by Black entrepreneurs experience bankruptcy within 36 months, and approximately 95% of Black-owned firms operate under sole ownership rather than as partnerships or corporations (Pinkney, 1993). Most Black-owned businesses operate with no full-time paid employees other than the owner. Less than 1% (0.3%) of all Black-owned firms gross receipts of more than one million dollars with an average of $37,392 in annual gross receipts (Pinkney, 1993). The major Black-owned businesses tend to concentrate in large urban areas with large Black populations (Hacker, 1992). The future of Black-owned businesses in small towns in which the respondents lived was not promising. Furthermore, 80% of all Black men who start their own businesses work 16 hours or more each day, which can cause considerable marital strain (Marable, 1994).

The Unemployment of Wives

The unemployment of wives emerged as a central source of marital discord and subsequent divorce. The experience of Luke, a 35-year-old building contractor, illustrates the relationship between spousal unemployment and marital instability. Luke's father played an important role as a strong male figure who took a great interest in the development of his son. He taught Luke the importance of being a responsible man and to value close relationships. Luke explained the reasons for his marriage:

> I had known my ex-wife, Dawn, for 3 years before we married and married her because I thought I was in love. I had just graduated from college a year earlier and had just moved to a new city, new job, and was starting out on my own.

Luke married a young woman whom he characterized as "liking to do the same things I like. We would go driving a lot and would do silly things." Luke's ex-wife, Dawn, was a nurse; she contributed 60% to the couple's monthly income. He reported, "The happiest times of my marriage were when Dawn and I were working; we were putting things together and building our lives." He vividly recalled the circumstances of Dawn's unemployment that led to their divorce after 7 years of marriage:

> After Dawn hurt her back from lifting patients, she had to quit work and had trouble resuming her nursing career. She was also blackballed by hospitals because they saw her as a troublemaker. She defended patients and confronted physicians who often would not recommend the same treatments for Blacks as for Whites. For 3 years, she put in applications all over the city without any success and then gave up. The bills started to pile up, and bill collectors called, demanding their money. At the same time, we were audited by the IRS [Internal Revenue Service] and owed back taxes. The marriage went downhill from there because I could not be the sole provider with a house payment, three kids to raise, two car payments, and pay[ing the] IRS. We lost our ability to talk. Instead, we argued.

Luke said that Dawn accused him of being selfish, irresponsible, and lazy. He remarked, "It was clear to me then that we were two very different people whose outlooks on life, values, and goals were so dissimilar. During those times, we had drag-out fights."

One month after the divorce, Dawn was diagnosed with myasthenia gravis, a relatively rare and grave disease of unknown cause. Luke was confused because Dawn decompensated postdivorce. Subsequently, he suffered extreme guilt postdivorce over an inability to support his family solely on his income and was, therefore, confronted with a sick ex-wife and a failed marriage. He felt a continued obligation to help Dawn, and he periodically gave her money. As a result, Luke felt no subsequent relief or sense of closure following the divorce.

Other men also identified the unemployment of wives as a significant marital stressor that contributed to divorce. Roscoe, a 38-year-old construction worker, explained,

> I was in love and wanted to settle down. I was 29 and my ex-wife was 20 years old when we married. I wanted a family of my own, and Cynthia seemed like the perfect woman to marry. I married a woman who was "my best friend" because we grew up together. She knew me better than any person on this earth, and I knew she was a little stubborn, but I believed we would be married for the rest of our lives.

Cynthia was a postal worker, and he explained the circumstances that led to the divorce, which involved the birth of his son and the subsequent unemployment of his wife:

> After our son was born, Cynthia quit work [and] the marriage fell apart because I could not give her all the things she needed at that time. I wanted her to be happy, but I could not afford a washer and dryer or even baby furniture. . . . She became frustrated because I could not provide the things she needed, and our marriage went downhill. After the baby was born, all communication was gone. Even though money can't buy love, Cynthia felt like she could find somebody else who could give her the material things she needed.

Peter, a 39-year-old factory worker divorced for 4 years, recalled,

> I was paying installments on a large medical bill when my ex-wife, Jackie, was fired. . . . What a blow to our economic base. Because she could not find work, I borrowed $10,000 to help with bills, and to repay the loan I worked more. . . . We argued constantly about money, and the arguments worsened over time. I saw a cold side of her that I'd never seen before. Jackie's unemployment marked the beginning of the deterioration of the marriage, and it slowly fell apart.

Peter further noted,

> After the jobs, I felt tired, but I hated to go home. I hated to argue constantly about bills, and it got to the point where Jackie was always coming at me about bills accumulating and bill collectors demanding money.

On the other hand, Matt, a 42-year-old emergency room technician, reported that when his ex-wife began to work in an effort to acquire the material possessions that Matt was unable to afford, his marriage subsequently deteriorated:

> My ex-wife, Hazel, was not happy with our financial situation, even though I worked two jobs. She wanted more than what I was able to give her. She joined the military to get money to buy a house and get some other things she wanted. We had a beautiful relationship until then; we were there for each other. While I worked, cooked, and got my kids ready for school, Hazel was in another city. After a year of this arrangement, she decided that she did not want the responsibility of a husband and kids. So, she never returned home, and [she] purchased a house in another city.

Black women have participated in the labor force at a higher rate than have White women due to the uncertain conditions that characterize the earnings of Black men. For example, two incomes often are necessary to equal that of one White breadwinner. Thus, wives' unemployment often precipitates disagreements over which bills to pay, which bills to defer, and which items to purchase, suggesting that wives' unemployment generates marital discord in what husbands described as compatible marriages. The response to the unemployment of former spouses ricocheted into marital distress and subsequent divorce. This finding reinforces the argument that the stability of the Black family structure and the employment pattern of Black wives are inextricably linked.

Consumerism Incompatibility

Evidence suggests that divergent attitudes about money are the most frequent areas of marital disagreement (Spanier & Thompson, 1987). Without exception, men complained that their former wives spent too much money on children, and some resented their wives' spending money on extravagant items such as fur coats and expensive jewelry. In their opinion, these spending habits made their marriages irrevocably unsalvageable. For example, Curtis, whose marriage ended after 6 years, reported that his wife, Julie, spent considerably more money on clothes than he could accept. Curtis always had worked and believed that hard work and saving money were virtues. His comments illustrate the influence of divergent spending practices on marital stability:

> I married my high school sweetheart and best friend, Julie. I would have been married to her today if we could agree on money issues. We both worked two jobs because we had two children to raise. Julie had a daughter when I married her. When I received a better job, Julie got overboard with spending money. The marriage changed drastically.

Although Curtis's family operated on a small income even after he received a "better" job, the family still was faced with numerous spending decisions. In fact, he said,

> Our arguments were always about money . . . and the money was not enough for Julie. She wanted my 5-year-old son to wear tennis shoes that cost over $100, and we purchased a large-screen television set that cost over $3,000. We were over our heads in debt.

Lennie, a 41-year-old high school teacher, also revealed that divergent values about consumerism subsequently led to divorce. Despite his former spouse's desire for a fur coat, he refused to invest money in an item he considered extravagant. Although he admitted that his former wife had expensive tastes and grew up in an "upper class southern family," Lennie's opposition to the purchase of a fur coat led to intensive marital distress and subsequent divorce:

> I made it clear that I was not going to buy my ex-wife, Cheryl, a mink because it seemed extravagant. We had numerous arguments about this. I had no qualms about spending $3,000 or $4,000 on her, but I would not spend that much money on a mink coat.

In explaining his values in regard to consumerism, Lennie noted,

> I would spend a couple of thousand dollars on something that we could get some pleasure out of—like a boat—whereas a mink coat represents that I am better than other folks. I would not contribute to that. My marriage deteriorated because Cheryl was unhappy about my refusal to buy her a mink coat.

For Lennie, the fur coat represented bragging of one's economic accomplishments, which symbolized superiority over others and offended his basic sense of egalitarianism. Lennie believed that a fur coat would elevate him to a higher plane and would remove him from the community of Black brotherhood. Lennie's tie to Blackness here rarely was perceived as the militant self-conscious pride of being Black; rather, it was perceived as deeper, more profound ties to beloved figures of childhood.

On the other hand, Cheryl believed that the fur coat represented social status in the context of social marginality. Thus, the conflict in Lennie's marriage involved dissimilarity in consumerism values. Other men also reported marital conflict involving divergent views about the purchases of houses, automobiles, and furnishings.

AUTOCRATIC SPENDING DECISIONS

Marriages frequently were disrupted when former spouses spent money without the respondents' knowledge. The men described their wives' compulsive shopping as a "spending addiction" that further exacerbated marital problems. As Roger, who had been married for 10 years and divorced for 3 years, explained,

> My ex-wife Doris's biggest problem was that she loved to spend money. She would buy clothes and hide them over at her play mother's house and bring them in slowly so I would not see them. She's got to have clothes . . . I mean [a] closet full of clothes with tags on them. I encouraged her to save money, stick to the budget, and we argued constantly about this. Doris would write checks without telling me, and that really upset me.

Roger also reported that Doris failed to pay bills on time and accumulated a huge debt.

In half of the interviews, the men complained that the spending practices of ex-spouses caused them considerable physiological as well as marital distress. This was a representative remark by the men interviewed:

> I have had upset stomachs, headaches, and high blood pressure because my ex-wife saw what Whites had and spent considerable money trying to keep up with them. Because I could not provide things she believed were needed, this created numerous problems.

The consumer practices of some Blacks may be related to the way in which they cope with being perceived as culturally disadvantaged, intellectually inferior, and linguistically deprived by a large number of Whites (Wilkinson, 1977). In fact, according to one study, Black households spend a larger proportion of their incomes on fashion than does any other group, spending more than $18 billion for clothes and accessories and another $748 million for cosmetics in 1993 (hooks, 1990).

Indeed, the social marginality and discrediting of Blacks often is manifest in the excessive use of designer clothing, expensive jewelry, and elaborate furnishings (Wilkinson, 1977). For innumerable Blacks, extravagant clothing conveys social acceptance by symbolizing participation in a White consumer-oriented culture. It is probable that in coping with social subordination, Blacks often use expensive clothing to acquire a sense of self-worth. Operating in this manner, clothes often elevate the self-images of Blacks. Paradoxically, whereas such attire provides increased self-esteem, it may weaken marital cohesiveness because few Black families can afford expensive consumption patterns.

Moreover, Black families are affected by American mass culture models of conspicuous consumption. The need to possess, consume, and purchase new items is a reflection of the influence of the dominant society on Black marriages. Due to exposure to a capitalistic system that emphasizes material success rather than human qualities, Black marriages often are transformed into an institution with an emphasis on the acquisition of more and better material goods. However, this philosophy is detrimental to Black marriages because money has not given Blacks a sense of mastery over conditions similar to those of Whites.

The respondents believed that their former spouses' autocratic spending decisions challenged their authority as heads of their households. The men's demand for domestic respect reflects how the system of race and class oppression shapes the context in which men construct gender ideology. For example, Black marriages often are characterized as more egalitarian than White marriages. Black husbands are more likely than their White counterparts to share housework and child care. However, there is a common folk notion that Black men ought to have domestic authority because it validates their identities in the context of social marginality. Brent's comments illustrate this:

I was really hurt when my wife did not take my advice about saving money. The home is the only place where my words, as a Black man, are worth listening to. As a Black man, I received very little respect in the broader society, but I expected my wife to treat me with respect by honoring my decisions about spending money.

Other men also reported that when their wives failed to consider their economic advice, it affected their self-esteem and undermined the stability of their marriages. They reasoned that if not at home, then where is a Black man who constantly is socially discredited to experience himself as a person whose words have weight and who is worth listening to?

THE IMPORTANCE OF DEMOCRATIC SPENDING DECISIONS

Honor and respect from wives become more important, and humiliation becomes more unbearable, for Black men because they confront the task of establishing families in a nation in which they encounter a latter-day version of problems endured by slave families. The question is, how can one build a family when the institutional structure of the nation makes it difficult for families in general, and Black families in particular, to serve its primary purpose—the protection of family members?

Black fathers often cannot protect their children from exposure to criminal elements in their neighborhoods because law enforcement authorities show little capability for the suppression of crime in Black neighborhoods. Despite paying hefty taxes, these fathers often are unable to improve the quality of their children's educations because educational boards generally are more responsive to White parents than to Black parents.

Consequently, for a large number of Black men, it is not so much a matter of overcoming the impediments of obtaining manhood as it is a constant struggle to feel it as their own. Whereas White men regard their manhood as an ordained right, Black men often are engaged in a struggle for its possession. For example, some Black men are born into families in which daily survival has been problematic. Because they often have seen their parents' struggle to survive, their work lives generally are not planned; they happen due to necessity.

By contrast, White men are entitled to manhood at birth and by the possession of their skin color. This affirms their masculinity, and whatever their individual limitations, America will not systematically erect barriers to their economic achievement. For a White man born into a middle class family, the sky is the limit; his dreams are not barricaded by constraints. As he grows, he observes men who work at prestigious jobs. At home, at school, and in the neighborhood, he is encouraged to test the limits of his ability and to reach for the stars. He has personal contacts to help push his career along and to plan for the future. Thus, the need for some Black men to exert domestic control represents a response to their lack of power, wealth, prestige, and status in a capitalistic society, and these factors are inextricably interwoven with definitions of masculinity. Although Black male domestic domination increases the self-esteem of Black males, household domination frequently results in marital failure. Consequently, Black male domination on the personal level is intertwined with social disenfranchisement on the structural level to influence the stability of Black marriages.

Too Many Family Demands

The continuation of bonds with members of the family of origin also provoked marital discord. For example, Larry, a 34-year-old city administrator, spent too much time with his sick mother, and his ex-wife, Pat, subsequently filed for divorce. Because Larry's mother was diagnosed with colon cancer 6 months after the marriage, he struggled with a conflict between a personal obligation toward his sick mother and the wishes of his wife. He vividly conveyed a sense of frustration:

> I wasn't spending time with Pat but [rather was spending it] with my mother. I stayed in the hospital with my mom for 10 days. Pat divorced me; she could not understand that my mother's cancer really upset me. I only have one mother. Pat would say this is not a marriage. Then I would say, maybe it is not a marriage. At that time, I just felt that Pat lost respect for my mother.

He further noted,

> I guess another woman broke up my marriage because I was in love with my mother. Since I only have one mother, I had to be with her during her

hospitalization. I was afraid she might die, and I didn't want her to die alone.

Larry also believed that Pat lost respect for his mother:

I felt that Pat should have accepted the whole package, my mother and me. Pat refused to visit the hospital with me. If she could not accept my mother, then she could not respect me. The key point was that I was not with another lady.

Consequently, Larry developed a generalized disinterest in the marriage and believed that Pat should have informed him of her views about his family before marriage and that Pat failed to understand the importance of his mother in his life.

EXTENSIVE FAMILY INVOLVEMENT

Similarly, extensive involvement of kin in family decisions created intense marital distress. Lawrence, a 36-year-old probation officer, explained, "My ex-wife's family was close and had such a strong presence in our affairs that I felt like I was being debunked all the time." For instance, despite Lawrence's desire to name his daughter Harriet after Harriet Tubman, his ex-wife's family made it clear that the baby would be named Laquita. Lawrence explained, "After the conflict over my daughter's name, I knew I was in for a bitter power struggle with Frances' family that would last for years. And it eventually led to a divorce." Similarly, Leon was asked the causes of his divorce, and he said,

My mother-in-law and I couldn't do anything about it. When I objected, Carol and I had arguments. Carol allowed her mother and sisters to make crucial decisions in our marriage that created extreme marital distress.

Truman also reported,

I think the straw that broke the camel's back was when Barbara's sister showed up with her child—unemployed and [with] no intentions of getting a job. She wanted me to take care of her and her child in addition to trying to run my own household. Barbara, of course, sided with her sister.

Barbara's family represented the kin-base cooperative network preva-lent in a large number of Black families. Truman, therefore, continued to maintain a sense of loyalty toward Barbara's sister by supporting her and the child for 3 years. Even after the divorce, Truman contin-ued to support his sister-in-law's child. He explained,

> The kid has had a rough life. At 9 years old, he was picked up for vandalizing, and I paid for the damages he caused. Since then, he's been in and out of foster care, and nobody really cares about him; he really has nobody except me. I really feel for him because he's been through a lot, and I try to give him as much support as I can because I don't want him to end up in jail.

The respondents also provided financial and emotional support to their own family members; thus, their wives accused them of placing the needs of their families of origin above those of present family members. Other men reported tensions inherent in extensive familial bonds including difficulty finding time to spend with kin, problems in allocation of financial support to extended family members, exposure to the increased number of problems of family members who also were coping with economic and social marginality, coping with unwelcome and unsolicited advice from kin, and confronting the incongruence of views with respect to the socialization of children.

Studies of Black kinship networks indicate that they are more exten-sive and significant to the Black community than to the White commu-nity because they help to cushion the effects of social disenfranchisement by providing valuable supportive and instrumental functions. The ser-vices provided by Black extended families include sharing of economic resources, child care, and advice. in addition, Black extended family members have assisted in socializing children and have been a source of strength for generations. Despite the resources provided by kin net-works, extended family members can create strain within Black mar-riages already stressed by unstable economic and social conditions.

Personality Incompatibility

According to the men, the jealous behavior of former spouses was the most frequent behavioral characteristic that created marital distress.

Actions characterized by jealousy were associated with pervasive distrust in the relationships. Gerald depicted the following pattern: "Molly always accused me of seeing other women, but she could not tell me who those women were. As a result, I stopped playing tennis or jogging to counteract her unreasonable jealousy."

Prior to the divorce, Gerald separated for 1 year, thinking that Molly's jealousy would cease. However, Gerald looked out of his window one day and saw Molly standing across the street watching him. On another occasion, Molly showed up unannounced at midnight to see whether he had been dating someone else. Over time, the behavior of Molly developed into a disturbing pattern, and he subsequently filed for divorce because he felt imprisoned by Molly's "insane" jealousy.

Other men also reported that former spouses doubted their commitment to marriage. For example, Maurice reported,

> The bottom line is that I'm a Black male, and Black women frequently believe the stereotypes society have about Black men such as being womanizers who are by nature destined to be uncommitted to marriage. So, Elaine often became jealous when I had business meetings with women, talked to them on the phone, and consulted about buying cars.

In assessing the situation, Maurice stated,

> The truth was, I felt obligated to Elaine and my son and daughter in a way I can't explain. I felt an obligation so strong that I would feel ashamed sneaking around with other women, so Elaine's irrational ideas frightened me.

Constant surveillance of the men's movements by former spouses also demonstrated the lack of trust in their relationships. Todd explained the actions of his former spouse, Rachael: "To determine if I was at work, Rachael called constantly. This drove the secretary crazy. Even if I was in a meeting, Rachael expected me to answer the phone to confirm my presence and to have long conversations with her." Other men reported that former spouses called restaurants to determine whether they were in business meetings, secured friends to spy on their behavior after work, and doubted their fidelity. Black women's perceptions of their husbands' betrayal might be explained, in part, by the sex ratio hypothesis. The imbalanced sex ratio (i.e., the number of men per 100 women) remains about 5 points below that of Whites, even when corrected for an undercount of Black men. In other words, there are approximately 1.4 million more Black females than Black males in the United States. For those Black women in the 22- to 25-year age range, the male-to-female ratio is as low as 85.6 males per 100 females, compared to 100.5 for Whites in the same age range.

The imbalance in the sex ratio is due to a number of factors. Black young men have comparatively high mortality rates, and many are confined to prisons. The high homicide rate affecting Black men, combined with the disproportionate number of deaths of Black males from cancer, heart disease, strokes, cirrhosis of the liver, and accidents, also contributes to the severe Black sex ratio imbalance. The increased number of Black men who are attracted to non-Black women for potential mates further reduces the pool of available men for Black women. In 1985, the number of Black male-White female couples in the United States was more than eight times greater than that of Black female-White male couples (Williams, 1983). Moreover, Black men constitute approximately 6% of the general population but represent 50% of male prisoners in local, state, and federal jails. Approximately 46% of Black men between 16 and 62 years of age are not in the labor force, and 32% of Black working men have incomes below the poverty level (Staples, 1985).

Considering the number of Black men who are gay, already married, or unacceptable as mates, the male-to-female ratio for Blacks is further reduced. In fact, Staples (1978a) suggests that in practical terms, there might be no more than one Black man for every five single Black women in the United States. Divorce rates are higher when the ratio of women to men is higher. The male shortage in the Black population has been a major contributor to marital decline, adultery, out-of-wedlock births, and less commitment among Black men to relationships.

One presumable consequence of the low supply of Black men is the erosion of basic trust in marriages that erupts through possessive jealousy. A Black jealous wife might be conforming to societal pressure for a monogamous marriage while expressing resentment and frustration with the shortage of Black men as well as the lack of desirable men with whom to form monogamous marriages.

It is possible that, given the quality of the Black marriageable pool, the respondents' wives might have felt pressured to "hold onto" their employed husbands. As Larry poignantly expressed, "Black women are depressed because there aren't nearly enough eligible and sane Black men to go around, and that critical shortage is making them desperate and jealous."

INTIMACY VERSUS AUTONOMY

Another personality characteristic associated with marital distress involved the degree to which wives expected intimacy versus the respondents' need for autonomy. Edward, who had been married for 8 years and divorced for 1 year, explained,

> I left my ex-wife, Delores, because I was making her miserable. I left thinking she would find somebody because I was gone all the time. I was ripping and running and knew I wasn't going to quit. I thought I was having fun. I left and went to California, Florida, and New Jersey to work on various construction jobs. The money was good, and I liked doing construction work. Delores wanted more of a stable home than I could give.

Other men reported that the ability to meet their wives' expectations for companionship was prohibited not only by their work schedules but also by an inability to make sacrifices for their marriages. They often indicated that it was difficult for them to subordinate their needs to those of their partners, as represented by the statement, "A Black man's got to do what a Black man's got to do to survive in a hostile world."

Failure to Negotiate Conflict

Violent solutions to marital problems have been incorporated into the mainstream culture of the United States. One terrifying aspect of this fact of American life is that the incidence of domestic violence increases every year. In Atlanta, Georgia, a predominantly Black city, 60% of all police calls on the night shift are domestic disputes. Black male-female conflict leads to the assault and murder of Black females at a greater rate than do the intimate relationships of any other racial/ethnic group in the United States (Gullattee, 1979). Black women are more likely to strike back at their abusive husbands, whereas Black husbands are more likely to assault their wives and cause bodily harm (Plass, 1993).

Identifying the correlates of intimate violence among Blacks, Gullattee (1979) points to the escalating violence in the general population. Violent acts intrude into Black homes through television. Surveys show that acts of violence occur every 3½ minutes on television. During prime-time evening hours, Blacks have their choices of endless depictions of death and violence. According to Gerbner (1990), Blacks watch television 39% more than do all other American households. The cumulative message of television is that solutions to marital disputes should involve violence.

In this study, the most common violent situation involved both partners and included verbal and physical abuse. The following represents a typical case. Alvin, a 36-year-old auto mechanic, emphasized that his ex-wife, Maria, was a "loving, intelligent woman who overreacted to trivial events." He viewed his race as creating particular stress for his Puerto Rican wife because her family objected to the marriage. "The first 2 years of my marriage were really good because Maria was willing to do whatever needed to be done," he asserted. Alvin described an act of violence that centered around a car. To Alvin, a new car symbolized achievement of the American dream:

> We had just bought a $15,000 car. I had experienced layoffs for the past 3 years of my marriage. I worked two jobs, and sometimes three jobs, so that we could have a new car. I wanted a car that was loaded with everything—a CD player, sunroof, you know, the works.

Alvin suffered from a legacy of deprivation and remembered begging for food at a local grocery store as a regular part of his childhood. He quit school to work and to provide for his younger siblings. For a period in his life, he said, "I went crazy, got a girl pregnant who later had an abortion, and hung in the streets." One day, he realized that "I didn't want to end up like my friends in the neighborhood who were in prison or dead. I knew I had to set my own direction." Alvin received his high school GED and became an automobile mechanic. To Alvin, a new car symbolized achievement of the American dream.

Alvin recalled reactions when his ex-wife, Maria, broke the high beams in the car:

> Maria flickered the high beams of the car off and on. She finally broke it. Since I'm paying for this car by working two full-time jobs, I asked her not to do that car like that. Maria grabbed my shirt and was fighting. I hit her. Maria called the police, and we separated for 1 month, then later got back together.

Alvin reported that he felt guilty about beating Maria and was conciliatory the following 6 months. Although they still had arguments, he stated, "I never laid a hand on her again." Two years later, when the couple had a heated argument in the kitchen, Maria grabbed a knife and stabbed him, resulting in Alvin being disabled. Other men pointed to scars and bruises caused by domestic violence. Several men referred to scars on their foreheads; others revealed old bullet wounds, described swollen eyes, and revealed lost teeth.

In several cases, minor attacks escalated into major physical assaults, and experiencing domestic violence once often made it easier for couples to do it again. For example, Vince recalled an abusive incident in which his ex-wife, Sandy, threw a model airplane, one of his cherished possessions, at him. He recalled,

> Sandy I were arguing, then she threw my model airplane and broke it. Few Blacks or Whites own that model. She grabbed me and tore off my shirt. Afterward, I grabbed her by the throat, lifted her off the ground and threw her. I felt so bad, I felt like an animal. I cried and cried because I was taught never to hit a woman. I grew up around five sisters and was taught never to hit a woman. So, I knew at this point that the marriage was over.

Then Vince told Sandy, "I plan to file for a divorce." He left town to visit relatives in another state—without her. Sandy packed up their 7- and 8-year-old daughters and took them to stay with relatives for a few days. On Vince's return, Sandy met him at the door and shot him in the shoulder. In analyzing the incident, Vince said,

Sandy shot me to show that she really did not love me. I wanted the marriage to work, but she wanted to get out of the marriage. That was the only option Sandy believed she had. Sandy just couldn't tell me she didn't want to be married anymore.

Philip, a 47-year-old who worked in real estate, reported,

We got into an argument over something very insignificant. Pam, my ex-wife, grabbed a lamp and hit me hard over the head. Then she took the stereo and pushed it on my hand. I knew that I had a temper and if I hit her, she'd call the cops and I would get locked up, and I didn't want to get a criminal record. All my life, as a Black man, I have tried to avoid any involvement with the police. They target Black men for abuse. Plus, I work in real estate and didn't want my reputation messed up over a domestic problem.

Philip explained further that the altercation he had with Pam eventually led to her calling the police. He said,

Pam kept swinging. I grabbed her wrists to keep her from hitting me. Then she took a bottle and gashed me in the head. I got madder and slapped her in the face. She ran to the phone and called the police while the children screamed. The police took me to the hospital to get stitches and then to jail. I stayed in jail for 5 days.

Afterward, Philip found a lawyer and filed for divorce. Philip assumed much of the blame for the incident, and even after filing for a divorce he tried to dissuade Pam from leaving him and asked that she forgive him. "It takes two to fight. I was just as much of the blame. There [are] always two sides of the story. I still love Pam. We grew up together and have known each other all of our lives," he said.

The violence caused over a trivial event represents, in part, an attempt to establish an identity in the context of race and class oppression. Domestic violence in the Black community can be viewed as an attempt to cope with long-term frustration associated with social subordination. Black men and women often believe the promise that if they make sure they are qualified and work twice as hard as Whites, then Blacks can be anything they want to be in mainstream America. However, the promise often is not kept, even though some Black men change their appearances and personalities to try to assimilate. Thus, Black men often feel that although they are unable to control how society treats them, they should be able to control their women. A large number of Black men view violence as a means by which they can demonstrate their masculinity because most conventional channels of achievement are blocked.

Gelles (1984) notes that in most cases, a marriage license also functions as a hitting license. As John noted, "Some of my friends told me to give Rita a good beating to put her in her place." Numerous incidents of violence between married partners often are considered by couples to be normal, routine, and generally acceptable. Moreover, the patriarchal system allows a man the right of ownership to some degree over the property and people that comprise his household. John remarked, "It is scary because it is almost normative for Black men to use physical force to control Black women, and until Black men redefine what it means to be a man, there always will be domestic violence."

Similarly, Millette (1993) reports that among West Indian men who migrated to the United States, some use threats of violence, withhold economic support, and/or employ blackmail to control their wives.

BATTERED HUSBANDS

Several men believed that they were battered husbands, experiencing physical and verbal abuse from former spouses. They indicated that there is little emotional support for abused Black husbands because men are perceived as being tough, strong, and prone to be physically abusive. These men often believed that they were perceived as henpecked husbands when revealing physical abuse. Vincent said,

> I made a conscious decision not to hit Sally because I did not want to be charged as an abuser. But Sally certainly abused me. On one occasion, she took a lamp and hit me in the back when I tried to leave. On another occasion, she put sugar in my gas tank and broke my car windows when I tried to move out. I guess she wanted to hurt something that I cherished.

Bernie, who assumed a martyr complex during his marriage, said,

> I was actually afraid of Shelia. But who would believe that a Black man would act in self-defense? So, I tolerated her name-calling and tendency to punish me when I did not do what she wanted. Like, she cut my tires, slapped me in the face, and tried to poison me when I refused to do what

she wanted. Hitting Shelia was something that never crossed my mind. I was clear that I would never have a knock-down, drag-out fight. Even though Shelia and I had drag-out arguments, I said what I had to say and left the house.

AN EXPLANATION FOR BLACK
MARITAL CONFLICT

Conflict is common in most marriages and often leads to clarification of issues and to extension of the relationship into new areas. Thus, the question is not whether disputes occur in marriages but rather why Black spouses often fail to compromise and to resolve conflict. One reason might be that noncompromising behavior and a "stubborn attitude" have symbolized strength for some Blacks. For example, Ben stated,

> White people have a way out when things go sour and don't seem to hit rock-bottom. They always have somebody to rescue them and to make excuses for their behavior. I've had to be tough and noncompromising to gain respect in this society. Society is about making Black men feel like second-class citizens.

Allen also explained,

> I pay a price for integrating into mainstream academia. That price is humiliation. When I slip, White colleagues often say, "See, we gave him a chance, but he is incompetent." In coping with a hostile world, it affects the way I relate to women.

Allen recalled of a number of Black professors who were denied tenure, even though they had the same qualifications as Whites who were granted tenure. He elaborated,

> Black Ph.D.'s are leaving academia because their self-confidence has been eroded. Success in academia is tied directly to one's psychological state. But when Black men are constantly battling racial myths that require a huge psychological expenditure of energy, they are tired and angry. Black men may be noncompromising because they just don't have the energy to do otherwise. Unlike White women, much more is required of Black women, or of a woman who is involved with a Black man, since they are judged by their skin color with numerous stereotypes rather than by their educational attainment and job skills.

Finally, Brent reported,

> It is hard to be a sensitive Black man because there are so many stressors, like having to be twice as good as a mediocre White man to acquire the same job. To cope, I've had to be noncompromising to get building contracts from the state and city governments. So for me, it has been difficult to compromise on a personal level.

A defiant behavioral style, characterized by a refusal to accept the subservient position allocated to Blacks, has been a response to racial stereotyping and institutional discrimination. Because Whites have a racial privilege whereby American society conveys the message that their race is valued, Blacks often have developed obstinate attitudes to reconcile their racial status with feelings of dignity and self-worth (Genovese, 1976; Grier & Cobb, 1968).

Even though noncompromising behavior has been a survival strategy used to cope with being socially discredited, it also has been associated with the deterioration of marriages (Gottman & Krotkoff, 1989). For the men in this study, the paradox of adopting survival strategies to maintain self-worth and dignity and their effects on marital stability often was at the center of marital distress and contributed to divorce.

Differences in Values

SPIRITUAL INCOMPATIBILITY

According to the respondents, differences in religious practices also affected marital stability. For example, Ben's desire for spiritual freedom and autonomy clashed with his wife's emphasis on church attendance as an expression of spirituality. Ben, who also described himself as a religious person, explained,

> I realized that I had selected a mate not taking into account whether or not my spiritual values would conflict with her values. In fact, when I reclaimed a higher spiritual consciousness, the marriage ended. I saw that materialism was the basis for Etta's values versus the religious values in my life.

Solomon, who evaluated his former wife, Kaye, on her potential to
mother, stated,

> I have God in my life, but Kaye did not; therefore, she did not know how
> to treat someone like me, who really loved her. Our differences in
> commitment to God and what that means certainly strained the marriage.

Willy, who married because it was something to do, also illustrated
the dissimilarity of religious commitment and its effects on marital
stability:

> When Donna joined a fundamental religious sect, the Church of God, she
> stopped socializing and wanted me to stop smoking and drinking and [to]
> join the church. I felt frustrated, like I was giving up my life, which created
> a number of arguments. One day, I got tired of her nagging me to go to
> church and moved out.

Church attendance historically has been an important source of
support for a number of Blacks. The Black church has reinforced
values and behaviors leading to fulfillment of expectations regarding
conjugal behavior. Blacks also share a religious tradition dating to
Africa, where the sacred and secular are inseparable. However, the
inability of spouses to appreciate differences in spiritual expressions
and practices contributed to disagreements and marital disruptions.

VALUE INCOMPATIBILITY

In addition, some men expressed a lack of personal fulfillment and
marital happiness because their value systems differed vastly from those
of their spouses. Stanley, who stated in Chapter 2 that he assessed a
woman's maternal potential as a characteristic in a future mate, said,

> The only concern Paula had was raising children. She occupied her mind
> with the latest makeup and fashions. She could not or did not want to
> understand the world around her. We were two different people. We had
> arguments about this, and she could not understand my need to read, to
> visit art galleries, and to visit libraries, and I could not understand her
> need to watch TV talk shows, wear the latest fashion trends, and dance
> at trendy nightclubs. We drifted further and further apart, battling against
> extreme differences.

In commenting on value differences in his marriage, Clyde noted, "I am a very ambitious person. I believe a woman should always strive to better herself, and Betty did not want to do that. So, we ended up not wanting the same things." Variations on this theme expressed by other men included "I grew professionally and knew where I was going in life, and my ex-wife did not."

On the other hand, Vance, who viewed love as no hassles, could not understand Ella's need to engage in political and sociological discussions, to visit the library, and to read. Ella accused him of having no knowledge of his potential to grow and to expand intellectually. He explained,

> My main goal was to finish high school and go to trade school to be a hospital technician. As far as the future was concerned, I had no desire to go to college, and Ella wanted a college-educated man. She wanted a "buppie," a single Black heterosexual male with a job, a white-collar job, so she left me.

In assessing his divorce experience, Vance said,

> Ella talked about her career all the time, like [it was] all there was to life. She liked to hang around her White friends, dress up, go to fancy restaurants, and drink white wine. I liked to barbecue, invite people over, drink beer, and watch TV westerns. I socialized mostly with my family, and she socialized with people from work. We started going out alone, and that heightened tensions even more in our home. Our clash in values caused frequent arguments and distress, and one day we both realized that we were making each other miserable. There was nothing we could talk about, and I think that my ex-wife just got tired of me, so she took the kids and left.

Similarly, Ernell, who retired from the military, reported,

> My marriage ended due to conflicts over values. Dee devoted a lot of energy to get me to cooperate with her game plan, that is, how to get me secured in some professional career that included a Ph.D. and relocating to the East Coast with a lifestyle that included designer furniture and a vacation home. She was recruiting me for certain middle class qualities that included an Ivy League education and a high-status professional career. We argued about this because I was happy being a sergeant in the military.

REASONS FOR VALUE INCOMPATIBILITY

Although a spouse with a college degree has been highly desirable, a generation of Black men and women have married from varying class backgrounds. This situation has been attributed to the importance placed on teaching as an ideal career for Black women and the lack of professional career opportunities for Black men. In fact, during the Jim Crow era, a number of Black men with professional law degrees worked in the post office, and great promising Black talent was locked out of professional careers.

Whereas few Blacks in the past expected to marry doctors or lawyers, their ideal mates were "good" men or women who worked in stable blue-collar jobs. In fact, during segregation, Black couples often married each other with no money and few resources, believing that the capacity to appreciate and give love was the legitimate measure of a person's worth. As Blacks assimilated into the economic market, similar status has become a prerequisite to forming and continuing an intimate relationship.

Summary

Clarification of the divorce experience of Black men is important in understanding the nature of divorce. Such identification highlights how the divorce experience of Blacks is both similar to and different from that of the non-Black population; that is, there are distinctive patterns of the Black male divorce experience that have emerged here. Most striking are patterns that involve socioeconomic variables. The struggle to maintain economic stability and consumer incompatibility had a profound effect on marital stability. These patterns suggest that the influence of other socioeconomic-related factors, rather than simply the lack of income, affects the stability of Black marriages. This finding also suggests that variables related to finances such as consumerism incompatibility, autocratic spending decisions, and debt accumulation may create more strain on Black marriages than on White marriages because money has not given Blacks a sense of mastery over conditions similar to those of Whites.

In the area of personality incompatibility, we find that marriage instability is more likely to occur when the former spouses exhibit extreme jealous behavior and in circumstances where the husbands' need for autonomy clashes with the wives' need for intimacy. This assumes more significance when the composition of Black households is considered, as a much larger percentage of Blacks are divorced compared to Whites. The fact that a group already plagued by marital instability should have a higher risk of marital distress due to spouses' jealous behavior and husbands' need for autonomy is significant.

The most striking factor of the men's divorce experience related to the number of violent episodes that contributed to divorce. There may be several reasons for the violence that the men reported in their marriages. First, the use of the police to mediate domestic disputes is less common among Blacks. Moreover, Black men and women are reluctant to call the police to have their husbands or wives arrested and jailed because of the racial injustice in the criminal justice system. The unwillingness of Black men and women to use a White-dominated system of social control may increase the likelihood of the occurrence of marital violence.

Second, Blacks are less likely to use organizations for men's and women's groups for divorce. Blacks often view these services as run by and for Whites and as addressing issues pertaining to Whites. Given that counseling services have been found to reduce marital conflict (Lamanna & Riedmann, 1994), the reluctance or inability of Blacks to use this resource might be a contributing factor as to why conflict erupts into acts of violence.

Of interest is the finding that religious incompatibility strained marriages. This finding is significant when the historical importance of the Black church is considered. The Black church has been the most important positive force among Blacks and has provided opportunities for Black men to assume leadership roles denied them in the larger society. Furthermore, it has provided the constituency necessary for Black male political and social leaders in mainstream society. The fact that an institution that historically has provided Blacks a mechanism for survival and coping with social marginality creates marital strain is important. This pattern suggests the possible influence of factors such as a widening Black gender gap in the importance attached to religious beliefs and practices. In fact, Tinney (1981) argues that the Black church is a women's institution, as women compose the largest proportion of its membership and an even larger proportion of its active participants.

Value incompatibility underscores the complex nature of Black relationships in a postmodern racist capitalistic society. Similar to Whites, Blacks are influenced by the American way of life of the reduction of individuals to objects. Mass consumption has transformed marriages in general, and Black marriages in particular, into commodities. In a postmodern capitalistic society, marriages in general have become essentially those of alienated spouses. As Fromm (1956) observes, American capitalism has promoted a hedonistic culture that promises materialism and luxury sustained by the way of life of the marketing system of business.

The market perspective of relationships eliminates the traditional Black way of life of care and service to others, where racial cooperation was emphasized instead of individual ethos. As one respondent expressed, "People should go back to their ancestors because they are lost in a White culture." Indeed, the traditional values of the Black experience were based on the equality of people irrespective of status. The ideal of all men's and women's equality was at the center of Blacks' basic human philosophy, and it extended to the selection of marital partners. For generations, the concept of equality functioned to obscure Black class differences, to promote racial solidarity, and to deemphasize Black marital status heterogeneity.

Because Blacks have a recent history of relative economic deprivation, they might place an emphasis on material success. As a result, the car one drives, the clothes one wears, the residence where one lives, and the education degrees one obtains often are translated into requirements for marriage and are viewed as prerequisites for marital stability. The saturation of a market morality and a history of relative financial deprivation often eliminated the nonmarket values of love, care, and sacrifice for others, which eventually created marital dissatisfaction and then led to divorce.

5

Divorce-Related Stressors

*I pay for my children's health insurance and day care. So, I have
very little money for myself. Most Black men are bankrupted after a
divorce because their salaries are low before the divorce and they
can't support two families. That my credit would be ruined for the
next 5 years was also a major stressor.*

—Todd

Research has primarily focused on characteristics of divorcing couples rather than on descriptions of the psychological turmoil of
divorce. This chapter describes issues that are particularly stressful for
divorcing Black men. Topics explored include reactions to divorce,
stressors associated with child support, and beliefs that make the
breakup of marriages traumatic. Finally, the reactions of men who
initiated their divorces are examined. The discussion begins with an
overview of factors that have been noted to create particular stress
during the divorce process.

Economic Stressors

Divorce consistently has been inversely related to a woman's economic status. Weitzman (1985) found that the income of women and
children decreased 40%, whereas that of men decreased 15%. Unless a

93

woman remarried, her standard of living did not improve 5 years postdivorce. One reason that women experience downward social mobility postdivorce is that divorced mothers are thrust into the job market without skills or experience. Even divorced college or professional educated women experience difficulty in earning enough to support families (Weitzman, 1985).

Previous research has assumed that the economic situation of divorced men is nonproblematic. However, there has been limited research on the financial strain of Black divorced men. Because they are disadvantaged economically predivorce, financial strain may be a major postdivorce stressor. Moreover, two Black incomes often are necessary to equal the income of one White breadwinner. Thus, postdivorce economic stressors may be exacerbated for Black men.

Child Support

Child support policies often discriminate against Black mothers and fathers (Hill, 1989). Child support awards vary according to marital status. Approximately 77% of divorced mothers, 48% of separated mothers, and 24% of never-married mothers are awarded child support. Because those separated or never married are disproportionately Black, they are less likely to receive child support. Low-income fathers often pay a higher proportion of their incomes for child support than do fathers in the middle class. Black noncustodial fathers, therefore, are more adversely affected by the current child support policies than are White noncustodial fathers (Hill, 1989). Low-income noncustodial fathers are more likely to be arrested for nonpayment of child support than are their higher income counterparts (Hill, 1989, 1993). Because a large number of Black men are in the lower socioeconomic classes, they are adversely affected by biased and inequitable child support policies (Hill, 1989, 1993).

Psychosocial Stressors

Divorce produces numerous physiological responses including anger, depression, and ambivalence (Albrecht, 1980; Kitson & Morgan, 1990;

Weiss, 1975). Divorced individuals are more likely to die from a variety of diseases including cirrhosis of the liver, pneumonia, and tuberculosis than are their married or single counterparts. They are more frequent users of psychotropic drugs; are prone to motor vehicle accidents; and are more likely to die from accidents, homicides, and suicides (Bloom, Asher, & White, 1978; Kisker & Goldman, 1987; Mergenhagen, Lee, & Gove, 1985). Divorce produces emotional distress irrespective of the quality of the marriage or desire for its termination (Weiss, 1975).

Assessing Responses to Divorce

GENDER DIFFERENCES

Research on gender differences in response to divorce is mixed. Epidemiological studies indicate that separated and divorced males have higher rates of psychological and morbidity than do females (Reissman & Gerstel, 1985). Bloom and Clement (1984) report that women experience higher levels of psychological symptoms prior to separation, whereas men experience higher levels of distress in the postsepartion period. Because women are able to elicit supportive networks, their emotional distress decreases postdivorce (Chiriboga & Culter, 1977; Reissman, 1990). Divorced men's psychological distress intensifies postdivorce, and they report more suicidal thoughts than do women (Asher & Bloom, 1983; Reissman & Gerstel, 1985; Rosengren, Wedel, & Wilhelmsen, 1989).

The initiation of divorce has been associated with decreased postdivorce emotional distress (Kurdek & Blisk, 1983; Wallerstein, 1986). Perhaps women who initiate divorce have begun the detachment process earlier than have men. Thus, noninitiation of divorce may inhibit men's adjustment. However, it is unknown whether these findings can be generalized to Black men.

Blacks and Whites differ in their responses to divorce (Gove & Shin, 1989). For example, Black divorced females adjust more positively to living in single-parent families than do their White counterparts (Brown, Perry, & Hamburg, 1977). The literature provides inconsistent results on the response to divorce among Black men. Gove and Shin (1989) found no racial differences in response to divorce among men. Studies also have reported that Black divorced men experience lower anxiety postdivorce than do their White counterparts (Thoits, 1986).

Previous studies on divorce have failed to (a) exclusively focus on the responses of Black men, (b) include Black divorced fathers, and (c) adequately explain reasons for the different racial patterns of responses to divorce and subsequent postdivorce adjustment.

The following discussion examines divorce-related stressors. Peter's experience highlights the role of financial strain in the process of postdivorce adjustment.

Financial Strain

Peter called and asked to be interviewed. We drove to Peter's house. It was a three-room house in a pleasant suburb. Children were bicycling in the street, but the place had the deserted and worn-out look of many Black suburbs. There were old trees left behind by the builder. As we approached Peter's house, we noticed something—a notice of some sort—tacked onto the door; it was a notice of repossession signed by the sheriff's office. Repossession? We rang the bell and Peter answered the door.

"Hi, come in," Peter said as he stood looking at us, wearing an old t-shirt and pants. His face was haggard.

"I am glad you called to be interviewed." The house was full of boxes. "You're moving?"

"I have no choice," Peter's said acidly.

Peter told his story as if he needed to tell it. He lingered over every detail. It was his epic, etched in his memory by sheer pain. It started years ago, soon after Peter and his ex-wife, Jackie, moved from Louisville, Kentucky. "But we didn't tell anyone about our problems. Pride, I guess. It seemed too shameful," he said.

Peter had lost his job, and it took him months to find another. Peter and Jackie had gone into debt. Jackie worked, trying to keep food on the table and to pay the bills, but then Jackie was fired when the couple was paying installments on a medical bill. Eventually, Peter found a job, but they still were impoverished, trying to pay back the debts. Then Peter's teeth needed repair, and Jackie needed minor eye surgery. Peter lost his job again. This time, he found another before too long, but he was beginning to feel worn down, even doomed. Peter and Jackie saved on everything, but they never were able to break even. Then Peter lost his job again. "There were arguments," he said, adding,

> Jackie wanted me to stop working in factories, but the money was good when I was working. I made more than a teacher. But Jackie wanted me to go into another field. She thought I would make a good junior high teacher since I had a college degree.

Peter could substitute teach and take come college courses and eventually get a teaching job. But he was adamant that factory work— the automobile plant—represented economic potential because it was unionized. He reasoned that one day he would become a supervisor. He said,

> I got so disgusted and sat around the house poring through the newspaper and wouldn't go for an interview unless I saw an interesting ad. I just knew the Ford plant would recall some of the workers back to work. I was underfoot all the time, and we were living on a tiny unemployment check.

Peter paused and cleared his throat. He continued,

> The situation was aggravated by Jackie coming home every night to find me sitting and not making an effort to find a job, but I was so tired of hearing perspective employers say, "We found someone else more qualified." Jackie thought I could have taken a job pumping gas, anything at all, to feed the kids. Then checks started to bounce. The mortgage payments went further and further into default.

He cleared his throat again and continued,

> It got to be so bad, every night Jackie would come home and scream at me. The kids stayed with relatives and never came home if they could help it. It was terrible. Jackie couldn't stand it anymore, so she left and immediately filed for a divorce, saying she did not want any reminders of the marriage.

Peter went to the kitchen and poured a glass of water. When he returned, he continued his story:

The other day, the sheriff came. I got mad and tried to keep them from nailing that thing to my door. The neighbors knew. There is nothing left to lose. I don't know where to go. When I was packing, I cleaned out the closet. There were some boxes on the shelf, and behind that was a stack of papers. Bills. All bills. Some of them were 2 years old. Most I had never opened. They were just stuck up there as if they'd go away by themselves.

Peter smoked a cigarette and inhaled deeply. "I've given up," he said and explained,

The thing is that I found that I owed about $20,000. Can you imagine that? I can't. I'm only 39, and the rest of my life is already signed over to debt. Unless I can come up with $3,000, I am on the street as of Friday. My parents can't help. My father died last winter. His retirement annuity ended with his death. My mother is living on social security and his insurance; he didn't have much. She barely gets by, and I had been sending her money when I worked. I haven't told her any of this. It would upset her. Besides, she has a bad heart, and there is nothing that she can do.

After all the points in the interview were addressed, Peter smiled tiredly and said, "Listen, thanks for coming over and listening to my sad tale of my financial disaster. I guess it is the divorced Black man's lament."

The respondents expressed a profound concern over their financial situations. For example, they purchased new household furnishings and paid for two living spaces as well as legal and counseling fees. Consequently, they complained of limited financial resources as they reestablished their lives.

Each study participant was asked, "What was the major stressor during your divorce?" Without exception, the men reported that financial strain was a major stressor. These problems included responsibility for tremendous debt accumulated during their marriages and often financial support of extended family members. As a consequence of reduced income, the men experienced drastic decreases in their standard of living. Truman summarized his postdivorce economic situation: "The main stressor after my divorce was financial since I paid for the divorce, paid the bills Barbara created, and supported her sister's child. I'm still recovering financially. I have bill collectors calling and had my phone disconnected." In agreement with Truman, Todd, divorced for 5 years, commented,

I pay for my children's health insurance and day care, so I have very little money for myself. Most Black man are bankrupted after a divorce because their salaries are low before the divorce and they can't support two families. That my credit would be ruined for the next 5 years was also a major stressor.

REASONS FOR FINANCIAL STRAIN

The respondents' financial strain also was exacerbated because they believed that former spouses should receive all common marital assets. Approximately 83% of the men in this study relinquished to former wives houses, furnishings, and cars because their ex-wives were appointed custody of the children. For example, Bernie, divorced for 3 years, recalled his experience of leaving marital assets to Shelia:

I walked out of the house and gave Shelia everything. I viewed it as giving to my sons. I believe my needs should come last and the needs of my children should come first. So, I told the judge I did not want any marital assets.

Similarly, Kenneth lived in his car and in the police station, where he showered and dressed, until he was financially able to afford an apartment. He felt an obligation to make sacrifices for his children:

I suffered so my children could live in the house because I did not want my children to grow up on welfare. I felt the responsibility to bear the brunt financially and to start all over again because my former spouse, Mary, had custody of my 16-year-old daughter and 9-year-old son. I told Mary to take it all because I looked at it as giving to my children. I told Mary to take the car, take it all. I walked or used the police car to get to work each morning because I gave her the car for the children. When I was not working, I walked to grocery stores or took the bus.

WELFARE IS NOT AN OPTION

The men reported that preventing former wives from seeking public assistance was a major factor for relinquishing all common marital property. "I didn't want my children to grow up on welfare because I've seen children tore up by a system that mistreats and labels them" was a representative comment. Indeed, child support payments have been found to be a major determinant as to whether a woman applies for public assistance (Weitzman, 1985). Approximately 38% of women who do not receive child support apply for public assistance, compared to only 13% of women who receive child support (Weitzman, 1985).

Child Support Stressors

The respondents identified periodical court attendance to assess child support increases as a profound stressor. They questioned the circumstances required to warrant child support increases and reported that child support evaluations created extreme economic hardships. For example, Bronson, divorced for 2 years, described the frustration and humiliation he experienced with the reevaluation of child support:

> I went back and forth to court. That is losing time from work and money that could have been spent on the kids. I paid child support the best I could. Even when I did not have enough money for myself, I paid child support and even paid child support for my 12-year-old stepson. Then, after working two jobs to buy a car, Sara took me back to court again. The judge took the money that I budgeted for the car payment. I only had $150 a month for myself.

Taylor also recalled his courtroom experience:

> I remember sitting in court with my head hurting and palms sweating and ask[ing] my lawyer, "What am I supposed to do, go live on the street?" He said, "You have got to pay the increase or they will throw you in jail." I said, "I want to support my children, but I just can't pay the amount ordered." He just looked back at me and said, "That is just the way it is." Joanne's lawyer tried to make it look like I did not want to support my children. It was a very naked feeling when I sat in court and was stripped of my dignity and humanity. I would do anything for my kids and have always paid child support and given them my time. The court did not take that into consideration.

Taylor further noted,

> When I got behind in child support payments, Joanne filed an action to take me to court. Each time I went to court, I lost time off from work and

lost money that could have been used to help catch up on my support payments. I was caught in a cycle until I exhausted all of my meager savings and had gone deep into debt. I had no money to live on and borrowed money from friends, family members, banks, and credit unions. I even considered selling drugs to get money to catch up on my support payments.

Although Taylor and other respondents reported that they regularly paid child support, they also complained that periodic increases of support payments created severe financial hardships that exacerbated distress postdivorce.

RACIAL BIASES IN
CHILD SUPPORT DETERMINATIONS

Another reason that child support payments were stressful involved the respondents' perceptions that racial biases exist in the allocation of the amount of child support. Respondents emphasized that judges were more likely to enforce compliance of child support by attaching wages and withholding tax refunds of Black men than of White men. Gerald claimed that judges were excessively lenient and more apt to excuse money owed for past child support by White men than by Black men:

I talked with several of my White male friends who pay a fraction of what I'm paying. These men earn the same amount of money as I do and have the same number of children. I feel that judges punish Blacks to send the message that nonsupport of Black children will not be tolerated.

According to Graham, judges provided numerous opportunities for his White friends to make payments before imprisonment, whereas his Black friends were imprisoned immediately for failure to pay child support. Curtis blamed child support payments on the deterioration of Black relationships:

The majority of Black men are paying child support, but they have low-paying jobs. So, child support payments take most of their money, and they don't have money to live on. Eventually, they find another woman to depend on and who can take care of them. For these men, an intimate relationship is not a dream but a practical strategy to survive.

Men in this study believed that judges require Black men to pay more of their net incomes in child support. In fact, the percentage of a husband's income awarded in child support varies based on the husband's income level, with lower income men typically being required to pay a greater proportion of their incomes in child support (Weitzman, 1985).

Psychosocial Stressors

The men experienced a sense of loss that prompted psychological symptoms as well as self-destructive behavioral patterns including alcohol abuse, drug use, increase smoking, and suicidal and homicidal ideas. Bert represents a typical case. Bert and his ex-wife, Norma, lived together for 1 year and then had an "African wedding." Divorced for 3 years, the following comments reveal Bert's response to the divorce:

> I loved Norma and still loved what she once was. I was hurt every minute during the first year of the divorce and wanted it to be a nightmare. I went wild to dull the pain, smoking, drinking, and engaging in self-destructive behavior. I felt like a walking, breathing, living dead man. Drugs were everywhere, and I thought if I just smoke some pot, I could escape the pain. I had to smoke a joint every day, sometimes twice a day, thinking that I could handle it and that it would make my pain go away.

The men initially used alcohol and drugs to cope with the impact of divorce. They indicated that alcohol and illicit drugs created a false sense of well-being to avoid the negative feelings of divorce. Studies have shown that men typically repudiate feelings of loss by engaging in self-destructive behavior (Reissman, 1990). Paradoxically, although substance abuse relieved the respondents' emotional pain, at the same time it resulted in adverse consequences. The negative consequences of alcohol and illicit drug use included homicides, illnesses, accidents, family conflicts, assaults, and arrests (Harper, 1976; Staples, 1985).

A SUICIDE ATTEMPT

Vance, who was married for 10 years and divorced for 3 years, attempted suicide following the breakup of his marriage. He was the next to youngest of eight children, and at 5 years of age, he witnessed his father being killed by a neighbor. He reported,

> I can see it before me as if it happened yesterday. At the time of my father's death, my mother was pregnant with the eighth child, and she raised eight children alone because we had no one who could help us. So, my older brothers and sisters had to start working at an early age, scrubbing pots and pans and mopping floors. They helped to raise all the younger kids.

Early Sunday morning in January, huge wet flakes of snow were falling continuously—a kind of soft, quiet, and relentless snow. Vance aimed a gun at his head to kill himself. He said,

> I walked around with my head throbbing and furious that Ella wanted a divorce. We had a beautiful relationship, and we were there for each other. Plus, we both had a great appetite for sex, and she made me feel so good. I said to myself, "With all the problems you've got, all you got to do is pull a trigger and you won't have to worry." I wanted out so bad. So, I put the gun to my head while my two sons laid in the bed next to me. I just wanted to kill myself. I fired the gun and accidently shot myself in the neck. My pride was hurt. I felt like I couldn't even kill myself right. I should have known how to kill myself because I'm a trained respiratory tech[nician]. I called my mother, [and] she came over and called the ambulance. My mom took the kids.

During a 5-day hospitalization, Vance reported that he thought constantly of suicide:

> I couldn't get from under the pain. I wouldn't want to go through that again. I have never felt such hurt like that in my life. I didn't have any goals and felt that there was no way out. My mom said a lot of hurt[ful] things to me; she called me a fool, she called me stupid and said a woman is not worth killing yourself for. My mother felt like Ella made a complete idiot out of me. I needed to hear mom's harsh words.

For one year, Vance drank daily to drown the pain and did nothing more than "hang out." "I felt so ashamed that I'd married someone who would just walk away from her kids," Vance said tearfully. He cried because of the loss of his father and wife. He considered his father's life to have been a tragedy; his father never obtained the education he wanted (or that Vance wanted for him). Vance gradually realized that much of his grief was over his unfulfilled dreams and mourned the loss of common bonds and shared collective memories. Other men also reported suicidal ideations and clinical depression.

BEHAVIORAL CHANGES

The respondents also reported loss of appetite, anxiety, insomnia, and impulsive behavioral patterns immediately following divorce. Some men indicated that they were unable to sleep and that when sleep finally came, they woke up at 4 a.m. or 5 a.m. Several men reported increased smoking and an inability to concentrate. Tasks requiring attention were difficult. Driving was less skillful, and several men described minor automobile, motorcycle, and bike accidents for the first times in their lives.

Some used alcohol, drugs, and beer to sleep and discovered that not even drugs would erase the emotional pain. Matt said,

> I didn't see the divorce coming—like a bomb. I was married for 8 years. Then, all of a sudden, Hazel felt like she had to go, and joining the military was one way to do that. I developed stomach ulcers, lost weight, and started using drugs to overcome depression. I thought Hazel was the only person I could love. I felt like I was losing my mind because I was losing her, and drugs did little to ease the pain. For weeks, my life stood still. I could not think or work on tasks that required mental concentration.

Other expressions of tension, including irritability, outbursts of anger, and irrational behavioral patterns, also were reported. For example, Henry, who was married for 12 years, tearfully verbalized numerous experiences of erratic behavior:

> After the divorce, I would catch myself driving past my old home three times daily. I'd just stare at the house. I sat in my car and stared out the window. I thought about all the happy times I had spent in that house during the holidays with my family, and I cried. Tears just rolled and rolled from my eyes when I thought of Linda and the kids.

William is another example of a man who struggled with profound postdivorce distress. William had a "whirlwind" romance through college. Marriage was inevitable during his senior year because "we talked about everything and everybody." His postdivorce reaction led him to seek counseling:

> It was a sickening feeling. My nerves fell apart. I developed stomach ulcers, lost weight, and felt really depressed. It was such a depression. I felt lower than the ground I walked on. It was difficult to face the morning. For months, I sat in my apartment and felt sorry for myself and cried. I was hurt so bad that I would catch myself crying. Then I had thoughts of attacking Carol for rejecting me and putting me through this pain. I had to cry to release the pressure because I believe that behind every successful man there is a woman pushing and supporting him. . . . I saw a counselor to get help with the pain.

PHYSIOLOGICAL PROBLEMS

Physiological reactions, including stomach problems, migraine headaches, dental problems, and eyesight and hearing problems, were common reactions. Hospitalizations and visits to the emergency room were postdivorce experiences. For example, Allen reported,

> The divorce caused frequent asthma attacks. I had stomach problems during the night. An inflamed abdomen led me straight to the hospital for 2 [or] 3 days at a time. I had migraine headaches which occurred weekly, and I went to the hospital to get relief. So, the stress of breaking up affected my health.

In agreement Barry said,

> I suffered from migraine headaches, and my allergies got worse. I didn't want to see anybody. I did not want to have sex with anybody. I just locked myself up and suffered and cried. Sometimes, a Black man must cry to release some pressure. I was diagnosed with peptic ulcers and an irritable colon and went to the emergency room several times.

Divorce has been associated with adverse health consequences. For example, studies have linked the stress of divorce to the precipitation of a variety of illnesses including cancer, diabetes, depression, heart disease, and alcoholism (Bloom et al., 1978; Chester, 1971). These effects appear to apply to all races and ethnic groups. In addition, divorced individuals tend to die earlier than do those in any other marital group. This finding applies to every age group (20 years or over) for both genders and races. Separated and divorced individuals also have higher physician contacts and longer hospitalizations than do those who are married (Bloom et al., 1978).

Reasons for Postdivorce Distress

Black men may be constricted by the traditional male gender role, which discourages them from sharing their pain with others and may increase distress postdivorce. According to Majors and Billson (1992), the socialization of Black males may produce a coping style in which they fail to acknowledge the personal vulnerability associated with divorce. Consequently, they may repress feelings by engaging in self-destructive behaviors. Furthermore, psychological and physiological reactions to divorce were associated with beliefs of marital permanence. James, who spent 3 years separated from his wife before their divorce, described his situation in this manner:

> I may not have lived with Ellen for 20 years, but I would not have divorced her. I believe when I make a commitment, I like to keep it until I die. My father used to say, "You stay with your family no matter what." So, I carried that belief with me as an adult. No matter what, I think people should stick [with] it through[out], especially if there are kids.

Divorce was traumatic because it subverted some men's absolute commitment to marriage. Thus, marital termination was morally inexcusable. This obligation to marital vows, in turn, led to increased emotional agony following divorce. In fact, only three respondents initiated their divorces.

THE MARRIAGE WOULD BE SALVAGED

Another reason why divorce was stressful was related to the denial of the marriage termination. Maurice consulted a marriage therapist for help to admit the termination of his marriage. He said,

> I believe that no matter how bad the marriage is, there is a chance to change it around. Even if the wife commits adultery, a husband should forgive her and just keep going. If a wife wants a divorce, I believe she should go and get one.

Other men admitted that they fantasized about returning to former spouses following long periods of separation and reported that they would not initiate divorces.

THE NEED TO DEFY THE RACIAL STEREOTYPES

In part, the men's reluctance to admit that their marriages had terminated was a response to cultural stereotyping. They perceived that a stable marriage counteracted the cultural stereotypes that Black men often abdicate family responsibilities.

A case in point was Edsel, a 49-year-old business executive who progressed from the ghetto of Harlem, New York, to earning $50,000 annually by cultivating a proper image. He trained himself to speak distinctively and to dress for success. Edsel perceived that a stable marriage elevated his social identity and contradicted the negative images of Black men:

> A stable marriage is a plus for Black men because few people expect it. Most of my business colleagues believe that Black men don't care about their families. I thought it would be a plus if I could have a marriage and a career to prove to society that I am different. To counteract the image of the ineffective Black family man, I did not want to admit that my marriage was over.

With fierceness, Douglas further noted, "The stereotype is that a Black man [doesn't] want to take responsibility. That is bull. My family was the most important thing to me." Ironically, whereas the denial of marital termination counteracted the negative images of Black men and elevated the respondents' social identities, it also led to increased emotional turmoil when their marriages subsequently were terminated.

Divorce Was for the Best

Approximately 20% ($n = 10$) of the respondents acknowledged that divorce was beneficial. Because they had been in emotionally draining marriages, they felt energized by their divorces. Bernie reported,

> When I signed the divorce papers, I felt relieved and that the weight of the world was lifted off me. I felt that this was a chance for me to have a better life—cut the losses and go on. The divorce was for the best.

SENSE OF FAILURE

Although a divorce was beneficial, it also provoked a sense of failure. For example, Barry was an auto mechanic, a contractor, and a roofer. Attracted by a photograph of a piece of furniture, he proceeded to replicate it in his home. He established his assumptive world with the notion that he could fix anything. He said,

> I hate to fail because I like to find solutions to problems. I don't give up on them. I try to work them out. I didn't want my sons to view their father as a failure. The marriage was a failure, and I felt like I had failed, even though I was relieved after the divorce.

Thus, a sense of failure also characterized the postdivorce experience of men who reported that their divorces were beneficial.

UNPREPARED REACTIONS

Although there was a sense of relief at the termination of marriages, the men often were unprepared for the psychological and physiological symptoms. Allen was a representative case. His former wife, Jean, refused to become pregnant a second time and had her tubes tied. Allen was devastated and marked this incident as the end of their marriage. Following frequent arguments, Allen moved out of the house. Six months later, he suffered a heart attack and had bypass surgery. The following comments describe his feelings: "The divorce was a mutual decision. Even though I initiated the divorce, I was unprepared for my anger and how my body reacted. I had dental problems [and] migraine headaches and was diagnosed with high blood pressure." Even though some men believed that the divorces were beneficial, they reported being unprepared for the psychological and physiological symptoms as well as a pervasive sense of failure postdivorce.

Postmodern Betrayal

Men who discovered that their ex-wives had intimate relationships before finalization of their divorces felt hurt, humiliated, and rejected, which often led to homicidal tendencies and suicidal fantasies. They used images of death and illness to convey the depth of their despair. For example, Bronson married during college and lived with Sara for 1 year before marriage. Following marriage, Sara found a job as a receptionist, but she felt frustrated because she was not having much of a social life. Bronson encouraged her to go to movies and to socialize with friends. He said,

> Sara eventually got addicted to nightlife, and she could not get out of it; she got addicted to it. She initiated and filed for a divorce, saying she did not want to be married anymore. She started dating a friend of mine before finalizing the divorce—and that hurt. I think the hurt was whom she started seeing—my friend. That's what hurt.

During the interview, Bronson cried for the loss of his wife and for the unrecoverable years. He also cried for the life he dreamed about but never lived.

Sam also reported that Velma, his ex-wife, had an affair before the divorce was final. He was caught unaware when Velma expressed profound unhappiness and wanted to separate:

> Velma started seeing a retired man who lived next door. All the neighbors knew. I wanted to scream at her and beat up her lover. Do you remember a story of a man who killed his wife by pouring gasoline on her? Horrible. Yet, I've often thought about that crime. I can understand how anger and rage toward a woman could lead to a crime like that.

Sam described the day Velma told him she was seeing another man:

> When Velma told me she was in love with another man, I remember grabbing and choking her. She passed out. The kids stopped me and

grabbed my pants. They said, "Daddy, don't hurt mommy." I picked Velma up from the floor and laid her on the couch and walked out of the house. A part of me wanted to kill her because of her involvement with the retired neighbor.

Even though Bronson, Sam, and others felt deceived by their former spouses, participant observation revealed that they had trouble directing their attention elsewhere when encountering their ex-wives at church activities, children's school programs, and community activities.

Although it is difficult to determine the number of Black men who believe that their wives betrayed them by the establishment of other intimate relationships, the men in this study felt hurt and angry when former wives became involved with friends or neighbors before finalization of their divorces, even though they were separated. They claimed that a wife's death would have been easier to accept than the reality of a wife being with another man.

Summary

As we have seen, divorce-related stressors included the following: (a) financial strain, (b) noncustodial parenting, (c) child support stressors, and (d) psychological and physiological distress.

Financial strain. The belief that wives should receive marital assets to prevent children from receiving welfare exacerbated financial strain. Of interest, the *amount* of child support rarely was perceived as a major stressor. Rather, periodic court attendance to assess child support caused profound emotional distress. The time required to attend court and the humiliation experienced in court resulted in considerable bitterness and depression.

Child support stressors. One unexpected and significant finding was the perception of racial biases in the allocation of child support payments that, in part, provided justification that child support increases were punitive and unnecessary.

Psychological and physiological reactions. Divorce had a profound psychological impact on the respondents including anger, depression, ambivalence, and a sense of loss. Consistent with previous research, the men initially used alcohol and drugs to cope with the impact of divorce. Physiological reactions included stomach problems, migraine headaches, dental problems, eyesight and hearing difficulties, and hypertension, which resulted in hospitalizations or visits to the emergency room.

Although these responses are not unique to Black men (Hetherington, Stanley-Hogan, & Anderson, 1976; Reissman, 1990), the contemplation of harm to self and violence directed toward former spouses is striking. This finding is critical because violence occurring in Black relationships often turns lethal (Plass, 1993). This finding points to the need for community-based self-help groups to meet the needs of Black divorced men. For example, for help with postdivorce counseling, some men consulted the director of the Urban League, ministers of Black churches, and Black men who owned businesses. Conducting a postdivorce counseling group with lay counselors following Sunday services at a Black church, coordinated with university-based counseling programs, could be one collaborative endeavor to address the psychological needs of Black divorced men.

Of interest, postdivorce distress was related to a belief in the permanence of marriage. This finding is consistent with Staples' (1994) argument that the ideology of most Blacks is in the direction of traditional family forms, although their family arrangements can mislead others to assume that Blacks are strongly in accord with alternative family lifestyles. In addition, adultery before finalization of the divorces created intense emotional distress, suggesting that relinquishing sexual exclusivity often was problematic.

Although some men viewed divorce as beneficial, it also provoked a sense of failure. Despite society's liberal attitudes toward divorce, its occurrence in the lives of the respondents was viewed as an admission of failure. Consequently, for some who initiated their divorces, postdivorce adjustment was as difficult as for noninitiators. In fact, those who initiated the divorces expressed greater physiological complaints than did noninitiators. Noninitiators expressed psychological symptoms, whereas those who initiated divorces complained of a variety of illnesses including hypertension, toothaches, and back pain, and some men received medical diagnoses and had surgical procedures.

6

Postmarital Relationships

I can forgive, but [I] can't forget. I don't trust Hazel. She may have learned some more tricks that will hurt me.

—Matt

In Chapter 5, we explored divorce-related stressors. However, the continuing attachment to former spouses may cause intense emotional distress. In this chapter, we turn to a key component in understanding divorce—postmarital relationships—to examine the paradoxical bonds that exist between former spouses. On the one hand, couples no longer are married; on the other, they often are intertwined with complicated parental roles. We address ambivalent, friendly, and negative postmarital relationships. We also identify barriers that prohibit or facilitate reconciliation and discuss postdivorce in-law relationships. We begin by reviewing the literature on the attachment process.

Attachment to Former Spouses

Weiss (1975) was the first to use "attachment" in the divorce literature, based on the Bowlby's (1969, 1973) infants and mothers attachment research. Bowlby (1969) suggests that attachment increases security and represents a natural reaction to a threat. Divorced individuals,

113

therefore, search for the familiar attachment of a former spouse. Furthermore, attachment to former spouses persists even though other heterosexual relationships may develop. As a result, the inaccessibility of former spouses leads to separation distress and continued ambivalent postmarital relationships.

A number of empirical studies have investigated attachment theory (Kitson, 1982; Kitson, Babri, & Roach, 1985). White men have reported a greater degree of attachment and desire to reconcile after divorce than have White women (Bloom & Kindle, 1985; Zeiss, Zeiss, & Johnson, 1980). Greater time since separation, development of new relationships, and being the initiator of the divorce have been associated with greater postdivorce attachment. Hetherington, Cox, and Cox (1977) found that 2 months following divorce, couples relied on each other during emergencies and frequently had intercourse.

Some research has not supported Weiss's (1975) attachment theory. For example, Spanier and Casto (1979) found that some couples showed no signs of attachment. Attachment also has been correlated with postdivorce adjustment. For example, Kitson (1982) developed a scale for postdivorce attachment consisting of four items: (a) wondering what the ex-spouse is doing, (b) spending a large amount of time thinking about the ex-spouse, (c) disbelief that the couple was getting a divorce, and (d) feeling that the person will not adjust to the divorce. Attached individuals demonstated postdivorce adjustment difficulties with living alone, role changes, and new relationships (Kitson, 1982). In addition, Berman (1985) defined attachment as preoccupation with intrusive thoughts about the ex-spouse and found that individuals who experienced conflictual postmarital relationships reported less attachment. Berman's study suggests that the quality of marital and postmarital relationships predicts postdivorce attachment.

One major criticism of the divorce attachment literature is the assumption that divorce should terminate relationships and that those that do exist are maladaptive. However, some postdivorce relationships between ex-spouses satisfy legitimate adult attachment needs such as friendship, shared history, and extended family networks (Ahrons & Wallish, 1987). In addition, there are varying definitions of attachment reported in the literature, ranging from cognitive to behavioral conceptualizations. Divorced persons may experience a range of feelings for ex-spouses that are not necessarily ambivalent.

Although the high Black divorce rate has been documented, there is limited research of Black postmarital relations including descriptive analyses to determine whether attachment exists among Black men. Furthermore, factors that prohibit or facilitate adjustment among Blacks rarely have been examined. The study of postdivorce relations has implications for understanding the development of Black coupling in which intimacy and estrangement may fluctuate over time.

Postmarital Relationships

ATTACHMENT

Approximately 80% of the respondents in our study reported attachment to former spouses during the first year postdivorce. However, attachment feelings and behaviors decreased over time. For example, Anton, divorced for 5 years, did not understand why Thelma filed for a divorce:

> Initially, I called about everything—to see if the car insurance had been paid, to see if the grass had been cut, or [to see] if the garbage had been taken out. After a year, I stopped calling and waited for Thelma to get in touch with me. In other words, the relationship just faded.

Unlike the Weiss study (1975), we observed a gender difference in the attachment process. Of interest, respondents reported that former spouses were more likely to display attachment behaviors 2 or 3 years postdivorce. Curtis, who had been divorced for 3 years, said,

> As recently as yesterday, Julie wanted me back, but I know it will not work. She will put me on a roller-coaster again, and I can't go through that again. I keep Julie at a distance. When I am friendly to Julie, she wants to know where the relationship is leading. I could not just have caring feelings for her. It had to be, okay, where are we going with this?

Derek, who had been divorced for 2 years, agreed:

> Joan calls me every day. She tells me that the divorce did not have to happen. She compliments me and seems to be my most ardent fan. She

no longer starts with "You did this or that"; she asks "What can I do to make things right?"

Respondents also indicated that although the legal bonds of their marriages were broken, former spouses remained attached to their families by visiting or by telephone. Clyde said,

> Betty told me that no matter what happens to our relationship, she would always remain close to my family. She visits my mother and talks to my sister frequently. She sends Easter and Christmas cards. In fact, Betty had Thanksgiving dinner with my family. Even though we have been divorced for 5 years, Betty refuses to let go.

In contrast to Weiss's (1975) research, ex-wives professed love for, and desired to interact with, the respondents, even though both might have developed other heterosexual relationships. This finding suggests that gender may be an important variable in the attachment process of Blacks. One explanation for this finding is that ex-wives may be more attached to Black family relationships rather than to ex-husbands (which is found in mostly White samples). Furthermore, Black women's attachment to ex-husbands can be explained by the imbalanced sex ratio. The result is a marked shortage of potential marriage partners for Black women. Ex-husbands may be viewed as particularly attractive for Black women given available options.

AMBIVALENT POSTMARITAL RELATIONSHIPS

Postmarital relationships were characterized by ambivalent feelings. For example, Kenneth found it comforting to see Mary, but his anger became too great and he asked her to stop calling. He said, "I still make efforts to find out how she is doing, but I'm still angry with her because she causes me so much pain." Ivan also expressed anger and a continued obligation toward Margaret. He remarked,

> I still have mixed feelings toward Margaret. It is hard to explain; some-times, I don't know whether to kiss or shoot her. I didn't want to sign the

papers, but she wanted it. Every time I called, she was concerned that I wanted something—and I did, but I didn't know what that was.

Consistent with previous research (Weiss, 1975), the men showed ambivalent feelings toward former spouses including obligation, affection, anger, and concern.

FRIENDLY POSTMARITAL RELATIONSHIPS

Postmarital relationships also were friendly and represented platonic bonding. Truman, who had been divorced for 6 years, said, "Barbara and I are friends, and I talked with her this morning. Believe it or not, in the last 2 years, I have seen Barbara more than I have seen my kids." Children were the primary reason for maintaining friendly relationships with former spouses. The men believed that their children needed contact with both parents. For example, Gerald said,

> I told Molly that I was going to be her friend whether she liked it or not. I told her that we had to put our anger aside for the sake of the children. But she needed to let go of the relationship and to move on. I told Molly that we needed to be sensible and try to be friends because our son did not need any more instability in his life.

Lennie also said that he had a positive relationship with Cheryl because he had visions that a gang member would approach his sons and then point a gun to their heads and start firing. Lennie made an extra effort to establish friendly relationships with Cheryl, even though he preferred to avoid her.

Overall, the findings show that Black divorced couples may offer each other company and solace within an environment perceived as hostile. For example, former spouses called the respondents to receive assistance with insensitive teachers and advice about coping with racist employers, absentee landlords, and incompetent auto mechanics. They also informed each other of family members' deaths and illnesses. Couples who had friendly postmarital relationships lived apart but entered into platonic friendships. In many instances, these relationships will remain until death. As Kenneth explained, "Mary will be in my life until I die.

We will even talk about our grandchildren and great-grandchildren, but there is no chance of us getting back together."

EX-WIVES AVOIDED

The idea of a friendly postmarital relationship seemed unnatural and repellent for some men. Edsel reported, "I could care less if April dropped off the face of the earth. At first, we continued to argue. Then the fights gradually ceased." A high degree of conflict initially prevailed between some ex-spouses; however, the level of conflict usually decreased over time. Some men avoided former spouses by moving to other states, or their former spouses decided to move away to avert continued contact. Peter said, "The town was too small for the both of us. I knew there was no chance of running into Jackie being 200 miles away."

Indeed, contact with former spouses and their new relationships frequently caused extreme distress. Larry, for example, was angry at Pat when she introduced him to her boyfriend. He said,

> I was in the club, and Pat introduced me to her boyfriend. I felt so angry and thought, "What is he doing with my wife?" Yet, I knew that she was devious and could not be trusted, but I felt she was still my wife on some level. And I was still angry at her for disrespecting my mother.

On the other hand, Henry reported that when he started a new relationship, his ex-wife showed up unannounced and sabotaged the relationship. Dating symbolized that the divorce was complete and that the other spouse had been replaced, which often precipitated a renewed sense of loss and behavioral reactions.

Consistent with Weiss (1975), there was a wide range of postmarital relationships. Whereas many were ambivalent and conflictual, others were friendly. Children were a major factor in continuation of friendly postmarital relationships. Literature has consistently indicated that cooperative postmarital relationships benefit parents and children (Arendell, 1992; Cherlin, 1992; Fine, 1992; Hetherington, 1989). Positive postmarital relationships reduce custodial parents' role overload and decrease noncustodial parents' estrangement from children (Hetherington et al., 1977; Weitzman, 1985).

Respondents' Views of Former Spouses'
Postdivorce Reactions

SYMPATHY FOR EX-WIVES

Of interest, some men expressed sympathy for ex-wives because they were custodial parents. Research consistently has reported that divorced mothers experience severe role overload and that their difficulties are aggravated by the high cost of child care (Campbell & Moen, 1992; Weitzman, 1985). Willy expressed extreme sympathy for his ex-wife, Donna:

> I feel sorry for Donna because there is no adult in the house to take over anytime. She can't say, "I want to lie down and not be bothered" and know she will not. The only way she goes to the store is to leave my 10-year-old daughter in charge. She has to supervise the children's homework [and] play and referee fights.

Men also reported that their former spouses suffered economically. For example, Bert said, "Norma is suffering because I gave her everything she needed. She is jealous of my life now. I have a home—something she always wanted—and a new car. Norma is living with her parents, taking the bus to work." Other men reported that ex-wives had increased medical problems while coping with economic, housing, and parent-child-related stressors.

Among the respondents, 10 men reported that former spouses demonstrated little emotional distress postdivorce. For example, Carl believed that Rita was happy being single. He explained,

> Rita loves living alone because she does not have to be responsive to my needs. The last time I talked with her, she was in heaven. She was appointed to a variety of boards in the community and was thinking about running for a public office.

Carl believed that Rita's individuality was submerged in the marriage and that she viewed the divorce as an opportunity to take back her life. Therefore, he perceived that Rita was not a divorce casualty; rather, she claimed her identity postdivorce.

The previous discussion has shown that some men believed that their ex-wives suffered downward social mobility postdivorce, whereas others reported that their ex-wives were adjusting with few problems. When children were present, respondents expressed empathy toward ex-wives. However, it was difficult to assess whether custody of children adversely affected postdivorce adjustment. Ambert (1989) found that children help to displace anxiety during divorce. This buffering effect may be offset by increased stress resulting from continued contact with an ex-spouse, a child's negative response to divorce, and/or a custodial parent's socioeconomic status.

RECONCILIATION

Although a large number of Black divorced couples consider reconciliation, Staples (1986) reports that Black reconciliations are unsuccessful and that repeated separations often occur. In the following sections, we focus on reconciliation and postmarital in-laws relationships.

For the majority of men, reconciliation often was considered but remained out of the question. As Eric remarked,

> After living with a woman for 1 year, I realized that I was very compatible with my ex-wife and have more in common with her than with most women I meet. The thought crossed my mind to try to establish a relationship with Mary, my ex-wife. I dismissed the thought and would never go back because we have the same communication patterns.

Approximately one of every eight couples reconciles in the period between filing for divorce and obtaining the divorce decree (Weiss, 1975). However, respondents reported that signing the divorce decree symbolized that their marriages were over and that reconciliation was out of the question.

Barriers to Reconciliation

BELIEFS

The beliefs illustrated in the following remark prevented reconciliation and attachment:

> Once I walk out [of the marriage], that is it; I am gone, [and] there is no way I'm going back. I realized that I had done everything humanly possible to try and correct the marital problem. Since it was not correctable, there was no way of going back. My perception of life is that I was not placed on earth to suffer. If I cannot maintain a wholesome relationship . . . , I cut it off.

The respondents' belief that "once it's over, it's over" can be viewed as resourceful way in which they have survived social and economic marginality. For example, Grier and Cobb (1969) suggest that Black men often develop defensive beliefs and behavioral patterns to adapt to their environments. They must be on guard to protect themselves from humiliation and outright mistreatment. Douglas, a news reporter, explained that the "once it's over, it's over" philosophy was adaptive in his work environment and unconsciously practiced such ideology in his marriage:

> At the TV station where I used to work, they didn't think Blacks were qualified to compete on their level. On some level, they thought, "Those Blacks can't write well, they can't speak well, and they can't theorize." Because of those myths, I could never settle [down] and relax, and I had trouble pushing stereotypes out of my mind. The brass had decided to get rid of me and tried to undermine my self-confidence. Before I let that happen, I decided to quit. Even though I was equal to every other person working at that station, I was treated so consistently inferior. So, I refused to accept that type of treatment, and I told myself it was over and that I would never return. I just quit; it was over. Unfortunately, this attitude carried over into my personal life. I tried in my marriage, and now I'm through with it.

Other men spoke of the "once it's over, it's over" philosophy as a survival mechanism as old as slavery and emphasized that Black men must quickly recognize the invisible barriers of racial prejudice that signify the space in which they live and work. This sixth sense of being able to recognize "once it's over, it's over and there is no need to negotiate" is imperative for their sanity. For example, studies have shown the retention of racial discrimination in employment, housing, education, and health care. One study reported that 75% of Black men seeking employment are discriminated against (Hill, 1989, 1993). Blacks face discrimination 56% of the times they seek to rent houses and 59% of the times they purchase houses (Leigh, 1993). According to Staples (1994), the number of studies showing racial discrimination in every facet of American life makes a mockery of the color-blind theory. He further notes that the color-blind theory is a smokescreen to mask the persistence of a racial hierarchy and persistent social discrediting in American life. Thus, the respondents' pragmatic reactions to racial prejudice became an instinctive response that permeated personal relationships and prohibited reconciliations.

ENTRY OF NEW RELATIONSHIPS

The entry of new relationships also was a barrier to reconciliation. Ivan revealed that his ex-wife married, divorced, and wanted to remarry him:

> I honestly still love Margaret, but I'm involved with someone else. She left me for another guy, took me to court, and proceeded to take all my money. She wants to divorce her current husband and to remarry me, but I can never go back. I will never go back.

Solomon, divorced for 6 years, said, "Even now after 6 years, Kaye asked me if we could get back together, but I started seeing somebody else. It was like, 'No, I don't think so.' It was too late, and [I] would not do anything to hurt my new girlfriend."

INABILITY TO TRUST

One of the most formidable barriers to reconciliation was the establishment of trust in the relationship. Matt explained, "I can forgive, but [I] can't forget. I don't trust Hazel. She may have learned some more tricks that will hurt me."

Derek also claimed that the damage from his marriage was unalterable and that the thought of reconciliation made him vomit. He reported that a reconciliation might prompt a chronic stress-related disease. He said that his health had improved after the divorce and that he viewed Joan as a health risk. Indeed, Renne (1971) found that unhappily married people are more likely to experience chronic illnesses, neuroses, depression, and isolation than are divorced people. Thus, an unhappy marriage is a social disability analogous to a physical disability (Renne, 1971).

FAMILIES' AND IN-LAWS' ENCOURAGEMENT TO RECONCILE

The respondents were more reluctant to report the end of their marriages to family members than to friends or neighbors because they feared that kin would encourage reconciliation. Solomon said,

> My family lived two blocks from me and knew the whole mess but tried to talk us into getting back together. They were hurt when we could not resume the marriage. And I thought about going back to the marriage to make my mother happy, but [I] decided that was an unacceptable reason to be married.

A majority of the men reported that family members strongly disapproved of their divorces and that parents tried to convince them to give the marriages another chance. Although parents found it bewildering that their daughters-in-law initiated divorces over frivolous matters, they desired reestablishment of the marriages. Larry said,

> My parents couldn't understand why Pat filed for a divorce. Since my mom was going through a hard time and I spent more time with her than with Pat, my parents could not understand Pat's actions. My mom said, "Larry, you did the best you could." My dad said, "Son, you didn't do anything wrong." They could not understand it because they encouraged me and my brothers and sisters to stick with a marriage.

Larry's parents had difficulty understanding the reasons why Pat initiated the divorce, and they frequently encouraged Pat "to try and work things out" by calling, writing letters, and inviting her to church.

Overall, the majority of respondents' parents viewed the divorces as devastating events. Even in homes characterized by intense emotional distress, parents encouraged reconciliation. A frequent comment was "Give the marriage another chance for the children's sake."

In-Law Relationships

Divorce forces an assessment of in-law relationships. Anaspach (1976) reported that 80% of divorced women decreased contact with members of their former spouses' families. Weiss (1975) found that divorced males ceased contact with in-laws completely, whereas women continued to maintain contact postdivorce, although at a lower level than predivorce.

A majority of respondents in our study maintained relations with in-laws postdivorce. Due to proximity and time, the most frequent contact included phone calls and letters. These relationships often were characterized as friendly with very strong ties. However, postmarital in-law relationships were based on the predivorce relationships. If respondents had hostile in-law relationships before the divorce, then often the relationships remained without close ties. For example, Ben described his in-law relationships:

> My in-laws never liked me. They attacked me and said the marriage and the divorce [were] my fault. They supported their daughter, right or wrong. I talk to them occasionally about the kids, but I try to have as little contact with them as possible.

Men who had positive predivorce in-law relationships reported that these relationships were close despite the divorces. Lennie said,

> I love my mother-in-law to death. I visit her every chance I get when I am in South Carolina. When I sing, she comes to my concerts to show her support. She blames her daughter for the breakup of the marriage. And to this day, she talks to me more than [she does to] her daughter.

Barry also reported that he often visits his mother-in-law and characterized the relationship as friendly. Other men reported calling their former mothers-in-law regularly, buying birthday and Christmas gifts and assisting them financially in times of crisis. In fact, Brent secured a loan to assist his former mother-in-law to purchase a house.

Unlike those reported with White samples, most in-law relationships remained postdivorce. The most frequent relationships were mother/son-in-law relationships. The men believed that such relations were valuable in their own right. This finding points to the endurance of the Black family and its ability to adapt to a divorce. In several cases, even when the respondents remarried, the bonds remained and former in-laws embraced the new wives.

GRANDPARENT RELATIONSHIPS

How does an adult child's divorce affect the grandparent relationship? Studies have shown that the effects of the divorce are different for the custodial grandparent (parent of the custodial parent) and the noncustodial grandparent (parent of the noncustodial parent). Cherlin and Furstenberg (1986) found that during the marital breakup, only 6% of custodial grandparents saw their grandchildren less often than they did predivorce, compared to 41% of noncustodial grandparents. This pattern persists for years following the divorce.

The men felt that children should retain ties with their parents. Indeed, Blacks have more contact with grandchildren than do their White counterparts. Taylor explained, "I think it is great my kids see their only grandparents monthly since both [of] Joanne's parents died. My daughters spend every summer with me and my parents."

Noncustodial grandparents provided valuable services to children such as imparting knowledge of their family histories and socialization to the families' value systems. Among other services grandparents provided were providing child care and purchasing needed items such as school clothes and supplies. In addition, grandparents were significant and important because children had others to relate to and from whom they could receive emotional support.

Summary

In this chapter, we explored postmarital relationships. For a large majority of respondents, postmarital relationships were characterized by a mixture of positive and negative feelings with varying levels of conflict that decreased over time. Although some of the men avoided former spouses by moving to other states, a majority maintained friendly relations with ex-wives because of their children. This finding suggests that divorce does not end the relationships for some Black couples; it merely changes the relationships. It also suggests that marital ties between Black divorced partners are not easily broken.

Attachment to former spouses occurred initially but decreased over time. In contrast to previous studies, former spouses behaved in ways to increase attachment. Although women were more likely to initiate divorce, they also were more likely to exhibit attachment behaviors than were men. This finding can be explained by the imbalanced sex ratio among Blacks. However, it must be pointed out that we do not have wives' assessments of their attachment behaviors.

In contrast to previous research (Weiss, 1975), the following factors prohibited reconciliation and attachment:

1. a respondent's belief that once a concerted effort is expended to correct a problem with poor results, there is no need to expend further energy to solve the problem;
2. the entry of a new relationship by one partner; and
3. an inability to trust a former spouse.

Divorce also forced reassessment of in-law relationships. Although postmarital in-law relationships were defined based on the relationships predivorce, a majority of men maintained in-law relationships when children were involved. A surprising and unexpected finding was the retained relationships between the respondents and mothers-in-law, compared to the most common White retained relationships between daughters and mothers-in-law. This might be explained by the key roles that men played in the provision of resources to their mothers-in-law. Although Black males experience employment instability, they provide human resources within their support systems. For example, a large number of men provided tangible support to in-laws that included repairing household appliances, mowing lawns, servicing cars, and painting houses as well as often providing economic and transportation resources. Moreover, due to their relatively higher status as males in the traditional social structure of many Black families, the relationships between men and in-laws, especially mothers-in-law, remained postdivorce. However, former wives also retained relationships with sisters-in-law and female members of the respondents' families.

Noncustodial grandparents remained significant in the lives of children. A possible reason for this finding is that grandmothers have assumed a variety of roles in Black families, ranging from parenting grandchildren to sharing child care. Indeed, at various points in their marriages, 20% of the respondents reported that their mothers lived with them. The increased involvement of noncustodial grandmothers predivorce created enduring bonds that survived postdivorce.

7

Strategies for Coping With Divorce

My ancestors suffered and believed that they would overcome oppression one day. My forefathers and foremothers kept on going, even though they were slaves. Knowledge of their strength has given me determination and inspiration to keep on going despite obstacles I face in trying to reestablish my life.

—Leon

What strategies do Black men use to cope with divorce? What activities do they use to facilitate a new lifestyle transition? What qualities do they desire in a future mate? In this chapter, we discuss the ways in which the respondents coped with divorce. The importance of family and friends support, religious involvement, and community participation is emphasized. Other issues explored include views on singlehood, qualities desired in a future mate, and beliefs about interracial remarriages.

Support of Family and Friends

Social support has been correlated with positive postdivorce adjustment. Divorced women, however, are more likely than divorced men to find satisfaction in their friendships and to seek social support (Albrecht, 1980; Amato & Booth, 1991). In a longitudinal study, Keith (1986) found that divorced men are more socially isolated than divorced women, indicating that women adjust to divorce better than do men due to supportive friendships.

The availability of social support may be particularly problematic during divorce. First, friendships often are changed during the disruption of a marriage. Second, a divorced individual might find that most friends engage in couple-oriented activities. Third, patterns of interactions with family and friends might be strained because they disapproved of the divorce (Miller, 1970). Fourth, friends might feel threatened because the marital dissolution of a close friend could cause an examination of their marriages. Other friends might remain aloof because they feel awkward and ambiguous about the situation (Spanier & Casto, 1979). Friends also might take sides out of loyalty to one of the divorcing spouses and reject the other (Weiss, 1975).

However, there are a number of weaknesses in most available studies on social support:

1. Studies often have ignored Black men. Culture-specific influences in the perception and acceptance of social support often are neglected.
2. Research often has compared Blacks and Whites without using ethnomethodological and descriptive research.
3. Few studies have included both working class and middle class Blacks in the study populations. Consequently, generalizations about low-income Blacks have been applied to all Blacks.
4. Typically, research is unidirectional. The focus generally is on the recipient of social support. There is an absence of research on those who provide social support. For example, Dressler (1985) found that kin support is beneficial for Black males. Females between 17 and 34 years of age received no benefit from extended kin support. This study neglected the age and gender of those who provided support. This presents an interesting question: Do some Blacks believe that it is more important to provide support to males than to females, and if so, then what factors account for those beliefs?

Social Participation

A number of community groups have been designed to minimize the distress of divorce. Such groups have targeted single mothers (Johnson,

1986), single fathers (Tedder, Scherman, & Sheridan, 1984), or older divorced women (Langelier & Duckert, 1980). Community self-help groups have been shown to minimize the negative impact of divorce and to facilitate self-development (Gray, 1978).

Social participation increases postdivorce, especially for males (Albrecht, 1980; Weiss, 1975). Whereas males become more involved with clubs and organizations, females have more contact with family members. Research has shown that social participation correlates with lower distress and better postdivorce adjustment (Ambert, 1988; Furstenberg & Spanier, 1984; Raschke, 1977, 1987; Raschke & Barringer, 1977).

Forming New Relationships

Forming postdivorce heterosexual relationships often is a difficult task due to unfamiliarity of a single lifestyle, which is especially significant for those married for a long period of time (Hetherington, Cox, & Cox, 1977; Wymard, 1994; Zeiss, Zeiss, & Johnson, 1980). Studies have reported that dating lowers postdivorce distress through several processes (Kitson & Morgan, 1990; Weiss, 1975). First, it familiarizes the divorce to the customs and values of singlehood. Second, it often results in needed self-appraisal (Wymard, 1994). Although dating a variety of people is as effective as forming a very close relationship, Raschke (1987) found that dating decreases postdivorce distress for males but not for females. However, Black men may have other disadvantages during the dating process compared to White men. First, they usually have less financial resources to spend on dates. Second, they might be constrained by work schedules because a large number work various shifts and part-time jobs. Third, fears of rejection also might prohibit some Black men from dating.

The previous discussion has shown that positive social support, community groups, social participation, and dating often moderate postdivorce distress. It is unknown whether these factors are influential in the adjustment process of Black men. The next section examines the respondents' supportive networks and the various strategies they used to cope with transition to a new lifestyle.

Positive Social Support and Divorce

Taylor reported that he has been dreaming every night:

Some days, I feel alive. Some days, I feel dead, treading out time. Once in a while, my mind slips and I think I'm back in my dream. The only thing that saved me was my friends and family. They were there for me. My sisters gathered together when they learned about my problems and did what they could. They made pots of greens, ham, cornbread, and rice. My uncles went fishing yesterday, and I'm drowning in bluefish. My work friends and I are going to a club tonight. They would say, "Why don't you come along with us?" The little things my family and friends did, like making sure they would pick me up for work, meant a lot. I will get over and survive the battlefield of my own life, with the help of the church and friends. It was Sam, my play brother, who sat with me until I got over the sense of betrayal and the awful hurting. He seemed to understand what I was going through. He would say, "I don't care where you are, if you feel this uptight, give me a call." It was nice knowing that if I needed someone, I could call.

In contrast to previous research with White male samples (Albrecht, 1980; White & Bloom, 1981), the men requested and relied on the support of friends and family members to cope with the psychological stress of divorce.

SUPPORT FROM MOTHERS

Of interest, the respondents reported that their mothers provided emotional and tangible support. Allen recalled, "My mother helped me by providing emotional support, and she took care of [the] kids until I returned from work." Gerald emphasized the financial support he received from his mother: "My mother got me a lawyer—the best lawyer in town—and paid for the divorce." Anton also underscored the moral support he received from his mother: "My mother gave me so much emotional support that helped me to cope with the divorce. She understood that I was losing a wife and that it would be painful. That helped a lot." Ivan's mother gave him a car. Matt lived with his mother and viewed it as practical, convenient, and temporary. He explained:

Mom believed that Black men have it harder than Black women in America, so she did everything in her power to help me. One day, Mom asked, "Have you tried praying?" I began to pray. I didn't know what to say, but I began to ask God to help me cope with all this anger, hurt, and pain. I regained strength by praying. From then on, Mom and I often read the Bible and prayed together. Mom provided such positive support, and it was a relief to know that she was there for me.

Participant observation revealed that the respondents' mothers and sisters volunteered to take their children to parks, sports activities, and church. Black family members, especially females, also provided child care, mutual aide, advice, therapeutic comfort, and tangible support. Mothers exercised authority coupled with love in ways that few studies have reported with White samples. Indeed, Black mothers were sources of strength and support to sons in ways largely unmatched by Whites, regardless of income.

SUPPORT GROUPS AND FRIENDS SUPPORT

The respondents also formed their own support groups. Lennie said, "I hand-picked my support group from friends who had been in a similar situation. These friends were open-minded and saw both sides of the situation. We met every week."

Elaborating on the specific actions of his friends, Curtis said,

I talked to my friends about the situation, and that helped me cope. They helped me to ponder the question [of] whether I was addicted to a cycle of turmoil. We talked about my deep-seated anxieties of no matter how close I was to establishing a successful life, I would eventually find a way to blow it. We also talked about the experiences of being a Black man in America. We have the same feelings of being restricted by forces beyond our control and having fears of never knowing what we could really be and do within the system that is not plagued by racism. Divorce compounds the stress of coping with racial stereotypes.

A large majority of the men (70%, $n = 35$) reported that male friends prevented some of them from experiencing loneliness. In fact, most of friends were present prior to the divorces and remained post-divorce. This was a representative comment: "My friends never left. They were the same friends that I hung out with during my marriage.

They basically wanted to see me okay; they wanted to see me through this ordeal."

Most respondents viewed male friends as supportive. Unlike the Weiss (1975) and Spanier and Casto (1979) studies, the respondents did not isolate themselves from friends feeling that they no longer fit in. Moreover, unlike findings reported on White samples (Weiss, 1975), friends *did not view* the respondents as a threat to their own marriages, sexual competitors, or reminders of possible marital failure. Although friends were married, they involved the respondents in card parties, cookouts, concerts, and vacations.

OPPOSITE-SEX FRIENDS

Among the respondents, 18 men mentioned the support of opposite-sex friends with whom they shared confidences and described them as stable and valuable. These friends provided an atmosphere in which the men could receive a "woman's view of the situation." The following is Barry's description of such a relationship:

> I have had this woman friend for about 20 years. Sometimes, we get together and I just talk to her. There is no romantic interest; it's nice that she is somebody nice to talk to since she is a woman and I can get her point of view. Besides, I like her company better than the company of most men I know. She understood and responded [more] sympathetically than most of my male friends.

Opposite-sex friends also provided housing, provided financial support, and assisted with child care. Previous research has shown that friends provide distinctive types of social support postdivorce (Gerstel, 1988).

Religious Support

Approximately 36% (*n* = 18) of the respondents reported that increased involvement in church activities and a religious community helped them cope with divorce. One benefit of religious participation was the increased social contact it provided. Arthur explained, "I pulled myself together and started going to church. The church community helped me to deal with the mess I was in." Bert emphasized the assistance from a pastor of a church and recalled reactions and help received from the pastor:

> I checked into an inpatient psychiatric program, and the pastor visited regularly and provided emotional support. The pastor was understanding and forgiving. I felt a tremendous relief telling him about my past. He didn't moralize; I didn't need that. He did not preach to me. He just listened, and I needed that so much.

Barry also explained the role of the church in facilitating adjustment postdivorce:

> I wanted to kill Jennifer, and the church pastor showed me if you have God in your life, you can conquer anything. We had weekly talks about the pain and hurt I felt. He does not know it, but he may have saved Jennifer's life. I had to acknowledge my hurt through a church community or I would have destroyed myself or killed Jennifer.

Other men reported that church pastors, members, and activities as well as prayer provided emotional support postdivorce, which moderated emotional distress. A religious social network also provided emotional support, instrumental support, and referrals to other sources of aid.

INVOLVEMENT IN CHURCH ACTIVITIES

Participant observation of church services added another dimension to the study. Whereas interviews enabled assessment of patterns of experiences, direct observation of church members' support allowed observation of the role churches played in moderating postdivorce distress. For example, ministers emphasized a need to love—to love one's neighbors, one's friends, and even one's enemies. In Sunday school, we listened to a poignant discussion in which the teacher told the story of a man whose wife committed adultery. The class was asked, "Is it possible for the man to love her?" One man answered, "Yes, it is possible, but it is hard." This opinion was shared by others, who talked about the problems of married life. The discussion ended with an admonition to "do good to those who mistreat you" and to "drive out hatred with love."

We also observed fervent prayers offered on behalf of the respondents. For example, a church member opened the church service by reading a chapter from the Bible. This was followed by a congregational hymn. The church member then prayed. She began each sentence with "Oh Holy Father" and asked Him to bless the respondent during his trials and tribulations. "We ask you, Holy Father, to look on him and to give him strength during these difficult days." The prayer was very personal; therefore, the respondent could regard himself as superior because he followed Christ's precepts better than those of his former spouse.

Several men reported "getting religion" after the divorces and even "shouted" in church. They said that the Lord had changed their lives. Before the divorces, their lives were "heavy with sin," and they prayed to God for forgiveness. Because their sins had been forgiven, they felt "light as a feather." This feeling propelled them to make behavioral and attitudinal changes such as abstaining from smoking, drinking, and examining priorities.

The men's church activities also included participation in church conventions, weekly revival meetings, discussion groups, and social events such as boat cruises, Broadway plays, and trips to health spas. The men also participated in church cookouts and planned events to pay off church debts, to help needy church members, and to beautify the church. For example, Stanley and Sam organized a bake sale to help the church purchase a new furnace. Lennie organized events during Black History Month, which included a father-son night and several speakers from the local university. These activities facilitated adjustment to divorce.

Increased Social Participation

Approximately 80% ($n = 40$) of the respondents coped with the divorces by increasing their time commitment to work and engaging in self-improvement activities. For example, Jim, Curtis, Leon, Kenneth, Willy, and Henry worked overtime; Todd, John, Jim, and Bernie worked part-time jobs; and Dwayne, Bronson, Stanley, and Barry worked evening full-time jobs. Also, Vincent enrolled in a weightlifting class; Eric and Graham learned to play golf; James coached a basketball team; Allen biked cross-country; and Clyde became a big brother. Henry detailed the benefits of work to cope with divorce:

> I used my job as a tool to cope with the divorce. I kept my mind busy, and over a period of time the pain wore off. I would tell any divorcing man to make sure he gets involved with work because if he does not, he might end up shooting himself or killing someone else. I also fished, hunted, and spent a lot of time on my boat.

Similarly, men in Hetherington's (1989) study reported spending more time at work. However, unlike previous samples of Whites (Albrecht 1980; Weiss, 1975), not one man in this study reported that his work suffered as a result of the divorce. It also appeared that work aided in postdivorce adjustment because it provided positive supportive social relationships. For example, Kenneth said,

> The men at the police department were so supportive. They really understood what I was going through. They recommended a good lawyer and made suggestions about how to deal with the hurt and pain, like introducing me to single women.

COMMUNITY INVOLVEMENT

The respondents also increased their involvement in social activities including Black fraternity events and political functions. Participant observation revealed that Lawrence, Graham, and Barry joined community committees that opposed school busing. John, Maurice, and Bert formed a group to repair parks in Black neighborhoods. Ernell, who formed the group, detailed his involvement:

> I wrote a letter to the park and recreation board when I saw Black kids playing in a park with broken swings and dangerous equipment. The city council asked me to attend a board meeting. The city had constructed a golf course that costs about $4 million in a White neighborhood and neglected to repair parks in Black neighborhoods. I spoke in front of the city's park and recreation commission and even met with the mayor about the need for better recreational facilities in Black neighborhoods.

Truman reported that he belonged to the Elks Club and was chair of a committee to increase scholarships for Black youths. He attributed these activities to the moderation of emotional pain following the divorce. He said, "I organized a fund-raising drive for scholarships to give to Black youths who want to go to college. I raised over $50,000 and received a plaque of appreciation and had my picture in the paper. This helped me adjust to living alone and the pain of the divorce."

Participation in Black community activities reinforced the postdivorce identities of the respondents as respectable and, thereby, enabled them to cope with the postdivorce emotional turmoil. Therefore, race-specific community activities increased the self-worth of Black divorced men and provided an antidote to their sense of failure. Other activities that moderated postdivorce distress included attending movies, traveling, visiting museums, collecting Black art, and enrolling in college courses. The energetic moving out in many directions seemed to moderate postdivorce distress.

Cognitive Style

The optimism of Blacks has been documented extensively by a number of scholars (Billinglsey, 1992; Hill, 1972; Staples, 1985). This cognitive style has been characterized as an unfaltering faith and a strong religious orientation. Historically, Blacks have believed in and practiced the paradox of faith—the certainty of the uncertainty. According to Hill (1972), this cognitive characteristic of Blacks represents a survival strategy used to cope with social and economic marginality. Blacks would not have survived unless a sense of optimism had existed. This outlook involves the belief that when life devastates Blacks, they will triumph. For example, Leon discussed his optimism in the context of the historical experiences of Blacks in America:

> My ancestors suffered and believed that they would overcome oppression one day. My forefathers and foremothers kept on going, even though they were slaves. Knowledge of their strength has given me determination and inspiration to keep on going despite obstacles I face in trying to reestablish my life.

Truman also said,

> I strongly believe that life has a way of working out because, as a Black man, I've had to believe that or I would have killed myself a long time ago. That was the theme of slaves, and they were eventually freed.

The men's sense of optimism represents a resilience to adapt to divorce. Although some respondents experienced much pain and had been economically bankrupted, they expressed a strong unfaltering faith that their situations would improve. According to Hill (1975), the spiritual beliefs and the history of coping with oppression underscore the strength of Blacks.

Grier and Cobb (1968) suggest that the survival skills of Blacks have been passed from generation to generation and continue as contemporary coping strategies. For example, optimism has helped Blacks to cope with an American ethos that includes the assumption that Blacks are inferior and are born for physical labor. However, in the struggle to survive, Blacks have developed a lifestyle that has influenced music and a broad canvas of creativity. As Bronson said,

> Take a look at Blacks, who as slaves took the leftover trash intestines that White folks gave them from the hog and turned it into a delicacy, chitterlings. Blacks took the painful experiences of slavery and created the blues and jazz that the White world loves.

This finding suggests that strategies that enabled men to cope with social marginality and discrediting were revised to cope with post-divorce psychological distress.

Another way of coping with divorce is involvement in new relationships. The following sections explore the ways in which the respondents formed new relationships, expectations for future partners, and adjustment to a new lifestyle.

Heterosexual Relationships

A majority of the respondents did not engage in "frenzied dating activity" because it was expensive and required energy and time to arrange. Approximately 70% (n = 35) of the respondents became involved in close relationships 1 year postdivorce, which often resulted in cohabitation. Although the men recognized that cohabitation was a major commitment, it seemed to happen casually. Brent said, "It took me about 1 year to even want to talk to another woman again. I went back to church and met this wonderful lady who loved me as me, and we started living together." Vince agreed:

> It took about a year to want to meet women because I had trouble trusting them. I don't believe in meeting women in bars. A friend introduced me to this woman with three children, and we moved in together. So, I went from living alone to adjusting to living with three small children.

Vince also asserted that the living arrangement was a prelude to marriage to "see if we could get along," and he merged into a collective identity with his mate. In addition, cohabitation was preferred over dating because the latter often was emotionally draining. Ben reported his experience with the dating scene:

> I met women who I thought were shallow. They seemed to be guided by their most basic needs and feelings. They talked about shopping sprees, hairstyles, makeup, and clothing. The professional women I met were smart and ambitious, but they liked to dress up on weekends and go to expensive restaurants. These women seemed uptight to find a man—any single, Black heterosexual man with a job.

In fact, not *one* respondent expressed positive views about living single, yet only one man was engaged to be married. The desire for a stable family life appeared to underlie the reason why men yearned for intense emotional relationships. "I enjoy the family life, that is, having one special person in my life rather than dating a number of women" was a recurrent comment.

Some men also became involved with women who had children because it provided them with a sense of belonging and served as a substitute for their own children. Gerald explained,

> I live with my girlfriend and her daughter. Since I can't raise my own daughters, I can protect and provide security for my girlfriend's daughter.

I always wanted to raise a daughter, so my girlfriend and her 2-year-old daughter live with me.

Participant observation revealed that social events reinforced the belief that marriage and romance were necessary prerequisites for personal fulfillment. For example, songs in the tradition of "soul music" such as the Temptations' *My Girl* and the melodies of Luther Vandross often played during social events, suggesting that relationships were extremely significant.

Black fraternity parties, family reunions, and church socials also emphasized the importance of conjugal relationships. For instance, men and women usually were introduced as the wives or husbands of other persons, and individuals who were single often sat together while those who were married formed their own social group. There was a high social status attached to being coupled. Compliments were paid to couples who had been together for a long time and who were celebrating a 25th wedding anniversary. In fact, in the respondents' social circle, wedding anniversaries were celebrated events, costing between $3,000 and $5,000 with professional caterers and live bands. Consequently, the men organized their postmarital lives with intimate friends who they could talk to, who they could go places with, and who were committed to the relationships.

There was no single and uncomplicated explanation that men expressed for not engaging in a frenzy of dating activity. The need to belong, the need to be loved, and the need to raise children were the primary reasons for desiring an intimate relationship.

Barriers to Intimacy

Because intimate relationships often were viewed as threatening, some men had difficulty with commitment. For example, Sam felt apprehensive about making a long-term emotional commitment for fear of being hurt or rejected. He said, "I told my girlfriend that I am holding my emotions back because I didn't want to go through more hurt and pain." Larry also restrained emotions in his current relationship:

I'm hard on women because of my marriage. I don't want to love anymore. As long as I don't put myself completely out there, my relationships go fine. Every time a woman thinks a man loves her, something goes off in her head. So, I have a hard time trusting women. I am clear that nothing lasts forever. I thought I would be married to Pat until death. Today, I am clear that there is no guarantee that a marriage will last.

Anton expanded on his inability to trust a relationship:

Even though I am involved in a close relationship, I always say, "Is she telling me the truth? Does she really care for me the way she says? Does she really understand what I need in a relationship? If I marry her, will the marriage end the way my first marriage ended?" I ask myself these questions constantly. I have a hard time believing women after the divorce.

Although some men were involved in intimate relationships, they were hesitant to totally entrust their well-being to women. They wondered whether their future marriages would remain vital and warm and whether their love would continue to excite other women forever. They also wondered whether they would sleep every night with their spouses and reach for them with the same desire and eagerness. Although they hoped that their marriages would endure forever, they wondered whether those hopes were fantasies.

NEW SENSE OF FREEDOM

Some men had difficulty establishing intimate relationships because they feared losing their newly acquired sense of autonomy. The divorces allowed them to establish routines without constraints. The following comments reveal Ivan's feeling of a new sense of freedom:

Living single is a dangerous situation. If I live single for a long period of time, I don't think I'll be able to live with anyone else. It feels good to know that when I go to sleep, my whole household goes to sleep; when I eat, my whole house eats; and when I want some noise, it is the noise I make. So, this is a very dangerous situation.

According to Ivan, the divorce allowed him to live alone for the first time in his life and liberated him from the demands of adjusting to a woman's plans. Other men also discovered that they were free to do what gave them pleasure and relished in being able to come and go as they pleased, and some even described divorce as "being released from prison." Similarly, Reissman (1990) found that a large number of divorced men described a sense of freedom following the termination of their marriages.

MINOR CHILDREN

The presence of minor children also served as a major barrier to relationship development. For example, a number of men said that their energy and attention were concentrated solely on their children. Eric said,

> Right now, I am pretty happy because all of my energy and attention [are] solely devoted to my sons. They are only ages 5, 9, and 10, and they need me now more than ever. I spend a lot of time taking them to parks, fishing, and just hanging out. I do things that will last in their memories.

Because Eric devoted a large amount time to his sons, he had insufficient time, energy, or money to become involved with a woman.

Edsel also said that his life was harried by taking his kids to basketball games, football practice, and community events and that he did not have time for an intimate relationship. Other men reported that children gave their lives structure and purpose, which bonded them to family members and to the community. As a result, children often provided a substitute for an intimate relationship. Of interest, some men indicated that they avoided relationships because of children's disapproval. For example, Todd said that his teenage daughter would reject both the relationship and him:

> I think that Cheryl, my daughter, don't like me because of the divorce. I don't want to give her another reason not to like me. I know she will hate any person I date and it will destroy our fragile relationship.

Some men proceeded with relationships pragmatically and slowly, fearing the effects they would have on children. As a result, coupling was viewed as preferable to no relationship but seldom evolved into marriage. Heterosexual relationships, however, seemed appealing because they involved few constraints and, therefore, men could function independently.

The Benefits of Divorce

Divorce has been viewed as a growth-promoting experience and may benefit some individuals (Kaffman & Talmon, 1984; Veevers, 1991). Divorce may be defined as a chance for growth and an opportunity for constructive change (Buchler & Langenbrunner, 1987). For example, a change in roles associated with divorce compelled some men to reevaluate their lifestyles, which in turn led to improved functioning. Several men reported working through identity issues, which improved heterosexual relationships. Willy, who stated that he married when he was young and foolish and because it was "something to do," said,

> The divorce made me aware that I was deficient in the way in which I relate to women. After the divorce, I assessed who I was and what I wanted out of life. After the divorce, I started all over again with a new identity and purpose in life. I am more responsive to women in my life, and I listen more to their concerns—something I never did in my marriage and regret that I was never a husband to Donna.

Carl said that for all his unhappiness over the past year, he had attained harmony with himself and his life. "Adjustment," Carl called it. He was at peace with himself to choose a heterosexual relationship more carefully and, thereby, escaped the continuing pains of incompatibility. He believed that he never would lose the sense of peace he attained and that he had achieved a sense of inner harmony to confront unresolved conflicts.

EVALUATION OF MACHO IMAGES

Other men reported that the divorces forced them to evaluate their macho images. Brent said,

> I had a macho thing of not wanting to show love. Before the divorce, I thought I was not supposed to tell any man or woman how I felt. I learned to express my feelings and stopped being so macho. Plus, since I have

never seen my parents show outward affection, I am not comfortable with that. Most women want to be told they are loved, and I am working on that.

As a result, some men learned from divorce to perform behaviors that former wives desired during their marriages. As Sam remarked,

I should have spent more time with my family. I was so occupied with making money. I was raised to believe that a good husband was a good provider. I also thought I could do anything I wanted in a marriage—and basically I did.

Divorce stimulated some men to reexamine intimate aspects of their personalities. Although it is commonly believed that Black men rarely are introspective, some men engaged in self-analysis to prevent repeated marital failures, suggesting that divorce may stimulate self-actualization and emotional growth for some Black men. This finding concurs with that of Sutton and Sprenkle (1985), who suggest that divorce can provide an opportunity for emotional growth.

Qualities in Future Mates

The respondents were asked what qualities they wanted in future mates. Overwhelmingly, they stressed independence. Todd expanded on the independence theme:

I like strong, aggressive, and independent women. Maybe it comes from being raised by my mother and being around my sister; they are strong and independent women. I like a woman who will say, "I don't like that, do it this way," but who will not get upset when I don't take her advice.

The majority of the men emphasized warmth, understanding, and trustworthiness to describe the characteristics they wanted in a future mate. Leon explained, "I want a woman who has a warm personality and a woman who is doing things with her life." Reiterating on the personality characteristics, Lawrence emphasized commitment and the ability to communicate: "I look for a woman who can love me for me and who understands that marriage is a commitment. My future wife must be a woman who I can talk [about] things with." Vance emphasized the rejection of negative stereotypes about Black men:

> I want a woman who understands that a Black man can really love and who does not buy into the negative images of Black men. I am looking for a woman who can love very hard, I mean, a woman who will be there for me because I will be there for her.

The preference for women who reject negative stereotypes of Black men was striking. Cazenave and Smith (1983) analyzed the acceptance or rejection of negative stereotypes of Black men and women. The sample consisted of 256 respondents, with more than two thirds female and a median age of 30 years. They found that respondents who accepted negative stereotypes about Black men and women had traditional views of gender roles. In addition, divorced and never-married statuses were associated with acceptance of negative stereotypes of Black men. These findings support the view of men in the present study that negative racial stereotypes exist among Blacks and, therefore, may prohibit positive Black male-female relationships.

SIMILAR RELIGIOUS BELIEFS AND PRACTICES

Most men emphasized the importance of finding women with similar religious beliefs and practices. This was a typical comment:

> I don't go to church every Sunday, even though I believe in God. I am not wrapped up in going to Gospel concerts or being actively involved in church. I want a woman who believes that commitment to a Higher Power means giving to others and treating others good, right, and kind rather than going to church.

WOMEN WHO DO NOT DESIRE MORE CHILDREN

Of interest, 60% ($n = 30$) of the men said that they wanted women who *did not want more children.* Ben elaborated,

> My girlfriend does not want any more children. She has a 13-year-old daughter, and she is tired of raising children. So, that made her more attractive to me because I am tired of raising children and tired of

providing for their needs by working three jobs. I am just tired. I don't
think young kids these days realize how much money it takes to raise a
child and the pain involved when you can't buy your child the things that
are needed.

Although some men reported that they did not want more children,
they refused to consider vasectomies for fear they would interfere with
their sexual performance. The emphasis on preferring women who
did not desire more children is significant because Blacks have higher
fertility rates than do Whites. This finding suggests that lack of
knowledge of the costs involved in raising children and ignorance of
parents' frustration when financial resources are limited might explain
the high Black fertility rate. An implication of this finding is that
programs to decrease early childbearing should emphasize the economic costs of child rearing as well as its implications for the self-
esteem of parents.

NONMATERIAL WOMEN

As observed in Chapter 3, a large number of men emphasized the
importance of finding partners who were "nonmaterial women." Larry
explained,

> A lot of Black women see Black men as meal tickets. I want a self-sufficient
> woman who will not ask me for a thing. The woman I am seeing takes
> me out to dinner occasionally and takes me to the movies every now and
> then. I have never had that, and it feels good.

Larry believed that the emphasis on materialism has resulted in many
Black men and women overlooking genuine human qualities in mates.

Overall, men were afraid that mistakes in their first marriages would
be repeated and, therefore, feared second divorces. Indeed, studies
dating back to the 1950s have found that remarriages are 10% more
likely to end in divorce than are first marriages (Furstenberg, 1987).
Furthermore, people tend to divorce earlier the second time than the
first time—about 6 years for a second divorce versus 7 years for a first
divorce (National Center for Health Statistics, 1995).

RACE MAKES A DIFFERENCE

For the majority of men, race was a factor in mate selection due to societal reactions to intermarriage. Stanley said, "My brothers are in interracial relationships, and they say it is uncomfortable going to restaurants. I think societal attitudes toward Black men dating White women have changed very little since slavery."

Interestingly, some men who had been in interracial marriages reported that they preferred to remarry Black women. For example, Taylor, an ex-marine who had been married for 5 years and divorced for 3 years, represented a typical case. He met his ex-wife, Joanne, in Germany. Taylor lived in his parents' basement for 3 years, depressed over the divorce and emotionally immobilized. He said,

> Of course, I did not go out looking for a White woman to marry. I fell in love with a woman who happened to be White. Our differences did not directly relate to race, but race played a part in her expectations of a husband. My ex-wife, Joanne, a military brat, wanted me to be more affectionate. I had trouble demonstrating affection in public, and Joanne wanted that. Plus, she was extremely dependent and insecure. She lacked self-confidence and would not go out and find a job—even a part-time job. I guess I've been raised by Black women who worked all their lives, and I expected that in a wife. The next woman I marry will be Black. Plus, on some level, I would rather get hurt by a Black woman than a White woman, so maybe I am racist.

Indeed, it cannot be assumed that partners entering interracial relationships are nonracist. According to Rosenblatt, Karis, and Powell (1995), couples can place their racism in the background while forming relationships with specific persons. This may result from couples being insulated from the attitudes and predispositions that composed racism.

However, racist attitudes and behaviors may later surface. Indeed, Taylor believed that race played a role in his divorce:

> I found that Joanne was more calculating than most of the Black women I've met. She had planned on leaving me about 2 years before she actually left. All the while, she pretended to be a good wife. Most Black women leave their marriages impulsively, during a heated argument. It is not calculated or planned. Unlike Black women, White women have a history

of planning and being very calculating to get what they want. So, I think race played a part indirectly. Perhaps if I had been a White man, I would have been more in tune to Joanne's calculating behavior.

Taylor's marriage cast a dark shadow on every aspect of his existence. He was filled with self-doubt and repeatedly asked, "What is wrong with me? Why didn't I see the signs that the marriage was doomed for failure? Maybe I was mesmerized by her white skin and fascinated by her White culture." This suggests that divorced men and women from interracial marriages may have special concerns and needs compared to their non-interracial divorced counterparts. Furthermore, because some friends and parents may disapprove of such marriages, the couples might receive little social support.

RACE MAKES NO DIFFERENCE IN MATE SELECTION

Some men reported that race would have little influence on selecting future mates and believed that society should not dictate a marital partner. This was a representative comment:

> I don't look at race. It does not make a difference to me if a woman is White, Black, or Hispanic. I don't look at color, and I don't think society should tell me who to marry. This is America, and I am American, so I should have the freedom to marry who I want.

Specifically, some men emphasized the color of a future mate as being less important than the quality of the relationship. Vincent commented on this belief: "As long as the relationship is healthy, the color of a person does not matter. The most important factor is whether two people love each other and can get along." Some men talked about race and mate selection in terms of a basic religious philosophy. The following was a representative remark:

> I would definitely marry a woman from another race. I am a religious person. If you read the Bible, it tells you that there is no difference in races. God created men and women, and that's it. Society places a distinction on color, not God.

According to Rosenblatt et al. (1995), although people talk about factors that influence them to enter interracial relationships, there might be other factors such as the relative sizes of the Black and White populations in their communities and the gender balances of Blacks and Whites. However, people who reject racism are more likely to enter any type of interracial relationship, and such people are more likely to be free from the constraints of those around them who are critical of interracial relationships (Rosenblatt et al., 1995). Wilkinson (1977) describes interracial coupling in terms of prolonged idolization and tabu surrounding the White female. From this perspective, the White female symbolizes both freedom and bondage in the minds of a number of Black males. Paradoxically, frequent interracial mating has had no measurable impact on the reduction of racist myths. Color exogamy has not decreased institutionalized White racism, and numerous personal problems still confront interracial couples (Wilkinson, 1977).

Difficulty in Finding Future Mates

The men were asked whether they had trouble finding the qualities they desired in women. This was a representative response:

> Most Black women are caring, and that quality is not hard to find. But it is hard to find a nonjealous woman. I have many women who are just friends, and it's hard for some Black women to accept that a Black man can just have female friends.

Interestingly, despite the imbalanced sex ratio among Blacks, most men had difficulty meeting women who desired committed relationships because many women assumed that they could find other male partners. Graham explained,

> It is hard to find a woman who wants to commit to a relationship. Many of them say, "I can find somebody else when the relationship runs into problems." In today's society, people in general and Black men and women in particular have short attention spans and leave relationships quickly.

The respondents indicated that the sex ratio might be statistically significant, but many Black women view the shortage of Black men as nonproblematic. As John reported,

> The media [have] sensationalized the shortage of Black men. Black women often consider men from Africa or the Caribbean. They are also forming relationships with White men, and some are seeing men who make less money than they do.

According to some men, the absence of a strong commitment to relationships that plagues Black coupling results from a lack of tenacity to form serious attachments rather than from the shortage of Black men.

Men also reported difficulty in finding Black women who could compromise. Roscoe explained, "I have difficulty finding women who can compromise. I want my next mate to be able to look at both sides of a situation, to give up her position if that is necessary, and to be flexible to adapt to any situation." Roscoe believed that bargaining and negotiation are important to resolve conflicts. Consistent with his perspective, Gottman (1979) found that happily married couples reach agreements rather quickly and that one partner gives in to the other without resentment.

Overall, the men believed that it was difficult to meet women who had the following qualities: (a) nonjealous, (b) committed to a relationship, and (c) ability to compromise.

FINDING THE RIGHT MATES

Several men indicated that they had found all the qualities they desired in their current mates. For example, Bernie, who remarried, said,

> The woman I married is interested in the way I think, and she is very sensitive to my needs. We are both turned off by having a lot of material things and "Where is the next adventure coming from?" She is the kind of woman that I can really talk to. She is my best friend. In fact, we really enjoy each other's company. And I don't feel like I have to be on all the time, looking for the next adventure.

4. the rejection of negative stereotypes of Black men;
5. nonjealous behavior;
6. nonmaterialistic; and
7. Black.

In Kitson's (1992) sample with a majority of White respondents, the following characteristics were indicated by divorced single males as most desirable in future mates:

1. "helpmate" partner;
2. sexual partner; and
3. someone to talk to.

This finding suggests that whereas Black men's assessments of future mates include personality and behavioral qualities, White men often express specific pragmatic qualities.

The finding that not one man in this study mentioned desiring a sexual partner also is significant because Black men often are depicted in terms of biogenetic dimensions and have sought to overcome deep-seated anxieties stemming from the reduction of their social selves to physical entities. The respondents' lack of consideration of potential mates' sexual prowess belies the stereotype of the super-sexual Black male.

Unexpectedly, the *presence of children* did not preclude a woman as a future mate. In contrast to White samples (Kitson, 1992), some men in this study even *preferred* women who had children. This finding may be explained, in part, by the high value placed on children and by the fact that most Black men desire at least one biological child, even if they adopt or rear others' children (Rodgers-Rose, 1980). However, in Kitson's (1992) sample, the absence of children made it easier for divorced men and women to find new partners.

Of significance, although most respondents would not eliminate women who had child-rearing responsibilities, they preferred women who did not desire *more children,* suggesting that the timing of births is significant to some Black men. This finding is significant because Black men are largely stereotyped as parenting by default.

The concerns of divorced men from interracial marriages are interesting and unexpected. These men experienced profound stress in psychologically separating from former spouses. Future researchers should pursue this line of inquiry and design studies of divorced noncustodial fathers from interracial marriages as well as from blended interracial marriages. This is crucial because interracial marriages have increased substantially since 1980 (Chatters, Taylor, & Jackson, 1986; Chatters, Taylor, & Neighbors, 1989).

8

The Construction of Fatherhood

I was very clear in my marriage that I did not want to be like my father. I wanted to feel the bond that fathers are supposed to feel with their children. I tried hard to have a broader view of the role of women and children in my life. I made up my mind that I did not want to be a detached, remote, and distant father.

—Dwayne

The definition of *fatherhood* has changed dramatically in the past 30 years (Frustenberg, 1988; Griswold, 1993; Marsiglio, 1995). The public discourse on fathering has been reinforced by the parents' household division of labor debate, children's public policy issues, and decreased marital permanence. Discussions of volunteer single parents, teenage parenting, reconstituted families, stable gay and lesbian relationships, dual-career couples, and single fathers have increased interest in the roles and perceptions of fathers.

Cultural images of fathers have been shaped by dichotomies of good dad/bad dad fathers (Furstenberg, 1988). Opposing portrayals of fatherhood consist of nurturing fathers versus uninvolved deadbeat fathers. These ideological distinctions of fatherhood have been reinforced by the high rates of divorce, the greater public awareness of sexual child abuse, and the media's attention to teenage pregnancies (Furstenberg, 1988).

Race and social class affect the differentiation of good dad/bad dad fathers (Marsiglio, 1993). In addition, the public view of Black fathers has been more negative than that of White fathers. Scholars also have perpetuated negative stereotypes of Black fathers by investigating primarily Black lower class fathers (McAdoo, 1981).

In Chapter 7, we explored strategies that Black men use to cope with divorce. In this chapter, we consider the ways in which men shaped their fatherhood identities according to various role models. Specifically, we ask the following. What role models influence the identity of fatherhood? To what extent do these role models influence enactment of fathering roles? How does a man reconcile his father's generation of being a good provider with the current expectations of the "new father," one who takes an active role in child rearing? The following example illustrates Eric's experience of an aloof father and how he departed from a traditional role to that of a "new father."

Aloof Fathers and Fatherhood Identities

Eric reported that he went to see his father with much ambivalence and uncertainty. Eric's Father was orderly. Mr. Nash, Eric's father, never had eaten breakfast in a robe. Nor had Eric, until last Christmas. Not only had Eric come downstairs in a robe, but he had sat around in a robe until noon. Mr. Nash was extremely shocked, but it seemed ridiculous to reprimand a 40-year-old son who visited only once a year.

For as long as Eric could remember, Mr. Nash had a fixed pattern. He had dinner at 5 p.m. Dinner always consisted of fried or baked chicken, baked potatoes or sweet potatoes, and perhaps some collard greens and corn. On Sundays, there always was cake afterward, which Mrs. Nash baked every Saturday as she had done for nearly 40 years.

Eric felt loved, but he believed that his father's house was too clean and orderly. The disorganization that Eric created caused his father physical pain. Eric was careful. He emptied his ashtrays at night. Mr. Nash did not complain, but Eric sensed his father's difficulty in accepting what felt to him like defilement. Eric violated Mr. Nash's narrow pattern of life.

Eric wanted to violate more. He wanted to talk to his father, but that was impossible. He said, "*You know, I just wanted to have a father-to-son talk with my old man, but I knew the rules guiding conversation [were] strictly abided by; my father never talked to me.*"

Eric, hardly a child, thought he might be granted his father's confidence as they sat in the living room. Eric asked, "Dad, tell me what it feels like being married to Mom?" With Mr. Nash's eye cocked toward the door, Eric understood that this topic should not be approached. When he was young, family conversations could include only certain stipulated topics. He could discuss his school projects, but there could be no mention of problems. He never could discuss carousing at night. He could mention friends but not their problems. The cost of school activities was okay to discuss, but difficulty in getting money for school was not. If Eric mentioned that on Saturday night his father had been drunk and started a fight at a club, the shock would be less at the deed itself than at the fact that Eric mentioned it.

When Eric arrived at home, there always were hugs and handshakes as well as a lunch offer from friends and relatives. "How was your trip? Much traffic? How is the car holding up? How is work?" Eric answered the questions in a monotone and humdrum voice that made the exchanges seem more like a formal interview. Mr. Nash could not understand why Eric was not making more money with a college degree and why he was not the supervisor. Mr. Nash believed that Eric could overcome social discrediting by "working hard."

"So, how long you gonna stay on this job?" Mr. Nash asked.

"As soon as I get enough money to move on to something better. I want to own my business one day and not work for Whites."

"I don't know why you just won't settle down."

Mr. Nash could not understand why Eric changed jobs so often. Eric said that his father had asked the same questions last year and would ask the same questions the next year. Eric said,

> I loved my father, but we never said that to each other. It was understood but never expressed. So, I knew as a child that my father loved me, but I didn't know it [then]. I've always had a vague sense that there was something in life I was missing, but it seemed out of my reach.

Eric was silent for a minute, then said,

> Unlike my White male friends, I have never heard my friends say they wanted to be like their fathers when they grew up. Why would we want that when we knew our fathers were catching hell at work? My father

and his friends complained about Whites on his job being promoted over more qualified Blacks. My father drank a lot, and he usually got drunk on the day before it was time for him to go back to work. So, most of my friends wanted to be the opposite of their fathers. We didn't want to just work and work for the White man and end up like them.

Eric shrugged and added,

My dad was so downtrodden, so burdened and preoccupied with working for White folks, that he seldom talked much to me. He spent most of his life working and devoted most of his free time to working off steam built from counteracting and dealing with stereotypes. While his generation drowned their sorrows and stress in liquor, the younger generation is shooting drugs to escape the pain and confusion they feel inside.

Eric said that he could not understand how social experts on the Black family could discuss the problems of single-parent households without addressing the problems of two-parent families:

A two-parent home is good, but it is just as destructive as a single-parent home when the main breadwinner is frustrated, [is] oppressed, and has been beaten down by racism. I remember my dad feeling especially sad about a summer job contact. If he had any contact at all, [it] was for manual labor because he wanted my brother and me to work. Even then, my dad was not in a position to help me get a job because young White kids were getting those jobs before the openings were posted. He was hurt because he wanted us to work, but he had little control or influence.

As he observed his father, Eric thought that he did not look old—no older than he had ever been—and he could not remember him any other way. He recalled a photograph of his father taken in his Korean war uniform before he had gone overseas. He was slender and looked like Denzel Washington. What had happened to him? His life had been constricted to a mortgage payment, working for Whites, and raising children. Had simple physical survival in a racist society been so difficult for him that any other type of life was a luxury? Was his existence so hard? Perhaps it was the way in which he had to live in a world of racism and discrimination. Yet, going over this in his mind, Eric realized that his father had very few choices as a Black man growing up in the 1920s and 1930s. Eric could respect him for surviving the brutality of segregation and sticking by his family. He said,

> My old man paid his bills on time and had managed to keep the refrigerator full of food and a roof over the heads of five kids. That was a monumental task during his time, when a number of Black men were being lynched.

Mr. Nash rose the moment the news reporter said "good night" and turned off the television set. Eric turned to his father and said, "Good night, Dad." He stood and embraced him, really embraced him. Mr. Nash was surprised and a little stiffened. He smiled at Eric and could only say, "Remember to turn the thermostat down, son, won't you, Eric?" Mr. Nash never showed too much affection because it made him feel weak. And he hated feeling weak because it made him vulnerable. Who would be there to pick up the pieces if he let himself break down? At that moment, Eric could not remember his father ever hugging him or any of his brothers. He could not remember his father ever saying, "Son, I'm proud of you." Eric explained,

> My father was always critical of my behavior. He never encouraged me to do very much, and he never took me fishing or to play baseball. He has never known me as a person. He has never attended any of my graduations and doesn't even know that I was promoted to principal of my school.

Finally, Mr. Nash walked to the door and went upstairs. Eric said, "It's okay, I'll turn down the thermostat."

THE IMPORTANCE OF BEING AN INVOLVED FATHER

Eric reported that this father was aloof, which resulted in a desperate attempt to use that model for the type of father he *did not* want to become. Eric was devoted to his sons. He said,

> My father never got involved in his kids' lives. I wanted to try something different with my sons than my father tried with me. I took them to the movies, we went bowling, and we went shopping. While my sons were going through the divorce, they were fighting and taking knives to school.

They were not learning nothing in school. I was going back and forth to
social service agencies because they were acting out. I put my sons in a
mental hospital because I knew my kids were in trouble. I talked to them,
really talked to them, about their pain. We had sessions with a psychologist. I had to get past what my father thought was stigma—the idea that
counseling was for crazy people. I told them that I deeply loved them,
something my father never said to me.

According to Eric, his father was emotionally unavailable and aloof.
Without a strong model of an attentive, devoted, and vigilant father
to guide his behavior, he created a new model of fatherhood. He spoke
about being bonded to his children in a way that represented a
departure from his own father's behavior:

I was wounded by my father, not because he was evil or wished me harm
but because he was also wounded, like his father. My father's father was
mean to him. The pain in our family has drifted from generation to
generation, and each generation has been more alienated and lost. I finally
discovered that no amount of food or love would get rid of the hurt I felt
by a distant and aloof father. So, I made up my mind to be as involved
and interested in the lives of my children as possible. I didn't want my
children to experience the type of father I had. You know, all my life I
have felt deeply alone, that I had no one to count on but myself because
my father wasn't involved in my life. He wasn't there for me when I
needed him.

However, in presenting a role model that was different from that
of a previous generation, the respondent's new parenting style failed
to establish a new line of generational continuity that children would
want to imitate.

THE CONSEQUENCES OF
AN INVOLVED FATHER

Although the respondents practiced a different fathering style from
that of their fathers, their children often did not respond positively. For
example, Dwayne desired to bond with his daughter in a different way
from how his father had bonded with him. He was disappointed that
his daughter did not imitate his desire for a higher education. He
explained:

My old man came from the old school. Regardless of what was going on, he believed that a man and woman should stay married. He worked every day and drank on weekends. My mom realized that she didn't have [many] options with three kids. My father liked other women, so that was always an issue. Fridays, he would come home, take a bath, and go out and not come home until 3 or 4 in the morning. He would hang out with his friends in pool halls, and about the only day he stayed home was Sunday, to rest for work. He had very little interaction with me and my brothers. He didn't, and still does not, know us. He never showed up for our football games or college activities. He thought putting food on the table and providing a roof over our heads were his only responsibilities.

Trying to explain the reason for his father's behavior, Dwayne said,

My father had strict concepts of the role of women. He believed that a woman's role was to raise children, and the house was separate from life outside the home. He believed that a wife should play a subordinate role. My mother basically stayed home, had children, and took care of him. She couldn't go to the supermarket and get the food she wanted. She had to get the food he wanted. If she didn't, he would yell. She was strictly controlled in ways you would not believe. And when he came home, he expected meals to be ready and the children to be cleaned. The house should be neat, and that was the role of the wife, although he helped occasionally by doing the laundry. He was raised in the 1920s, and he adopted that thinking. So, he never discussed my dreams.

Dwayne emphasized that he wanted to be the opposite of his father:

I was very clear in my marriage that I did not want to be like my father. I wanted to feel the bond that fathers are supposed to feel with their children. I tried hard to have a broader view of the role of women and children in my life. I made up my mind that I did not want to be a detached, remote, and distant father.

Dwayne believed he had a good relationship with his daughter:

I did things with my daughter like my father never did with me. I sent my daughter to college, and she dropped out the second month. I paid her tuition and sent her money for living expenses. While in college, she was arrested for selling marijuana. She came back home and said, "I am grown and I am going to do what I want to do." I said, "Yea, you are grown but you can do it outside of this house." So, we argued for about a month or two. Then I showed her the door. I told her to get out because she sold reefer in my house and later she started to sell chemical drugs. Her friends were always trying to steal for drug money. She would get so high and stayed so tore up, I'd pray to God to bring her down.

Dwayne paused for a moment, then continued,

My daughter said drugs were like being in love with a man who is no good, but you can't let go. She was in jail for a while, and I supported her even then. At least when she went to jail, she seemed grateful. It gave her the opportunity to dry out, to thaw, and to think about the possibilities of what she could have become. She has two children and is on welfare, and she is happy. I am happy if she is happy. Of course, I would have preferred if she had a college degree, but if that is what she wanted, then that is okay. I feel comfortable with myself because she never felt unloved by me. Weekly, we talk on the phone.

Even though Dwayne wanted his daughter to be "like me, with a college degree," he was satisfied that he played an active and influential role in her life. He incorporated into his fathering repetoire values and standards such as expressing admiration and love for his daughter and providing advice. These behaviors were distinct from those of his father, who was present in the house but remained unapproachable and often indifferent.

Abusive Fathers and Fatherhood

Men who had abusive fathers described them in a manner such as this representative remark: "My old man was abusive, and he would yell at us for no reason." Ben recalled that he was determined not to be a verbal or physically abusive father or husband like his father:

I would never hit a woman. It was something my dad did, and I was clear I would never have a knock-down, drag-out fight with a woman. I would never pattern myself after my dad. My mother initiated the divorce, and she was pretty happy when it was over. My parents fought quite a bit. A few times, I remember the police coming to the house to break up a fight. They arrested my father. I remember my mother throwing skillets at him.

He hit her with his fists. They had a volatile and violent relationship. I saw the pain my father inflicted on my mother—the crying.

Ben felt that his father served as a negative role model because of the physical abuse he imposed on his mother. Ben subsequently instilled the values of a positive relationship in his children. Edward also emphasized that his father had a confrontational style in relating to his mother:

> I had to tell my father that I may not be the child he wanted, but don't harbor any bad feelings that may cause me to self-destruct. I grew up feeling out of it, or very different from people around me, because I was artistic. My view of marriage resulted from my parents' dysfunctional relationship. I had no notion that being married would have such an impact on whether or not I would be able to fulfill any aspirations that I had. I guess I just saw my father acting pretty much independently in pursuing his interests. My parents separated when I left for college, and before my dad left there was a lot of arguing. He bullied and intimidated my mother. So, even though I really didn't want to be like my father, I adopted his way of relating to women and behaving in a marriage.

In the absence of a strong role model, Edward expressed a fundamental anxiety about how he should act as a father. He was aware that his father was an inappropriate role model.

Other men also reported that they made sure that marital arguments did not occur in front of their children. For example, Douglas said, "My parents fought in front of me. I made it a point not to fight in front of my kids." For these men, there was a need to depart from the tendency to use physical violence in their relationships. However, without the benefit of a relevant comparison group of nonabusive fathers, fatherhood for some respondents was ambiguous and ill defined.

THE ABSENCE OF VIOLENT FATHERS

Interestingly, men who reported acts of violence in their marriages reported experiencing no violent behaviors in their parents' marriages. Alvin, who reported slapping his ex-wife "every now and then," indicated that his father never yelled in front of the kids or behaved violently toward his mother. He attributed marital arguments and subsequent violent behaviors to a temperament that included poor impulse control. Similarly, in explaining the violence that occurred in his marriage, Philip said,

> My temper flies off easily. The next thing I know, I'm swinging. Somebody has to keep a cool head and have enough sense not to argue and to walk away. Pam did not do that. She would argue back, [and] then my voice would rise. My kids understood that if their mother screamed at me, I would scream back.

Although some men were violent in their marriages, they believed that their children would not imitate their behavior because of an association to violence to a genetic predisposition. The following was a representative remark:

> I tell my children to do as I say and not as I do. I don't think they are harmed by my behavior. They know I can just fly off the handle. My former wife had a smart mouth. We argued a lot. But my kids didn't take that seriously. They would say, "I don't want to hear that." They knew I had a temper and would blow up in a minute. Then they saw that it would blow over. It never bothered them.

These comments suggest that some men viewed violent behavior as a personality defect or a genetic disability over which they had little control. In fact, Vince indicated that most men in his family were compassionate, kind, and nonviolent. However, he had inherited a "temper or a violent gene." Thus, he had little reason to believe that his children would be influenced by his violent marital behavior.

The Importance of Being a Nonalcoholic Father

Substance abuse has been associated with the disruption of Black marriages. Heavy drinking has been considered a norm as well as a characteristic of masculinity and camaraderie by many Black males. In fact, the Marlboro cigarette and heavy beer-drinking men are hyper-macho concepts that have been adopted by innumerable Black men (Staples, 1985). Because alcohol is both a depressive drug and one that releases inhibitions, it is closely linked to violent behaviors. Indeed, some respondents reported that alcohol contributed to the instability of their parents' marriages and, therefore, affected their fathers' parenting styles. Brent said,

> My parents are still together, but they argued a lot. When my father used alcohol, he would be unreasonable at times with the kids. He became loud and aggressive when he drank. He wanted to know why my grades were not better, [and] then he would yell, grab, or threaten me when I offered an explanation. I would say they had a pretty good marriage because they raised five kids and they all turned out pretty good. They have had problems, but they are still together. My father and I were never close, and I think alcohol was the cause of that.

Lennie also explained the role of alcohol in his parents' marriage:

> My father was an alcoholic. He was a good man and treated my mother well until he started to drink. He took his money and spent it in the streets. He was a gambler, a woman chaser, and he had babies by other women. I saw the way my mother was hurt and all the pain she went through with my father. So, I made up my mind that I would never inflict such pain on a woman. I remember one time when my father was drunk, he told me I wasn't his kid. He said that I was stupid and would not amount to a hill of beans. From then on, at age 12 [years], I decided that my father was clearly not the type of father I wanted to be. But my parents stayed together until he died.

There were a variety of contradictions that emerged from these fathers as they tried to reshape fatherhood into a different version from that of their own fathers. For example, although the men typically held their fathers accountable for drinking and neglecting the parental role, they usually were quite willing to excuse their fathers' behavior with statements such as "I survived the period when I needed him most" and "My father was dealing with segregation, Jim Crow, and racism, so it was difficult for him to be a father. As a result, he was broke, bored with life, and angry because life turned out to be such a disappointment."

Although the men were clear about not wanting to be like their fathers, they frequently expressed respect for their alcoholic fathers solely because the fathers remained married and refused to abandon their families. They were aware that society has institutionally subordinated their fathers and refused to allow them to fulfill the provider role. Thus, they respected fathers who lived with their families despite their alcoholism.

Absent Fathers and Fathering

Men have deserted families because of marital disagreements, alcoholism, and an inability to support families (Skarsten, 1974). This raises an important question: How do men construct fatherhood when they grow up without fathers?

One of the most striking findings was that men who were raised without fathers perceived their *mothers* as providing role models for fatherhood. They talked about the absence of any significant role models for becoming fathers except for their mothers. As Vance explained,

> My father could not relate to fatherhood. Although he thought children confirmed his manhood, he did not confront the challenge of keeping children clothed and fed. My mother is the one who taught me standards of proper behavior, and that is how I raised my son.

Vance paused and noted,

> I respect my mother because she disciplined all seven kids. I remember my mother waking me up at 3 a.m. if I left my socks under the bed. She wanted things to be in their proper place, and she stressed responsibility. So now, I try to teach my son the importance of being responsible around the house [such as] taking out the garbage and making up his bed.

As Vance's comments suggest, his mother was identified as the model of fatherhood who provided practical advice on how to raise and discipline children. Roscoe also noted,

> My mother made sure we ate and wore clean clothes to school. Even though we had to wash the same clothes out the previous night and iron them for school, my mother made sure we had clothes. That was a feat with seven kids. Today, I make sure my children have new school clothes every year and [that] they receive clothes for Christmas. I celebrate their

birthdays with a big party because my mom also baked a cake and had a party for all the kids' birthdays.

Roscoe noted poignantly, "Since I never had a father, my model of fatherhood comes from my mother because she raised us by herself. She suffered, she hurt, and she denied herself for us." Other men who were raised without fathers talked about learning to confront specific child-rearing situations from their mothers. Consequently, some men were unlikely to construct their fatherhood identities solely on the basis of male models.

Consistent with Chodorow (1978), these findings suggest that the absence of father models results in a stronger focus on mothers for guidance and identification of fatherhood. Several men who grew up with fathers made comments like the following:

> The kids in our family had more respect for our mom than for our dad. Mom disciplined us. We were not abused, but we got whippings when we did anything wrong. I remember my mom saying, "I don't care if you got as big as this house, I would jump off the house to discipline you." Mom would let us know when we were doing something wrong.

In fact, when the respondents were asked what Black women they admired most, without exception, they pointed to their mothers because their mothers expected responsible behavior.

According to Randolph (1995), one well-known gender-based adage about the child-rearing practices of Black mothers is that "they raise their daughters and love their sons." This suggests that Black females are socialized to take on adult roles at earlier ages than are Black males. Black mothers expect their daughters to be socially responsible, whereas sons are allowed to "do their own thing." However, men in the present study did not report that their mothers allowed them to "have their way." They viewed their mothers as excellent models for fatherhood because they taught proper morals and values and expected socially responsible behavior. Perhaps Randolph's observation represents a cohort effect among Black women. Indeed, some respondents reported that their wives pampered their sons while expecting responsible behavior from daughters.

FAMILY MODELS AND FATHERHOOD

Arthur described the nonrelationship he had with his father, which resulted in his aunt and uncle conveying a set of values and expectations for how he should raise his own son:

> My father was a married man [to another woman] and much older than my mother. After my mother got pregnant with me, my father wanted her to have an abortion. My father had given her money for an abortion, and she was supposed to have it the next day after school. My aunt went to the doctor's office, and when my mother entered the doctor's office, she pleaded with my mother not to have an abortion. My aunt said, "Just have the baby and give him to me. Give the baby to me, and I'll raise it like it is my own."

Arthur smoked a cigarette and continued,

> My aunt did just that. I was born at Cook County Hospital. My aunt came to the hospital, and she brought me home. My aunt was so protective and strict. She just didn't want anything to happen to me because she had a son who was hit by a car and killed. My dad was never involved with my life. I wanted to tell my father that the only riches I wanted were his friendship, his presence, and his time. Most of my memories of my father are painful. There was no tenderness between us and no sense of camaraderie. The only time I remember being with my dad was when I stayed with him and his wife when my aunt was sick. I have always resented my father because he didn't marry my mother, even after his wife died. But he said my mother was too bossy to live with. He said my mother wanted everything her way and it had to be her way. My dad said because he was a man, he would not be dominated by any woman. I do believe my mom and dad were really in love with each other. He died at age 51, and my mother died 2 weeks later. She was only 39 years old.

Arthur considered his father's behavior unacceptable because he failed to have a commitment to his upbringing. In discussing the influence of his father's absence on his parenting style, Arthur said,

> Because I was raised by my aunt and uncle, I remember happy times of fishing. I loved to put the bait on hooks. My uncle taught me how to cast out, and I'd put on gloves and try to take the fish off. We had a lot of family outings. We even went to Mississippi and Wisconsin on fishing

trips. I was never hungry, and there was always plenty of food, and any time I asked for money, I was given it.

Arthur paused and tearfully said,

> I regret my childhood. I wish that it could have been different. I would have liked to have been raised by my mother and father, although my aunt and uncle were the sweetest people in the world. There was always something missing in my life; that is, I belonged to an incomplete family. I had no man to really bond with, you know. So, I try very hard to bond with my son because I don't want him to come up the same way. It just never occurred to my dad that I might have needed him, even though we lived in the same city.

Whereas children often forgave geographically distant fathers who did not appear frequently, they were hurt by fathers who lived close but rarely visited (Weiss, 1975). Arthur was depressed because his biological father did not visit, even though he lived 20 minutes away.

Sam also emphasized that there was a missing aspect in his life because of his father's absence. He talked about being grateful for his uncle's presence in his life and expressed little difficulty in establishing an identity as a father. He said, "Fatherhood is not determined by genes or blood. Fatherhood is a state of mind. My uncle who raised me was my father." Lawrence voiced a similar concern:

> Without a father in my life, I became a grown man before my time. I wasn't happy inside. I felt like I had no future and felt lost, alone, and hurt. I just felt like something was missing in my life. I couldn't talk to my mother about the things that were eating me up inside. I needed a male figure in my life [who] I could just talk to. I was fortunate to have an uncle who I could relate to. Plus, I had an older brother who assumed a father role.

Consequently, Lawrence strongly believed that it was important to "be there" for his children because he was raised without a father. For Arthur, Sam, Lawrence, and other men who were raised without fathers, uncles, grandfathers, cousins, older brothers, and play kin were the reference groups that shaped their fatherhood identities.

Although respondents emulated desirable qualities from many fathers including uncles, grandfathers, and play fathers, these relations often failed to provide the "emotional intensity" the men desired. As Sam said,

> I wanted to tell my dad how smart I was in high school. I wanted to tell him about my new trumpet. I needed to know where I came from and who I was connected to. My father never met my son, and what's more, I had never laid eyes on my father's mother and father, even though they live 2 miles down the street.

The intergenerational transmission of divorce has been implicated in the increased rate of divorce. This perspective contends that divorce begets divorce. Several explanations have been advanced for this finding. First, personality problems of divorced parents produce similar problems in their children, and these lead to later marital instability. Second, an economic explanation posits that reduced family income and downward social mobility often associated with divorce reduce the type of marital mates available.

However, the transmission effect is consistent for Whites of both sexes and for Black females but is small for Black males (Kitson, Babri, & Roach, 1985). Black male kinship networks, including uncles and grandfathers, may reduce the transmission effect for Black men. This supposition is supported by evidence showing that greater involvement of same-sex family members may reduce the probability of divorce.

Positive Fathering and Fatherhood

Those men who held their fathers in high regard identified them as models of strength and pride. As Kenneth said,

> My dad has been the most positive and influential person in my life. My dad did not believe in disobedient children. I remember my brother stole a candy bar. My dad took my brother back to the store and made him take his money to pay for it. He gave my brother a whipping for lying to him about the candy bar. He was a very strong person. My dad would not

settle for any foolishness. . . . You have to be a good man to raise seven children by working two jobs all of your life.

As Kenneth's comments suggest, his father was viewed as a model for establishing moral principles. From this perspective, his father served as a model who ensured children's moral development and emphasized appropriate moral behavior. The idea of discipline and the communication of proper standards appeared to underscore Kenneth's relationship with his father. He recalled the feeling he had when his father died:

> My dad had always been a steady force in my life and gave me advice about what direction I should take with my life. When I heard the news of his death, I thought about all the things that were left unsaid and [that] I never gave him the pleasure of knowing that his faith in me was not wasted. When my dad died, I realized that death is so sad and that missing a person is so painful. I thought about [my] dad never asking for much in life; a beer every now and then, a baseball game on TV, some ham and collard greens every now and then, and he was fine. I supposed he never asked for the ceaseless toil of working all his life as a janitor so he could take care of his children, and sometimes he painted houses to put food on the table. He lived for 65 years. Yet, it seems like he never really lived. He was the type of man who is never seen on the news—the ordinary, everyday, hard-working Black man.

Graham also recalled the image of his father:

> My mother and father were poor, but there was so much love in our house. My father always worked two jobs. One was stripping tobacco, and the other was at an army depot as a laborer. My father taught me the real truth—that our strength comes from God. He always told me that it doesn't make any difference how much money you have to survive pain in life, but it is one' faith and strength in God. That advice has helped me to get through some hard times.

Men who perceived their fathers as positive models viewed them as being emotionally close, suggesting a strong alliance that neither could find elsewhere. They repeatedly talked about the ways in which their fathers represented "pillars of strength" that they were unable to find in other family relationships. As Robert explained,

My father gave me so much love and respect. He believed in me. His strength helped me cope with the death of my 4-year-old son, my own accident and later disability, and a house fire which was set by drug dealers because I gave their license number to the police.

Robert also indicated that his father's role extended beyond the traditional economic provider role to that of expressive involvement. Thus, he now relates to his 17-year-old son and 15-year-old daughter in a similar manner.

Stepfathers as Role Models

Men raised by stepfathers voiced particular concerns about integrating biological fathers and stepfathers to have a clear picture of fatherhood. Generally, their stepfathers provided central parental role models, whereas their biological fathers remained "shadowy and ethereal" figures who failed to provide positive models of manhood. The respondents' biological fathers were not involved in their lives until adulthood, resulting in the men reporting increased levels of stress when meeting them. Consequently, stepfathers shaped their fatherhood identities. Solomon, who was 3 years old when his mother married, reported, "I traveled to different places as a child, which helped to expand my experiences. My stepdad was stationed in Japan. I would not have had those experiences without my stepfather." However, Solomon acknowledged that he never emotionally connected with his stepfather:

We had little communication because we simply looked at life differently. I remember feeling that I wanted to see my biological father. Perhaps there could be some connection. I visited my dad, Mouse, and we seemed to get along. I wanted him to know that I made it in life without him and without his help. As I talked to him, I told him that I missed some things while growing up. He asked me to come back to visit and do some of those things. I was shocked and amazed that he assumed that we could form an ongoing relationship after all these years. He seemed completely unaware that I needed him as a child. We were total strangers.

Solomon paused, crossed his legs, and added,

When I left his house, Mouse said, "Call when you want to do something." I thought the few times in my life when I've seen him has been when I called. I decided that if he wanted to see me, he would need to call me. I have not seen him in 15 years. I've decided that my real father is my stepfather who has been there for me, who has disciplined, encouraged, and loved me.

Although Solomon respected his stepfather for "raising another man's children," he also was haunted by fears of fatherhood from his father:

There was always an uneasy silence between my stepfather and me. I still could not express my deepest emotions to him and could not really tell him all the things that were bothering me, like wondering about my own biological father. Maybe that is why I withdrew from fatherhood. I did not have a relationship with my father.

The experience of having stepfathers was a key issue in which some men developed models of fatherhood. Although Solomon had difficulty identifying concrete figures whom he could emulate, he readily identified values and standards from his stepfather to incorporate into a model of fatherhood. Whether expressing admiration for the way in which his stepfather handled discipline or for the way in which he gave advice, Solomon's model of fatherhood was represented by his stepfather. Other men raised by stepfathers reported similar experiences. This was a representative remark: "Real fathers are fathers who play an active role in the lives of children, not simply [men] who father [children]."

Conceptualization of Fatherhood

Social learning theory emphasizes how individuals develop appropriate behaviors through observation and imitation of models (Thompson & Walker, 1989). Although there is little research on how Black men learn to be fathers, the men in this study believed that their children would imitate them and would resemble the same-sex parent more than the other parent. Thus, they reported that being a positive role model was significant and important to the development of their children. Role modeling was emphasized when men referred to their sons. For example, Derek emphasized the importance of role modeling to prevent his son from being involved with a street culture:

Being a role model is one of the most important elements for my son to grow up to escape the destruction of the streets. I have a good relationship with my son because most of the things he does, he talks them over with me. He wants my point of view.

THE IMPORTANCE OF EDUCATION

For these men, fatherhood also involved teaching children the importance of an education. Lennie said,

I taught my sons to survive in the world. I told them to work hard, [to] respect the rights of others, and by all means to get an education. I want them to have a better start in life than I had. I told my son that boys who are White may drop out of school and may end up being your boss, or they might get the job before you. It's all because of the color of your skin. So, you must achieve more.

Eric visited the public library weekly with his sons to encourage them to read. He also stressed the importance of education as a mechanism for Black upward mobility. Thus, he advocated educational attainment to protect his sons from the detrimental outcomes of racial occupational segregation.

Indeed, education has been viewed historically by a number of Blacks as an effective strategy for upward mobility. Because there is a deep cultural belief in the efficacy of education, Blacks have sought education in every conceivable manner and at every level (Billingsley, 1992). For example, they built their own institutions, in part, because they were prevented from attending mainstream institutions. Blacks also confronted White institutions demanding entrance and acceptance (Billingsley, 1992).

Consequently, when the respondents' children modeled their behavior, especially graduating from college, it was a much-celebrated event. Truman described his feelings when his son, who was born out of wedlock, graduated from college:

On commencement day, I sat proudly in the school auditorium. His mother had notified relatives and distant relatives who lived on the east and west coasts. I invited friends from the church I attended as a child in Alabama. I took pictures of friends and relatives. We we were hugging, crying, celebrating. My son was the only person who graduated from college out of my parents' 19 grandchildren.

THE IMPORTANCE OF FAMILY VALUES

The men also believed that instilling good family values was an important aspect of fatherhood. "I needed to be in the home to make sure my kids were being raised with values and morals" was a representative comment. In many instances, "good family values" focused on teaching caring and love for family members. For example, Curtis said,

> It is important to raise children with love and to teach them that it is important to support family members. Often, there is hate in Black families since the father may have been in prison. The father may pass his hate on to his children. Children then are unable to love each other. I teach my children to love those who hate you and to be there and support their brothers and sisters.

THE SIGNIFICANCE OF SURVIVAL SKILLS

Another aspect of fatherhood involved the belief that children need to learn survival skills including knowledge of automobiles, information on sex education, and devotion to a Higher Power. Jim and Bernie said that they taught their sons about cars. Anton reported that he taught his son, Shawn, the importance of using condoms:

> I told Shawn, "Don't get a girl pregnant. You take the responsibility to prevent a pregnancy and use condoms." I also tell him that the relationship should be based on caring instead of sex. His hormones are raging, and I try to stress the importance of sexual control.

Others said that they taught their children the importance of spirituality. Roscoe said,

> I tell my children, "Prayer will get you through rough times. No matter how bad it gets, you can reach out to God because when you do, God will be there to receive you." My kids listen, especially when I tell them if I had placed God as head of my life, my life would have been easier.

These comments suggest that the men believed in providing practical strategies to assist their children in surviving, which included being aware of exploitation in car repairs, avoiding early pregnancies, and deferring to a Higher Power. Perhaps this reflects the men's attempt to help their children cope with the difficulties Black men confront in acquiring self-confidence and self-esteem in a racist technological society.

PROPER RESPONSES TO POLICE OFFICERS

From the respondents' perspective, teaching children—especially sons—the proper responses to police officers was a major component of their fathering role. The respondents had observed police officers beat, jail, shoot, and use various types of violence toward Black men. Thus, some respondents believed that it was necessary to teach their sons interaction strategies in dealing with police officers. Robert explained,

> I tell my son if he ever gets stopped for any reason by the police, to say, "Yes, sir" or "No, sir." The police will hurt kids if they think they are smarting off at the mouth. I tell them to be nice and to respect [police officers'] authority instead of making them angry. I also tell my son, don't say the wrong things to police, and look them in the eye when they are talking to [his son]. If [he doesn't], the police might hurt [him].

Indeed, for some men, the world was perceived as a dangerous place. Thus, they believed that it was their responsibility to teach their sons skills that will help them to survive. Other survival skills included avoiding school fights (particularly those involving gangs), not buying expensive or flashy clothes that might cause jealously, and speaking with deference to police officers.

Although the respondents taught their sons skills to survive in a hostile and violent world, they still were anxious about their sons' safety. As Henry said, "Every time I read a news story about some teenage boy being gunned down by a policeman or killed in a drive-by shooting, I had visions of my son." Without exception, men believed that parenting was a tremendous responsibility in a postmodern society. For example, Bronson said,

It's hard to raise kids today with all the gangs, drugs, racism, violence, AIDS, and teenage pregnanc[ies]. Black fathers must be strong. It is scary because many parents feel helpless in competing with the pressures that kids are exposed to today. The TV has taken the place of parents, and kids listen to friends now more than [they do to] their parents.

The men constantly emphasized the ambiguity of living simultaneously in two worlds—the world of the Black community and the world of mainstream society—a phenomenon unique and often hostile to Black men.

Stepfathers of Minor Children

The increased number of births to unmarried women, rising divorce rates, remarriages, cohabitation of women with children, and maternal child custody patterns have resulted in a growing number of Blacks raising nonbiological children (Hernandez, 1988; Miller & Moorman, 1989). Estimates using the 1987-1988 National Survey of Families and Households suggest that 4 million stepfathers live with minor stepchildren (Larson, 1992).

In this study, a large proportion of the respondents married women who had previous births outside of marriage or who were widowed with at least one child. In fact, most respondents believed that "most Black women will have at least one child before marriage." The respondents reported that they loved and raised nonrelated children similar to how they loved and raised biological children. Ben detailed the relationship he had with his stepdaughters. "I raised my ex-wife's child like my own" was a representative remark. In fact, these men had sympathy for their ex-wives, who often experienced pregnancies without partners or who were abandoned by their partners when their children were infants. Curtis explained,

Julie had an 8-year-old daughter, and I considered her as my own child. Julie went through a lot with her first husband who left her. He didn't consider family life important. So, I was very close to my stepdaughter.

Most biological fathers were not involved in their children's lives; thus, the respondents viewed themselves as "real fathers." Edsel said,

"I taught my stepdaughter to ride her bike, to count money, and to write her name. There is nothing I would not do for her. I checked her homework and visited her school for parent-teacher conferences."

Marsiglio (1995) indicates that stepfathers who report feeling more like real father to the children are more likely to have better relationships with them. However, it is not clear how the quality of this relationship affects children as adults.

Because most of the stepchildren were young when the respondents married the children's mothers, the children did not react negatively to the discipline of stepfathers. Men reported considerable power in everyday decisions in their stepchildren's lives. However, respondents who married women with adolescent children reported considerable distress over their stepfather role. For example, Vincent said that his stepdaughter resented the marriage, and frequent arguments occurred when he disciplined his stepdaughter:

> My stepdaughter disliked me from Day 1. She was 14 when I married her mother. She would do things that I did not approve of, like stay out late at night. So, when I tried to set limits on her behavior, that pulled Donna and me apart.

Similarly, Taylor, who had a White stepdaughter, said,

> I guess I'm old-fashioned. I think teenagers should have curfews. When I told my 15-year-old stepdaughter [that] she had to be in the house by 11 p.m. and had to stop talking on the phone at 9 p.m. on weeknights, [it] caused frequent arguments between me and Joanne. My stepdaughter did not approve of her mother marrying a Black man.

Vincent and Taylor reported that they were uncomfortable because their views of family life differed from those of their ex-wives. For example, Vincent's stepdaughter participated in decision making in a single-parent family and, therefore, was unwilling to be supervised by a male. He viewed her as a "spoiled brat" rather than as a mature individual capable of making decisions, which resulted in the deterioration of the stepfather-stepdaughter bond.

Adolescent stepchildren may lack a desire to see their parents' marriages work. Teenagers often harbor fantasies that their original parents will reunite. Wallerstein and Kelly (1980) found that 5 years after divorce, 30% of children whose parents remarried during adolescence still disapproved of their parents' marriages. In addition, children who wanted their natural parents to remarry often sabotaged the new relationships to achieve that goal.

A Need to Contradict Black Fatherhood Stereotypes

Because there is an absence of positive images of Black fathers, several men were profoundly distressed about the stereotypes of Black fathers. Leon's following remark was a representative comment:

> There is nothing that I would not do for my kids—absolutely nothing. Most people think that Black men do not care about their children, but we do. Just because there [are] no fathers in the [homes] doesn't mean that fathers are not involved in the lives of their children.

Leon emphasized the following as his voice became louder. It was quite clear that he felt intense emotional pain about the negative stereotypes of Black fathers:

> Black fathers don't get the recognition they deserve. I have contributed a great deal as a father. Not only was I a househusband, but I helped my daughter with her schoolwork and shared all household responsibilities. In the midst of the public effort to call attention to deadbeat fathers, the public has lost sight of Black fathers who enjoy their roles and who are involved in their children's lives.

Throughout the interviews, the men frequently said, "I regret my marriage, but I don't regret having my kids" and believed that the myth of the ineffective Black father is designed to perpetuate racial subjugation. Although the respondents refused to accept the negative social definitions of Black fathers, they could not comprehend why society has chosen to view and define them as impotent fathers. They believed that social scientists should ask why mainstream society continues to perpetuate myths about Black men in general and Black fathers in particular and to ask what purposes those myths serve. Without exception, the men asserted that the media should focus on Black men who accept parental responsibilities and publicize those who actively participate in the lives of their children.

Summary

Black fathers employ various models to construct fatherhood. Men who were raised without attentive, devoted, and vigilant fathers to guide their behavior created new models of fatherhood that included emotional bonding to children. Men who grew up with abusive fathers were concerned and anxious about the role of fathering. Of interest, abusive men who experienced no acts of violence from fathers believed that tempers resulted from a genetic predisposition.

Surprisingly, some respondents reported that their fathers were alcoholics but were willing to excuse their fathers' drinking and respected fathers who lived with their families despite their alcoholism. From the respondents' perspective, the deepest expression of love was that their fathers kept their families together and did the best they could in a world in which the cards were stacked against them. Thus, alcoholic fathers were viewed as "doing the best they could under those circumstances."

Notably, men who grew up in single-parent households perceived their mothers as providing role models for fatherhood. In addition, some men shaped their identities as fathers from uncles, grandfathers, older brothers, and/or play fathers. Those men who had positive fathers identified them as models of strength and pride and viewed their relationships as emotionally close.

Men raised by stepfathers voiced concerns about integrating biological fathers and stepfathers to have a clear picture of fatherhood. Generally, stepfathers provided a central parental role model for the respondents' construction of fatherhood, whereas their biological fathers remained nebulous figures in their lives.

The respondents' definition of fathering consisted of the following:

1. being appropriate role models;
2. teaching children the importance of an education;
3. imparting the significance of good family values; and
4. providing practical survival strategies including appropriate responses to police officers and sex education as well as spiritual teachings.

Stepfathers expressed various perceptions of their roles. Men who married when their stepchildren were young reported considerable power in the lives of their stepchildren and reported extreme psychological distress over the loss of their stepchildren. However, men who married women with adolescent children believed that the children often sabotaged the marriages. Because the stepfathers entered households headed by mothers and children, the stepfathers had to work their way into closed groups. Gaining entry for stepfathers was complicated when adolescents were involved. First, teenagers resented sharing family decision power. According to Giles-Sims and Crosbie-Burnett (1989), stepfathers have less power relative to adolescent stepchildren when they move into mother-child homes.

Second, stepfathers often have different perspectives of family life. After living as single-parent families, mothers and children developed a consensus of family rules such as curfews, attending parties, and male visitation. Although stepfathers had varying views about established household rules and discipline, they reacted to these difficulties in different ways. Some men were driven away, whereas others established themselves as undisputed heads of the household and forced the former single-parent families to accommodate their preferences. A majority, however, assimilated into families with relatively little influence in family decisions but tried to negotiate new perspectives of family life. In addition, men refused to accept negative social definitions of Black fathers and believed that discrediting them superiorizes the social position of Whites.

9

Divorce and Fatherhood

My sons went through so much hurt and pain. I told both my sons
that I will be there to help them.

—Matt

In Chapter 8, we focused on acquiring fatherhood identities, which were influenced by family and community models. In this chapter, we turn to the role that fathers play as noncustodial parents, explore barriers that prevent father-child involvement, examine reactions of children to divorce, and discuss problems of noncustodial stepfathers and fathers from interracial marriages. Finally, we explore the future of Black fatherhood and propose solutions to strengthen father-child bonds.

Impact of Divorce on Fatherhood

Divorce changes the structure of fathering (Arendell, 1995; Marsiglio, 1991; Weiss, 1979). First, and most important, there are no norms for noncustodial fathering; thus, these fathers often are uncertain about their roles as disciplinarians versus weekend friends (Seltzer, 1991; Weiss, 1975). Second, divorced men no longer have wives to encourage and to facilitate father-child interactions. Third, noncustodial fathers often are unprepared to accept sole responsibility for supervising young children because mothers usually care for young children (Umberson, 1992). Studies have found that divorced fathers often disengage from parenting roles over time (Furstenberg & Nord, 1985). Approximately 23% of children 11 to 16 years of age have no contact with their fathers, and 25% have bimonthly contact with their fathers postdivorce (Furstenberg, Morgan, & Allison, 1987). Of interest, fathers who are divorced longer are more likely to be disengaged from children (Furstenberg et al., 1987).

Various explanations have been postulated as to reasons why noncustodial fathers withdraw from their children. First, postdivorce withdrawal has been related to continued antagonism with former wives (Arendell, 1995; Weiss, 1975). The lack of cooperation from ex-wives about children's education and upbringing impel men to decrease father-child interactions (Fulton, 1979; Grief, 1985; Gutmann, 1987). Second, work conflicts, inadequate incomes, and geographical distance have been associated with noncustodial father withdrawal (Arendell, 1995). Fourth, an interesting theory for the absence of noncustodial fathers has been posited by Ihinger-Tallman and Pasley (1989). These researchers suggest that withdrawal may be a response to feeling unappreciated or rejected by children, particularly older children.

Custody Issues and Visitation

Approximately 53% of couples who divorce have children under 18 years of age, and in 90% of cases, the mother has custody by agreement or default (National Center for Health Statistics, 1991). According to Lamanna and Riedmann (1994), child custody has been an extension of the basic exchange principle; divorced fathers have legal responsibility for support, whereas divorced mothers continue daily child care.

The controversy has been centered on joint custody. In joint custody, both divorced parents assume equal responsibility for child rearing. However, it is difficult to maintain joint legal custody of children when one parent has sole physical custody. One problem with joint physical custody is geographic distance when children divide the year between two different communities and schools. In addition, joint custody is expensive, with each parent maintaining housing, equipment, toys, and separate clothing for children. Furthermore, research has not supported the assumption that joint custody is best for divorced parents and for children (Kline, Tschann, Johnston, & Wallerstein, 1989).

VISITATION

Fathers often feel out of touch with their children because contact weekly or every other weekend does not provide the same relationship with children as does living within the same household. Consequently, noncustodial fathers experience a sense of extreme loss. Ironically, more emotionally involved fathers before their divorces visit their children *less* often (Kruk, 1991). Evidence suggests that this also applies to stepfathers and men in cohabitation relationships (Dullea, 1987).

Children's Reactions to Divorce

The impact of divorce on children has been documented extensively (Glenn, 1987). Children from divorced parents acquire less education, marry earlier, tend to have out-of-wedlock births, and are more likely to divorce (see, e.g., Keith & Finlay, 1988; McLanahan & Bumpass, 1988). On the other hand, Amato and Booth (1991) conclude that children of divorce are little different from children of intact marriages and that the negative impact of divorce on children might be overstated. Similarly, Spanier (1989) argues that children who experience family disruption possess a strong commitment to family life.

Nevertheless, both optimistic and pessimistic views of the impact of divorce on children often have failed to explore the impact of divorce on racial/ethnic minority children. The following discussion explores telling children of divorce.

Children as a Reason to Remain Married

From the back porch, James watched his two sons play. He wanted to call them and say, " 'I'm sorry I turned your world upside down.' I then felt the divorce was real." James could hear himself breathing and tears seemed suspended as he attempted to tell his children about the marital breakup. He explained, "The children seemed so happy, and I hated to upset them. I told them to obey their mother and grandmother and I would [go] away for a while. 'It's just that your mother and me can't live together anymore.' "

"Where are you going?" James's oldest son asked.

"I'll be in the next state and will see you every month. Plus, we will talk on the phone every day."

"Daddy, do you have to go? What are we supposed to do?"

These words struck James like a bullet that would remain lodged inside his chest forever. He explained, "The divorce was painful, but knowing that I had disappointed my two sons was more painful. I felt that it was important to be in their lives daily as they deal with living in White America."

As James and his children walked back to the house, a pain as sharp as that of an ax blade split his skull into two pieces. The thought of missing the precious moments of his sons' lives resulted in tears streaming softly at first and then in a gradual crescendo that seemed destined to never end. Most men indicated that they regreted their divorces because of the decreased contact with their children. They often believed that in leaving the marriages, they abandoned their children. "The divorce was hard because I hated leaving my children" was a representative comment.

The distress of divorce was heightened for the respondents because they viewed children as the brightest aspects of their marriages. Compared to their own fathers and those of earlier generations, they were extremely involved fathers. The predominant father-child relationship was nurturant, warm, and loving. Predivorce, 10 men coached sports teams and 5 taught Sunday school in which their children took part. Thus, due to geographical distance, some men complained about exclusion from opportunities to interact with their children postdivorce.

Telling Children

Research has shown that children should be informed of divorce. For example, Wallerstein and Kelly (1979) found that children who were told that their fathers were planning to live elsewhere appeared less distraught than did those whose fathers disappeared without any explanations. Without exception, fathers reported that they informed children of the divorces through short explanations. Bernie said, "I simply told my son that his mother and I just changed so much, and it was impossible for us to live together. He seemed satisfied with that explanation." Bronson explained how he informed his biological sons and stepsons of the divorce to prevent them from adopting a negative view of marriage:

> I took my sons took to their favorite restaurant, the Pizza Hut, and after we had finished eating, I said, "Your mother and I took marriage seriously, but sometimes marriages don't work. That does not mean we love you less; if anything, we love you more. When you grow up and marry, you will make it work."

The respondents also informed their children of the divorces without discrediting their ex-wives. For example, Brent said, "I told my kids that their mother and me just had some problems we could not work out." Overall, most men emphasized that it was important to be supportive of their children's mothers and often told their children that their mothers were not to blame for the divorces. However, several respondents reported that ex-wives often defamed them in front of their children. Leon said,

> Carol told my children that I did not care about them. She also told them that I did not want to see them. Carol tried to turn my children against me and called me derogatory names in front of them. Children pay attention to that stuff, and now I think my daughter is ashamed of me.

Barry also reported intense emotional pain because Jennifer made negative comments about him to his sons. He perceived those comments as destroying the relationship with his children:

> Jennifer has always said negative things about me in front of the children. That hurts because my children have a tendency to avoid me. My son said, "Dad, Mom told me you were no good and didn't care about us." He made no effort to see or call me because he was under Jennifer's spell.

Barry struggled through tears stating that most people are unaware of the problems divorced Black men endure with ex-wives and the deep hurt they feel from missing their children. As a result, their relationships with children often were a source of pain and frustration. Whereas respondents coped with being inaccessible to their children and endured the pain that they no longer had genuine authority in their children's lives, the tendency of ex-wives to discredit and berate them to their children generated much distress and agony.

Fathers' Perceptions of Children's Reactions

Black children also are more likely than White children to live with divorced parents. How do separation and divorce affect Black children? Experts disagree. The men in this study reported that during and, for a period of time, following divorce, their children were depressed and anxious and displayed behavioral problems.

PRESCHOOL AND SCHOOL-AGE CHILDREN

Fathers of preschool children reported that the children exhibited numerous behavioral problems including bed-wetting, hyperactivity, thumb-sucking, and withdrawal. Jim said, "My 5-year-old started to wet his bed and fought kids in his preschool. He was obviously affected by the divorce."

Fathers of school-age children also believed that their divorces negatively affected their children. For example, Douglas said,

> My son started acting out in school. He started to fight other kids after the divorce. I had to go to his school several times to talk to teachers. Can you imagine a 6-year-old being suspended from school? He really hurt another boy in school, and I'm trying to get some help for him.

According to the respondents, school-age children appeared to experience more psychological distress than did preschool children 1 year postdivorce.

PREADOLESCENT AND ADOLESCENT CHILDREN

Children in their preadolescence and adolescence years appeared to be overwhelmed by the stresses of divorce. They also felt abandoned by their mothers, who were overwhelmed by supporting and managing households alone.

Matt described a sad story of his son's reaction to the divorce. His sons were 11 and 15 years old when he divorced. The youngest son, Dameon, immediately reacted to the divorce with a sense of detachment. Matt explained,

> Dameon was going through so much hurt and pain. He was withdrawn and fighting. He started to steal, and I could not put up with it anymore. I put him in a treatment center for juveniles. The only thing I wanted him to do was to live a normal life. Dameon stayed at the center for 1 year and then went to Job Corps at age 13. He came home from Job Corps, and I was actually afraid of him. He got involved in street gangs. He did not want to do anything. I said, "You are going to school." We got into a fight. He ran out the house and returned with four other guys. They all had .25 automatics. I called my brother to come over to my house. I got my pistol. Dameon and his friends were coming toward my door shooting. I shot the gun up in the air to scare them. I just wanted to scare them away. The police came, and I explained to them the situation. I had to lock Dameon in detention for a couple of months. When he got out of detention, I told him that we could not live together. I said, "Two men can't live together. One of them must be the father, and the other must be the son, and I am not gonna be your son. I brought you into this world." He left and went back to Job Corps. He calls my mother often. He is lost, confused, and in pain, wandering through life with no hope for a better future.

Tears rolled from Matt's eyes when he described his oldest son's problems:

> My oldest son, Marcus, is in prison. He was at a dangerous age at the time of the divorce. . . . Marcus loved his mother, you know. One day, 6 months after the divorce, Hazel was beaten and robbed. She was beaten so badly that two ribs were broken and all of her teeth were knocked out. They took her money, her clothes, and even her shoes. Marcus knew the boys who did this. One afternoon, Marcus bought a gun and shot the boys who beat his mother. He was in a state of shock and hadn't realized that he had killed them. Blood was gushing out like a waterfall as they crumpled

over on the floor. Marcus suddenly felt sorry for them. Police cars were pulling up, lighting up the driveway, and the sirens and red flashing lights brought all the neighbors out. Marcus was arrested. I didn't have money to get him a good lawyer, but I paid $1,000 for the lawyers. They sentenced him to 10 years in prison. My mother sobbed in disbelief when the bailiffs led Marcus from the courtroom in handcuffs.

Matt said that the divorce contributed to his son's behavior:

> My sons went through so much hurt and pain. I told both my sons that I will be there to help them. I told Marcus that it wasn't all his fault. I told him I don't know what I would do if I had been in his situation, seeing someone beat my mother. I understand that when someone disrespects your mother, a man has to do what he has to do. I didn't want to tell Marcus that if Hazel had stayed married, this probably wouldn't have happened, because I think Hazel's boyfriend instigated the whole incident.

Other men also reported that children adopted destructive behavioral patterns following their divorces. For example, Maurice reported that his teenage daughter became sexually active following the divorce and believed that she was encouraged by his dating to act on her sexual impulses. Other respondents reported that children displayed similar behavior when their ex-wives dated. As Carl explained, "When Rita started to date male friends, my 13-year-old daughter became absolutely boy crazy. She asked me if she could kiss and have a boyfriend."

There has been a lack of research on the relationship between growing up in a mother-headed household and Black female adolescent sexual development. From the respondents' perspective, preteen daughters often were more desirous of masculine attention and approval postdivorce. An interesting research question concerns the relationship, if any, between divorced mothers' dating and subsequent teenage pregnancy among Black adolescents. Men also reported that their sons became resentful of their ex-wives' dates. For example, Derek explained, "My 12-year-old son was so angry when he met Joan's boyfriend. He left home and stayed over at a friend's house because Joan was dating. My son complains that Joan's boyfriend tries to discipline him and to tell him what to do."

Men also reported that preadolescent and adolescent children were troubled by a lingering sorrow that resulted in self-destructive behavioral patterns including engaging in the drug culture, becoming pregnant, and skipping school. Some men said that their children were angry at them for disrupting their homes and believed that the divorces were childish. Wallerstein and Kelly (1979) identify this process as "precipitous de-idealization of the parent" in which the adolescent feels disappointed and lost without moral guidance.

Perhaps the cultural pull of pseudo-macho hip-hop fads are powerful inducements for Black preadolescent and adolescent children of divorce because these children often experience the loss of daily interaction with their fathers. Indeed, there is a younger generation of Blacks who are more alienated than were previous generations. Thus, these children might be in even greater need of fathering and might be even more adversely affected by divorce than were previous generations of Black children.

Child Custody

The respondents believed that there is a gender bias in the U.S. child custody laws due to maternal preference in custody awards. Therefore, without exception, fathers reported extreme psychological distress because courts automatically assume that women should be awarded custody of children. A case in point was Henry, who described his reaction when the judge awarded maternal custody:

> I wanted joint custody, and the judge said because I had been separated from my spouse for 1 year, my daughter and son should live with Linda. I was sick to my stomach for months, I couldn't sleep or eat for weeks because I am a better parent than Linda. I tried to tell the judge that Linda was depressed and was not capable of being a good mother because she was being emotionally ripped apart at work by racism. But Linda was awarded sole custody.

The men reported extreme difficulty adjusting to the reduced involvement in their children's lives. For example, Leon was exuberant at the birth of his daughter. He pointed out the stress of noncustodial parenting:

> I was involved as much as possible with my daughter from birth. Because
> I had experienced little warmth from my father, I wanted to be the
> opposite of him. I attended prenatal appointments and child birth classes.
> I was in the delivery room when she was born. As I held my newborn
> daughter, nothing could prepare me for the love I felt. All of a sudden,
> the world changed and I wanted to protect her. When I cut the umbilical
> cord, I experienced the greatest moment of my life.

Leon's daughter was 3 years old when he and his wife divorced. He emphasized, "I regret not being part of my daughter's life on a daily basis. Anything that reminds me of her makes me cry, even a child on TV commercials, like the Kodak commercials with fathers and daughters." Brent also said, "The greatest stressor is not being there when my daughter returns from dates. Since I want her to marry a man like me, I want to meet her dates and be there when she returns." During the interview, Brent cried, expressing the grief he felt at leaving his daughter. He thought about buying a home "where my daughter would live when she reaches age 18." He even coached his daughter's basketball team to spend time with her and expressed considerable pain over seeing his daughter only intermittently.

For the respondents, their absence from their homes was particularly stressful given the presence of gangs and the high rates of homicides, adolescent pregnancies, and illicit drug use among Black youths. For example, they became anxious at indications that their children were succumbing to a negative teen subculture. As Anton explained,

> I was afraid of the subtle changes in my son Shawn's behavior. He was
> becoming defiant toward his teachers and stepfather. He behaved in a way
> that nobody understood. He bopped liked the kids who lived in the 'hood.
> He started to let his baggy jeans fall lower on his behind. He suddenly
> resisted authority and displayed an arrogant body language that teenagers
> do to tell grown-ups they are the boss. It drove me up the wall that I
> couldn't have more influence or control over his life. I felt powerless.

Respondents also reported numerous difficulties with maintaining contact with teenage children. Kenneth expressed the intense frustration of his failed attempts to contact his daughter. He explained, "When I call my 16-year-old daughter, she's too busy to talk. She's busy with friends, at a dance class, or at the mall with her friends. It seems like she has no time for me." He also indicated that he felt abandoned when his daughter failed to acknowledge a birthday or a holiday. Kenneth tearfully stated, "My daughter didn't call to wish me happy birthday, nor did she wish me happy Father's Day. It's like she hates me. I keep telling Mary to tell my daughter to call me." In the past, Kenneth contributed to family discussions with the assurance that his viewpoint would be seriously considered. Now, he felt like an outsider. His point of view often was voiced only as a criticism of the mother's opinion.

Todd also vividly expressed the lack of influence in his daughter's life:

> I am trying to make Cheryl understand and to figure out what she wants to be. Her favorite words are "my friends." Rachael lets Cheryl have her own way and to do her own things. Rachael wants to be friends [with] Cheryl. So, what I think does not count. In the final analysis, Rachael's opinion is what counts.

Although the respondents reported that they saw their children in accordance with the divorce decrees, they underscored that these visits reminded them that they were losing influence over their children. Although they pursued independent relationships with their children, in many instances, ex-wives defined and orchestrated father-child relationships.

Visitation and Child Support

Most men retained relationships with their children, even if they lived in other geographical regions. Fathers who remained in the children's localities maintained a regular schedule of visits. However, they encountered a number of problems. One problem involved ex-wives' non-cooperativeness. According to Ivan, he was allowed to see his children only when it was convenient for his ex-wife. Similar to Arendell's (1995) study, Ivan and other men frequently complained that ex-wives used visitation to pursue their activities without having to pay for babysitting.

Men indicated that although they might send child support payments to their wives, they often were viewed merely as income sources, like employers or social security. Thus, the following was a representative comment among the men: "Ex-wives often fail to recognize how valuable a father is for the development and growth of children. They see fathers only as a money source." Visitation sometimes was directly linked to child support; if men did not pay child support, then some wives would not permit visitation or contact with children. Clyde described an incident in which Betty had him arrested because he failed to pay child support:

> I called Betty and asked if I could see the children. I was really looking forward to seeing my daughters, Futima and Tamekia. I planned to take them to the children's museum and to eat pizza. I thought about all the things I wanted to ask them. Driving on the street, I noticed that the apartment was dark. I had talked with Betty a couple of hours before, so she was expecting me. Then I heard footsteps behind me. It was a policeman. I stood still and put my hands up. He shoved me into the backseat of a police car and said, "There's been a felony warrant issued for your arrest." I was in shock. Betty had arranged this so I could go to jail—and to destroy me. I had fallen behind on my $1,000-a-month child support, even though I had gotten loans, sold my car, [and] pawned all of my stereo and photography equipment to comply with child support payments.

Clyde emphasized that no one understood that he was doing his best with child support. He told his attorney about his plight, but the attorney only asked for another installment on his bill. Clyde could not understand why Betty linked child visitation rights to his child support obligations, especially considering she remained close to his family. After spending 2 days in jail, he pondered eliminating contact with his children to avoid Betty:

> For a while, I stopped picking my kids up on weekends because I was so ashamed [that] I didn't have any money. I felt like less than a man. I thought of just giving up and tried to tell myself just to let them go, but I couldn't abandon my babies.

Clyde and other men considered withdrawing from children to avoid contact with ex-wives.

COPING WITH NONCUSTODIAL PARENTING

Approximately 90% ($n = 45$) of the fathers coped with noncustodial parenting by increasing their involvement with their children. Stanley moved three blocks away from Paula and her husband to be near his children. He asserted that he participates biweekly in activities with his children including attending church and seeing movies. Willy reported that his children live with him every summer and during school vacations.

For the majority of men, spending time with their children was a priority for the following reasons. First, they were committed to raising their children. This was a representative comment: "There is absolutely nothing I would not do for my children. I want them to have a better life than I had." Second, they often received encouragement from family members to sustain contact with their children. "My mother and sister insist that they see my children every week" was another representative remark. Third, children often increased the respondents' self-esteem. Todd proclaimed, "When my daughter tells me I am a great father, and when she smiles upon seeing me, I feel 10 feet tall in a society where I am often treated as a second-class citizen."

Noncustodial fathering resulted in few benefits and little satisfaction, and it created profound emotional distress. The absence of daily interaction with children, difficulty in maintaining contact with teenage children, and conflictual postmarital relations made noncustodial fathering extremely stressful.

Interracial Children and Noncustodial Fathering

Men who were in interracial marriages reported particular stress with noncustodial parenting. Men often were concerned about their children's identification with a stepparent of a different race in that the children might develop serious identity problems. For example, Taylor agonized over being inaccessible to his son, who lived in another state. He explained,

> My sons are biracial and are struggling with identity issues, and I am the only one who can help them with this. They don't even know who they

are, and they are very angry and confused. They have been called racial names at school and [have] wondered why.

Graham also voiced profound frustration at being separated from his biracial daughter:

> My daughter is 12 years old, and when I see her during the summer months, I see how confused she is. . . . I feel so guilty because I can't help her sort out who she is. She is being raised by my ex-wife to be culturally White, but society treats her as Black. She is having trouble coping with racial stereotypes and prejudices. She doesn't even understand what it means to be Black in America. The hardest thing for me as a Black parent is to teach my daughter to live in a racist society.

Graham was convinced that his daughter would experience a better life living with him. Because Tina was considering marrying a man who had concerns about raising a biracial stepdaughter, Graham believed that he could provide a more normal life for his daughter by exposing her to a Black community.

Stepfathers in a Noncustodial Setting

The cultural norms of appropriate stepfather behavior are less precise than those pertaining to biological or adoptive fathers (Marsiglio, 1991). The norms for noncustodial stepparenting are even more ambiguous in Western societies. Therefore, stepfathers face increased adjustment problems postdivorce. For example, with trembling of his hands and tears streaming softly down his face, James reported intense frustration over the lack of daily contact with his stepdaughter: "I raised Ukemia from the age of 2. She was like my own daughter, and I miss her deeply. She was so devastated by the divorce, she is staying out late at night and getting into smoking and drinking." Because mothers usually retained custody of stepchildren, the respondents experienced profound distress and a sense of loss. Contact with stepchildren usually was by phone calls; however, as time passed, the number of phone calls decreased.

Stepchildren frequently requested to live with their stepfathers. In fact, Sam waged a court battle for joint custody of his stepdaughter, even though he lived with another woman. He reported, "My stepdaughter has always been with me from age 4. Her father died, so I feel like I have as much right to her as her mother." Sam visited his stepdaughter daily after the divorce.

Of interest, stepfathers encouraged biological fathers and other family members to become involved in the lives of their stepchildren. For example, Truman said,

> I saw how depressed my stepson, Ricky, was after the divorce. He'd call, cry, and tell me he was miserable. I told his biological father he needed to spend some time with him because he is at the age where he needs a father. He said he would try to call Ricky soon.

Stepfathers who married women with teenage children reported that there was no contact postdivorce. For instance, Arthur, who indicated that his stepdaughter was unwilling to accept a male authority figure said, "I don't see my stepdaughter. She left for college after the divorce, and I have not seen or heard from her. It has been 3 years." Taylor said,

> My stepdaughter and I have no contact. I wonder how she is doing, but I have not talked with her since I divorced her mother. My stepdaughter is relieved her mother divorced. She did not like having a Black stepfather.

STEPFATHERS AND VISITATION

Visitation was especially problematic with stepchildren. A large number of stepfathers were unable to visit their stepchildren unless they had biological children by the mothers. For example, James married a woman with a daughter, and they later had two sons. He was able to visit his stepdaughter while he visited his biological sons. However, Larry, who married a woman with two sons and had no subsequent children, relinquished contact with his stepsons. Larry's ex-wife, Pat, regarded marriage as a package deal. She could not separate Larry's relationship with her sons from the marriage. When the marriage ended, the stepfather-stepson bond withered. The rights of stepfathers and custody of stepchildren in the event of divorce is a crucial issue. Law in this area is rapidly changing, although it is unlikely that biological fathers will be legally replaced by stepfathers.

In the next section, we turn to respondents' views of the future of fatherhood and discuss recommendations to empower Black fathers. They were profoundly concerned about the current trends that are paralyzing the Black community and that are gradually spreading to all American families that are economically disadvantaged.

The Future of Black Fatherhood

The respondents were concerned about the high levels of marital instability and the plight of Black youths. As Maurice pointed out,

> What scares me is the younger generation of Black males who are angry. Their whole rap music is about abusing women. When I grew up in the 1960s, the music I listened to was about building a stronger relationship with women. The younger generation has little respect for their own lives and the lives of others.

Although some respondents presented dismal views of the state of Black America in general and of father-child relationships in particular, they believed that Black youths have been profoundly affected by the identity crisis of White youths and that the self-rejection of the total value system in which many Black youths have been socialized has been overshadowed by "a broader culture of pathology." Unlike previous generations of Blacks who had positive self-images that shaped their destinies, some men believed that the younger generation often lacked internal resources to cope with mainstream society.

DECREASE ECONOMIC MARGINALITY AND SOCIAL DISCREDITING

The men recommended complicated prescriptions for policymakers to alter the present situation. One such solution was to offer premarital counseling and family life education with job training programs. Whereas most men stated that material resources were problematic for a large proportion of Black males, others stated that emotional resources were equally problematic. As Matt explained,

Black men face a difficult time in establishing emotional connections because their image of manhood is directly tied to their marginal economic status in America, and most don't earn enough money to support their children. Some of my friends say they get tired of hearing "We are not hiring" when they look for jobs. Even if a Black man is hired, his employment is complicated by prejudice and distrust about whether he will be a good worker. He must prove himself constantly. So, it's hard for some Black men to be emotionally responsible fathers without jobs.

Matt also said that it is difficult for Black fathers to transmit high aspirations when they live in a society that often is hostile to Black aspirations:

America treated Jesse Jackson more like an outsider than a qualified presidential candidate. They assumed that a Black man could not want to be president of the United States. They couldn't understand a Black could have the mental strength, moral conviction, and intelligence to become a president.

According to Matt, solving some of the problems of Black fatherhood is translated into changing the attitudes of Whites toward Blacks. From the perspective of most men, the disengagement of Black fathers is the consequence of racial discrimination, cultural factors, and economic instability, which are inextricably linked. If America continues to sustain a racist culture, then there will be future generations of Black children who lack close relationships with their fathers.

PREMARITAL AND DRUG
REHABILITATION PROGRAMS

Several men also believed that premarital programs should be directly tied to effective drug rehabilitation programs. In their view, crack/cocaine has contributed to the deterioration of Black fatherhood. Many youths are using drugs or alcohol to escape and to remove themselves from problematic situations. Larry commented on the relationship between the use of crack and fatherhood:

It's hard being a drug dealer, but the money is good for a man who can make $1,000 to $3,000 a day versus $5.75 per hour. It is a demanding job that takes time and energy away from anything else. It's a round-the-clock hustle. Plus, you have to act ruthless or act like you are prepared to kill your friend or family. This attitude has created a different set of values among some Black men that prevents the development of the emotional sides of themselves.

Some men indicated that the seductive pull of the underground economy offers quick and easy money because there are few available jobs paying decent salaries. Thus, a future generation of Black fathers will have the attitude that women and children are burdens and that taking care of somebody else is devalued when it means having less for oneself.

NEW DEFINITIONS OF BLACK MASCULINITY

Other men indicated that it is important to change the definition of Black masculinity to change Black fatherhood. They believed that the socialization of Black men often emphasizes domination of women. This means that some Black men learn to function psychologically in ways to maintain their authority. Similar to White men, they suggested that Black men often strive to fit into male-dominated, hierarchically organized institutions through the adoption of aggressive behavior. Paradoxically, the socialization of Black men often is contrary to the dominant male preoccupation with power and competitiveness. As a result, Black youths often adopt an exaggerated and romanticized prototype of masculinity, which frequently is antithetical to enduring intimate relationships.

MALE SUPPORT GROUPS

Several men emphasized the need for support groups for young Black men who are anticipating fatherhood. Such a group could assist fathers in parent-child communication and could alert them to the effects of conflictual partner relationships on the development of children. A teenage male support group also would provide an outlet for men to discuss their problems and to generate solutions or strategies for coping with prospective problems of fatherhood. As Dwayne noted,

Men hurt, and there is nothing geared to Black men about fathering. They are disappointed and frustrated when they see the streets taking the lives of their children. Black women have magazines to help them to cope.

The respondents were concerned about the plight of future Black fathers and believed that children of involved fathers enjoyed a number of social, emotional, and intellectual advantages. They also were clear that given the competition from the media, peer groups, and a culture of drugs and violence, Black fathers can offer a unique contribution to children including love, care, and attention that promotes the optimum development of children. However, to effectively influence the future generation of Black fathers, mainstream society must tear down barriers imposed by race, erase stereotypes based on genetic background, and increase economic opportunities for Black men.

Summary

Children played a central role in the lives of biological fathers as well as stepfathers. Of importance, fathers viewed children as the most important reason to remain in an unhappy marriage, and they often delayed divorce. The most significant finding is that stepchildren and biological children were viewed as equals in vying for love and affection, suggesting that some stepfathers felt more like real fathers. However, it is unknown how the quality of these relationships affects stepchildren as adults.

There were a variety of stressors associated with noncustodial parenting as men sought to maintain contact with their children. For example, visitation often was hampered by ex-wives' noncooperation, maintaining consistent contact with teenage children was difficult, and uncertainty of the role of being a good noncustodial father compounded the stress inherent in noncustodial fathering.

Stepfathers encouraged biological fathers to increase interaction with their children. This might be a race-specific behavior and points to the respondents' emphasis on nurturing Black children. Thus, encouragement of biological connections symbolized stepfathers' love and concern.

The findings of the present study both support and refute past research on Black fatherhood. Psychological strain was evident in most of the noncustodial divorced fathers, a finding consistent with other studies (Carter & Glick, 1970; Goldberg, 1979; Gutmann, 1987; Zeiss, Zeiss, & Johnson, 1980). Compared to the men in Umberson and Williams' (1993) study, respondents in our study did not experience extreme distress associated with noncustodial parenting. There are several reasons why our results differ from those of the previous studies. First, most of the fathers recognized the impact that divorce played in their children's lives and developed strategies to maintain positive relationships including establishing positive relationships with ex-spouses, even at times when they would rather not. Other methods used by fathers included making sure that children were as comfortable with them as with their mothers. In fact, some fathers furnished rooms for their children in their houses or apartments similar to those provided by the mothers.

Consistent with Goldsmith's (1981) findings, several fathers believed that ex-wives purposely erected barriers to retard regular interaction with children and became more prominent following divorce. Similar to results reported by Arendell (1995), fathers felt cheated by the court system and ex-wives because of visitation privileges. The length of time divorced influenced whether conflict with ex-wives was a frustration; men who were divorced longer were less likely to perceive their former spouses as a source of strain.

The findings concur with Wilson and Clarke's (1992) conclusions that noncustodial Black fathers are involved in the development of their children. Without exception, fathers supported their children financially and emotionally. Few stated that they had ever been late paying child support; however, it must be remembered that this was a working/middle class sample.

The socialization of Black sons was especially relevant to the men in this study. One issue involved the value of training sons to aspire to be effective fathers in the context of social discrediting. Fathers encouraged sons to be autonomous and independent. This emphasis began during the marriage and extended postdivorce.

Of interest, previous research has documented that children brought into first marriages increase marital instability (Chan & Heaton, 1989; Trent & South, 1992). In the present study, stepchildren often increased marital stability. Some stepchildren were adopted by the respondents and received child support. However, the younger the children at the time of the marriage, the stronger the relationship postdivorce, suggesting that teenage children often may be mature enough to solely think of stepfathers as their mothers' husbands rather than as their stepfathers. In addition, stepchildren who were raised by stepfathers from a young age experienced divorce-related emotional distress similar to that of biological children.

There is a perception, fostered by the sensationalism of the mass media, that the Black family is dying. This perception was shared by respondents when they discussed the future of Black fatherhood. Although some problems that respondents mentioned might be appropriately viewed as community problems rather than as problems of the Black family, they certainly have a negative effect on the functioning of Black fathers. Contemporary young Black fathers are particularly vulnerable to stress due to adherence to traditional definitions of masculinity, lack of male support groups, inadequate economic resources, and lack of drug rehabilitation programs. These factors result in delinquency and criminal behavior that occur within the family as well as in the broader society. Thus, the building of more prisons and harsher punitive measures will not erase the feelings of alienation among a large number of future Black fathers.

10

Conclusion

I think there should be a mass media campaign to counteract the negative images of Blacks. We need to use the media to get across that everyday Black people are not criminals but [rather] hard-working people trying desperately to maintain satisfying relationships.
—a representative quote from the men

This study represents one of the few studies on Black divorced men based on interviews and participant observations in a community sample. We began with an analysis of marital formation based on social, personal, and cultural factors. Discussions of unique divorce-related stressors and postmarital relationships demonstrated the complexity of severing Black marital bonds. Strategies to cope with marital termination emphasized the importance of community support as well as family and friends support. Debunking the stereotypes of Black fathers, we addressed the roles that mothers, stepfathers, fathers, uncles, and other family members provided in the development of positive fatherhood identities. Positive, absent, aloof, and alcoholic fathers also were delineated in the construction of fatherhood. Discussions of the diverse conceptualizations of fatherhood identified issues that confront noncustodial fathers including stepfathers and fathers of biracial children.

Formation of Marital Bonds

Similar to other groups, love was the most significant reason for marriage in this sample. Despite its importance, definitions of love were confusing and perplexing. For example, provision of material and financial support, a need to rescue partners, an assessment of maternal potential, and the belief that love conquers all problems resulted in poor marital decisions.

Two explanations for marriage increased the likelihood of divorce. First was a belief that there was an appropriate time to marry, analogous to a biological clock women associate with childbearing. Second was a premarital pregnancy that resulted in rationalizations that the marriage was a trap. Thus, women often were blamed for pregnancy-inspired marriages, which increased marital instability. Because birth control was perceived as women's responsibility, not one man considered a vasectomy. Marrying because there was nothing better to do also increased marital instability because little consideration was given to the decisions. Therefore, trivial matters caused retreat from the marriages. These men often did not want to confront married life, which they viewed as giving women permission to determine how they spent their time.

The deterioration of marriages often involved several characteristics. First, there were frequent separations and numerous reconciliations. Second, there were long periods of anguish and mutual alienation. Third, a belief that wives had drastically changed, resulting in the failure to communicate, was a prominent theme. Following this period, feelings of pain and hurt surfaced. Consequently, an emphasis was placed on changing the popular assumption that Black men suffer little emotional distress following separations.

Correlates of Marital Separation and Divorce

Marriages were complicated by a number of structural conditions including (a) shift work, (b) working in jobs that require being away from home, and (c) work-related stressors of racial discrimination. In addition, the incarceration of Black men and women, social discrediting, economic marginality, and substance abuse were viewed as greater problems that destroy Black marital cohesiveness than is usually reported in the scholarly literature. The drug economy superimposed on existing gang networks with many young men unable to support families was perceived as especially destructive to Black family stability.

Marital instability also was influenced by consistently responding to negative images of Black men. Indeed, Black males expend an inordinate amount of mental energy to prove themselves respectable to others because dark skin has a special social meaning associated with deviant behavior and negative stereotypes. Whereas some wives employed a nonconfrontational style of handling overt discrimination, husbands challenged racism directly. As a result, disagreements about appropriate strategies to cope with racism generated marital discord, emotional strain, and a general feeling of marital frustration. Separations were different from those reported in previous studies. First, separations usually were longer. Second, separations were viewed as time contained and the first step toward a reconciliation to work through marital conflict—a "cooling-off period" or "taking a vacation from marriage."

The Divorce Experience

Distinctive patterns of the Black male divorce experience emerged. Most striking were maintenance of economic stability, consumer incompatibility, and autocratic spending decisions. Marital instability also occurred when wives exhibited extreme jealous behavior and in circumstances in which the husbands' need for autonomy clashed with the wives' need for intimacy. The number of violent marital incidents was striking and often involved both partners. Underlying these incidents were issues of control, with arguments and fights developing over trivial issues. Factors that increased the likelihood of physical and emotional abuse were the unwillingness of Blacks to use a White-dominated system of social control and a reluctance to use existing marital counseling resources.

A number of incompatibility issues strained marriages including values, religious interests, and educational dissimilarity. However, diversity of traits can be complementary when couples appreciate partners' variations and are compromising about their own interests. Often, it is not the opposition of traits that increases marital stability but rather an appreciation of those differences. Because few people are precisely matched, diversity of traits and interest will continue to disrupt Black marriages.

Divorce-Related Stressors

Divorce-related stressors were associated with (a) financial strain, (b) noncustodial parenting, (c) child support stressors, and (d) psychological and physiological distress. Underlying these sources of stressors was the belief that wives should receive marital assets to prevent children from receiving welfare. Furthermore, periodic court appearances for evaluation of child support created emotional distress to a greater extent than did an inability to pay child support. Economic resources was an important area for readjustment postdivorce. Whereas financial strain was a continuous stressor predivorce, separation and divorce complicated the struggle. The service economy, with past decades of inflation as well as limiting purchases of food and shelter, made postdivorce extremely stressful. Movement to less desirable residences often was required, which in turn altered social contacts and network patterns, increasing postdivorce distress.

Drugs and alcohol were used to cope with postdivorce distress. Consistent with Umberson's (1992) and Arendell's (1995) findings, these substances were perceived to temporarily relieve psychological distress. Substance abuse also was used to cope with feelings of failure. Even men who viewed divorce as beneficial admitted personal failures about the termination of their marriages. Consequently, postdivorce adjustment was as difficult for men who *initiated* the divorces as it was for those who *did not* initiate the divorces. Noninitiators expressed intense psychological symptomatology, whereas those who initiated divorces complained of physiological symptoms; both groups used drugs to numb thoughts and feelings.

Postmarital Relationships

Similar to Weiss's (1975) findings, postmarital relationships were characterized by a mixture of positive and negative feelings, with varying levels of conflict that decreased over time. Whereas some men avoided former spouses, a majority maintained friendly postmarital relationships, especially if there were children.

Of importance, there was little evidence of continued attachment to former spouses. The following factors prohibited attachment to former spouses: (a) a belief that once a concerted effort has been expended to correct a problem, there was little need to expend energy to solve a problem; (b) the entry of new relationships by one partner; and (c) an inability to trust former spouses. An unanticipated finding was the increased postdivorce distress associated with *attachment to former spouses*. Although Black women often initiated the divorces, they also exhibited attachment behaviors. Former wives' attachment behaviors were demonstrated by (a) attachment to female family members and (b) vindictive behaviors. This finding suggests that Black postdivorce attachment might be gender specific. However, we do not have former wives' assessments of attachment behaviors.

A surprising and unexpected finding was the retained relationships between husbands and mothers-in-law. This finding is in contrast to the most common retained relationships among Whites, those between wives and mothers-in-law. The key role that men played in the provision of resources to mothers-in-law often created bonds that survived postdivorce.

Strategies for Coping With Divorce

The availability of coping strategies was extensive and included (a) reliance on family and friends, (b) involvement in church-related activities, (c) increased social participation, (d) reliance on an optimistic cognitive style, and (e) formation of heterosexual relationships. Although most men received support from family and friends, most striking was the instrumental, emotional, and often economic support received from mothers. This support remained stable and often increased over time, suggesting that Black mothers provide considerable support to Black male adult children.

Postdivorce relationships were interesting. Most postdivorce heterosexual relationships were characterized by ambivalence. These relationships often involved cohabitation and being parental surrogates, which made easy exits from the relationships extremely difficult. Moreover, an emphasis was placed on future mates' personalities and behavioral characteristics, whereas White men often stress pragmatic and instrumental qualities. Unexpectedly, the presence of children did not preclude women as future mates, whereas White divorced single men often prefer women without family responsibilities. However, most men preferred women who did not desire *more* children. Unlike White samples of men, not one man in the present study mentioned sexual compatibility as a characteristic desired in a future mate. This finding is significant because stigmatization of Black males has placed an emphasis on their sexuality.

Previous research has suggested that separated and divorced men experience loneliness. In the present study, loneliness was viewed as nonproblematic. In fact, obtaining solitude was problematic given the relatively greater number of available Black women. Predivorce male and female friendships that remained postdivorce also prevented loneliness.

The Construction of Fatherhood

Black fathers employed various models to construct fatherhood including mothers, uncles, grandfathers, and play fathers. Of interest, men who were raised without fathers perceived their mothers as providing role models for fatherhood. Although some fathers were alcoholics, their drinking was excused. These fathers were respected and admired despite the alcoholism. In addition, stepfathers provided central models for fatherhood, whereas biological fathers remained nebulous figures. As a result, increased levels of stress occurred when respondents initially met biological fathers.

The conceptualization of fatherhood consisted of the following:

1. appropriate role modeling;
2. teaching children the importance of an education;
3. imparting appropriate family values; and
4. providing practical survival strategies that emphasized appropriate responses to police officers, sex education, and spiritual teaching.

Men who married women with young children had considerable influence and power in their households. However, those who married women with adolescent children experienced difficulty sharing family power and reacted in several ways. Whereas some were driven away, others established themselves as undisputed heads of household and forced the former single-parent families to accommodate their preferences. A majority, however, assimilated into the families with relatively little influence in family decisions and negotiated new perspectives of family life.

Divorce and Fatherhood

Children played a central role in the lives of both biological fathers and stepfathers. Fathers viewed children as the most important reason to remain in an unhappy marriage, which often delayed divorce. Without exception, noncustodial fathers supported their children financially, and few stated that they had been late paying child support.

Divorce profoundly affected children. School-age children exhibited a wide range of behavioral problems. Preadolescent and adolescent children retreated into self-destructive behaviors including drug use, sexual acting-out behaviors, and gang involvement. These findings suggest that the current generation of Black children of divorce might be more adversely affected by divorce than were previous generations of Black children.

Visitation was problematic for both biological fathers and stepfathers. One issue involved conflictual relationships with former spouses that resulted in decreased father-child interactions. Postmarital conflicts often centered on fathers' visitation rights. Because some former spouses linked nonpayment of child support to fathers' visitation rights, some fathers were denied access to their children. Nevertheless, stepfathers encouraged biological fathers to increase involvement with their children. This might be a race-specific behavior and points to the men's emphasis on nurturing and supporting Black children.

Without exception, respondents expressed concerns about future Black fathers and recommended complicated solutions to address their concerns. Solutions involved linking premarital counseling to drug rehabilitation services and altering definitions of Black masculinity. The need for support groups for young Black fathers to identify the positive aspects of fatherhood and to assist positive father-child interactions and communication was endorsed by a majority of men. Our basic perspective is that Black men experience a unique divorce experience linked to external and internal factors. External factors include social discrediting, economic marginality, pervasive drug use in communities, the Black sex ratio, and economic stress pre- and postdivorce. Internal factors such as relationships with biological fathers and stepfathers, noncustodial father-child interactions, conflictual postdivorce relationships, and enduring in-law bonds resulted in a distinctive divorce experience.

The relationship between social discrediting and economic marginality in Black family functioning is clear. For example, stable working class men are the least visible to journalists who collect information that makes sensational news and reinforces existing stereotypes. Complex, subtle portraits of Black divorced men who agonize over their lack of social mobility do not produce interesting sound bites. Therefore, a stigmatizing process has served to reaffirm the images of Black males as drug dealers and hustlers. While politicizing the identities of Black males, social discrediting has superiorized positions of White males and has blemished, perhaps permanently, the identities of a large number of Black divorced males, which has affected the functioning of Black families.

To address the issues of Black divorced men, it is important to develop three levels of interventions: (a) macro-level policies, (b) programs and services, and (c) micro-level support systems. These levels are interdependent, and a change in one level will have an impact on all other levels (Bronfenbrenner, 1979).

Macro-Level Policies

COMPREHENSIVE FAMILY POLICY

This level involves economic and political policies. To direct major changes in the structure and functioning of Black families, a comprehensive family policy that replaces the current antiquated welfare system is needed. Such a policy would guarantee minimum income, adequate housing, comprehensive health services, and opportunities for productive employment for all citizens. Because marital stability often is associated with economic resources, a full employment policy would contribute to the stability of Black families.

NO-FAULT LAW REFORM

According to Arendell (1995), fault grounds for divorce need to be abolished because they contribute to adversarial relations. Property division, child custody, and economic support policies must be more flexible. The objective is to create a legal framework for divorce that promotes nonconflictual relationships. In fact, Louisiana Governor Mike Foster recently signed a "covenant marriage bill." Married couples in Louisiana can decide against a no-fault marriage and elect a more binding legal union. Couples who agree on a covenant marriage agree to premarital and predivorce counseling and to accept a 2-year waiting period before obtaining no-fault divorces.

According to the sponsor of the bill, Representative Tony Perkins, covenant marriages focus attention on the meaning of American marriages and on the consideration of laws to achieve enduring families (Gallagher, 1997). Because a large percentage of divorce disputes are settled by couples, this law may assist in decreasing nonconflictual postmarital relations. Further study and evaluation of this law are needed.

CHILD CUSTODY REFORM

Child custody laws require policy evaluation and reform. For example, the "best interest of child policy" should be rejected due to its conceptual ambiguity (Furstenberg & Cherlin, 1991; Weitzman, 1985). First, attorneys and judges often do not have the necessary knowledge to determine the best interests of children. Second, judges often fail to assess parents' child-rearing skills and the quality of parent-child relationships. Third, mothers usually are awarded custody, although fathers might possess better parenting skills.

Chambers (1984) suggests that the United States should implement a primary caretaker policy, with the *primary caretaker* defined as the parent who has spent the most time caring for the child. According to Fineman (1991), the primary care policy would increase parental involvement predivorce, and the patriarchal prerogatives would be replaced by social ties and emotional bonds.

CHILD SUPPORT REFORM

The Family Support Act of 1988 directed states to establish uniform formulas to determine levels of child support and required states to institute collection and dispersal systems for payments. Although this has removed the exchange between parents and has increased child support payment compliance, the recent reforms do not address Black fathers, who often experience unemployment, underemployment, and frequent layoffs (Garfinkel & McLanahan, 1990; Martin, 1990). Garfinkel (1988) suggests adoption of a child support program as practiced by some European countries. Child support payments would be collected through payroll withholding and provided to the children. If a noncustodial parent refuses to pay, then the government would make up the difference, reducing poverty and welfare dependence. Clearly, revisions of the child support system alone are not adequate for a large number of Black children given that the present system aims at limited, short-term, deficient support. Effective leadership from the nation's capital is needed to enact policies that will enhance the economic well-being of children.

Programs and Services

MEDIATION PROGRAMS

Mediation counseling should be mandated for all Black divorced couples with minor children to develop conflict resolution and problem-solving skills (Vaughan, 1986). Divorce mediation is preferable to the traditional adversarial-based approach because it promotes cooperation through a structured process (Patrician, 1984).

PARENTING EDUCATION

Postdivorce parental education for Black men and women is urgently needed. Stepparenting educational courses, especially for stepfathers who marry women with teenage children, should be instituted.

An effective postdivorce parental education program mandated by the court is Focus on Kids at the University of Missouri–Columbia. The program reports that it has provided important information to divorced parents by offering age-related education about the impact of divorce. We suggest that the initiation of such a program in Black churches and Black community organizations with university-based partnerships might facilitate cooperative postmarital relationships and enhance the well-being of Black children of divorce.

MUTUAL SUPPORT GROUPS

Self-help groups can be effective resources for Black divorced men. In such groups, men meet others who have similar experiences, provide and receive emotional support, and work together toward solutions to problems. Because many Black men fail to find appropriate postdivorce counseling through the general health care system, removal of financial barriers to treatment and improved referral mechanisms are needed.

In addition, practitioners working to strengthen Black families can design interventions that involve individuals already known as helpers in the community. This strategy identifies lay helpers who customarily are relied on for informal assistance and involves them in postdivoce counseling training. For example, for help with postdivorce counseling, men in this study consulted the director of the Urban League, ministers of Black churches, and Black men who owned businesses. Conducting a postdivorce counseling group with lay counselors following Sunday services at a Black church, coordinated with university-based counseling programs, could be one collaborative endeavor to address the psycho-social needs of Black divorced men.

TRAINING COUNSELORS

Increased training of psychotherapists must be designed to enable therapists to enhance therapeutic skills to increase their effectiveness in counseling Black divorced men. According to Bernal and Castro (1994), the knowledge base that is essential for serving the mental health needs of racial/ethnic minority groups is limited. One consequence of the failure of counselors to recognize cultural, social, and historical facets of race has been a high attrition rate attributable to the therapists' racial ethnocentricity (Wilkinson, 1980). Thus, counselors for Black men must address the context in which they live and incorporate this perspective into their treatment efforts.

In fact, recent reports have documented that many applied graduate clinical and counseling programs currently do not provide experience in working with diverse populations (Allison, Crawford, Echemendia,

Robinson, & Knepp, 1994). Of 148 fully or provisionally accredited doctoral clinical psychology programs in the United States, 40% do not use clinical settings serving ethnic minorities as standard practicum placements for their students (Bernal & Castro, 1994).

PROGRAMS FOR PRISON AND MILITARY FAMILIES

Because a large number of Black men are in prisons and in the military, programs directed to such groups are urgently needed, especially those focusing on conflict-reducing strategies.

DRUG REHABILITATION/WORK PROGRAMS

Drug abuse disrupts a large number of Black families. Drug rehabilitation programs tied to partnerships with businesses that offer employment and marital counseling may be an effective method of reducing Black marital instability.

WORKPLACE PROGRAMS

To coordinate the demands of family and employment, it is important for employers to implement flexible work schedules, part-time employment with benefits, paternal leave, affordable child care provisions, and paid family leave (Garfinkel & McLanahan, 1990). Moreover, it would be advantageous to allow parents to arrange work schedules to accommodate children's school schedules. For example, there is no reason why work schedules must be from 9 a.m. to 5 p.m. Rearranging work hours that are compatible with elementary and high school schedules (i.e., 7 a.m. to 3 p.m.) would be desirable.

COMMUNITY PROGRAMS

Various initiatives to provide support to families of divorce are being undertaken by various groups such as the National Council of Negro Women, the Coalition of 100 Black Men, the International Black Women's Congress, the Urban League, and national sororities and fraternities. Support is provided to children and young adults in the form of tutoring, mentoring, and emotional support. It is important that these activities continue and focus on the special needs of Black divorced males with increased state, federal, and private funding.

Micro-Level Support Systems

PARENTS AND EDUCATORS

A concerted effort must be made by parents and educators to reinforce information to Black youths including the importance of personal effort, the significance of avoiding drugs, and the roles that Black families have played in America. Successful Black married couples must be willing to share their valuable advice and to serve as mentors for vulnerable families. Because many successful Black married couples have moved out of the inner cities and have loosened their ties with Black social and civic organizations, the least advantaged families do not have regular contact with happily married couples. These couples could participate in strengthening families through very specific activities such as offering advice on how their marriages have succeeded in the context of social discrediting and providing effective conflict resolution strategies. Individual efforts cannot be reinforced in a vacuum; rather, they must be linked to macro-level policies enhanced by community-based organizations and connected to employment opportunities.

Advice to Strengthen Black Families

According to Staples (1985), a number of social characteristics place Blacks at risk for divorce including higher rates of urbanization, earlier age at marriage, earlier fertility, higher education and income levels for the wife and lower income status for the husband, and the imbalanced sex ratio. The men in this study reported that although these factors are important in destabilizing Black marriages, there are unexplored issues that place Black families at risk for divorce. The following was a representative remark:

> I think there should be a mass media campaign to counteract the negative images of Blacks. We need to use the media to get across that everyday Black people are not criminals but [rather] hard-working people trying desperately to maintain satisfying relationships.

Consistent with this theme, some men commented on the need to reevaluate the socialization of Black men and encouraged Black men and women to take the initiative. This was another representative statement:

> Black men and women should demand more from their sons at a young age. My ex-wife made so many mistakes with my son because she pampered him. Now, at age 20, he doesn't know how to drive a car, [he] quit high school, and [he] sits at home watching television. He is doing absolutely nothing with his life.

Other men, however, believed that to strengthen Black marriages, Black women must stop sacrificing themselves to marital relationships. Sam said,

> Black women are often guilty of plunging wholeheartedly into the pursuits of their men, failing to focus on themselves. They often give all the physical, financial, and emotional support to their men without getting back any support. It is ironic that Black women are depicted as strong and tough but take care of men while risking their own personal well-being. This results in them being disappointed in dead-end relationships and fed up with heartaches and tears.

Overwhelmingly, the respondents reported that changing sex role stereotyping might strengthen Black families. For example, Brent said,

> I did not show Marilyn I was appreciative of her love. I would advise any man to show a woman that he really, really, cares. Wives need to know that husbands care, not just by doing things, but they need to hear it. Black men often have a difficult time saying "I love you." They think it is not macho.

Larry also noted that the decline of Black marriages results, in part, from many young Black males making permanent irreversible life decisions when they are immature in terms of self-awareness and development. A society interested in liberating Black men would not only provide jobs but also discourage young men from establishing permanent relationships early in life and discourage fathering until the identities of men and women are established. Most important, the men in this study indicated that the federal government must enact policies that will enhance life chances for youths. They also stated that education must be considered an important priority. Government and corporations should increase funding to public education for counselors. Teachers often are called on to perform social work tasks, resulting in high rates of teacher burnout and many youths dropping out of school.

Follow-Up of Some Respondents

This book has no ending. The lives of the respondents continue, and nobody knows what they will make of their world in 10 or 20 years. Some of the men interviewed called 1 year after the study to report on their progress. Peter decided to earn his teaching certificate, worked as a substitute teacher, and wondered when his life will improve. Most men were involved in committed relationships. For example, Barry remarried a woman whom he described as his "soulmate" and an answer to his prayers. Brent and Eric cohabitated with women, and Todd reported that he was in a committed relationship.

There were tragedies in the sample. Henry's hypertension became worse, and he experienced frequent hospitalizations. Graham was involved in a serious car accident that resulted in multiple physiological problems. His ex-wife, Tina, who had been diagnosed as schizophrenic, provided nursing care and emotional support. Several men were diagnosed with serious medical conditions. Jim developed hypertension and was diagnosed with kidney failure, Bronson was diagnosed with heart failure, and several men subsequently developed hypertension. Other stress-related conditions included ulcers, colitis, and recurrent pneumonia. Several men coped with the illnesses of ex-wives and family members. Willy's ex-wife, Donna, developed cancer 1 year postdivorce; Carl's ex-wife, Rita, was in a serious work-related accident; Peter's wife, Jackie, had a nervous breakdown 1 month after the study; Luke's ex-wife, Dawn, died; and Eric's father, Mr. Nash, had a stroke and was paralyzed.

Some respondents' children experienced difficulties postdivorce. For example, Eric's daughter began to use drugs again. Because he was distressed about the effects of drugs on Black youths, Eric started an organization called Black Men Against Drugs. James's stepdaughter, Ukemia, left home to live with a drug dealer. Matt's youngest son was

in prison on a murder charge, and his oldest son, Marcus, was anticipating parole. Truman, who continued to support the child of his
ex-wife's sister, reported that the child was killed by a gang. Bert's son,
Tabian, died from a sickle cell anemia attack. Dwayne's daughter gave
birth to a baby girl, and the baby's father was in prison. Dwayne said,
"I feel responsible for the choices my daughter made. I will invest energy
in trying to make my daughter's and granddaughter's lives better."

Meanwhile, the men dreamed of the future, a time when life will be
less stressful, when economic expenses will be fewer, and when they will
have time "to enjoy life and do what they want to do." They also
fantasized of a time when they no longer will have to constantly prove
themselves as respectable to others. Unfortunately, some of them will
not have the luxury of living carefree lives, with the demands of raising
children (and often grandchildren) to ensure their survival. Perhaps it
will be the strength of their forefathers and foremothers that will allow
them and their descendants to triumph over their shattered marriages.

The Interviewing Process

As stated in the beginning of this book, it took little encouragement
for men to discuss their feelings during the interviews. The probes that
were used during the interviews stimulated men to reflect on their
experiences, feelings, and attitudes. As Henry said, "It made me aware
of things that were affecting me and why I made the decisions I made."
Ivan said, "I never thought about this stuff, and I realized how much I
have to say." It was common for men to cry during the interviews as they
recalled the effects of divorce on their biological children and stepchildren. The following was a representative comment by the men: "I want
to read the book because it will be the first one to explore the lives and
experiences of Black divorced men."

It is worth noting that not one man said that the interviews involved
too much of his time. In fact, many of the interviews lasted much longer
than expected, some as long as 6 hours. Several men believed that the
study should have a 2-year follow-up as well as interviews with Black
divorced women. Furthermore, a few men requested specific counseling
referrals to provide assistance for the overwhelming emotional pain
associated with the dissolution of their marriages.

All of the men agreed to participate in the study due to a desire to increase understanding of the divorce experience of Black men. They believed that few people appreciate what it means for Black men to experience marital failure. This was verified when we talked with friends who were married. One Black man asked, "What makes the suffering of divorced men different from the suffering of others in miserable marriages? Why should they be entitled to special pain?" This was a representative remark by Black women:

> What about understanding the experiences of divorced Black women who are emotionally drained from caring for children [and] elderly parents; coping with sex and racial discrimination; and dealing with men who are demanding, unfaithful, [and] incapable of sacrificing their needs for a relationship?

Because there are "his-and-her divorces," perceptions of causes of divorce and postdivorce adjustment may be a different experience for Black women. Staples (1985) argues that the more education a woman has, the more likely she is to remarry deliberately or to decide to remain unmarried. This suggests that the benefits of divorce, as defined by Black women, may influence their attitudes about remarriage. In addition, some Black women might be afraid of marriage based on their unfulfilling marriage and divorce experiences. Black divorced women also might be reluctant to risk additional divorces, to live with their husbands' illnesses or deaths, and/or to entrust Black men with their feelings.

There is much to be learned about Black divorced women. What ideologies about marriage do they hold? Do they construct their postdivorce lives differently from those of Black men? What social support do they access from the larger culture? What reasons would they express as the causes of divorce? The number of divorced Black women warrants a detailed study of Black divorced women.

GENDER AND PERSPECTIVES

In making sense of divorce, the gender of the interviewer often influenced the information provided. For example, to the male interviewer, men often talked about divorce as a challenge as they developed more differentiated autonomous selves; to the female interviewer, men often talked about divorce in terms of relational and self-examination as their identities changed in the process. The interviews may have been occasions to celebrate independence and to express solidarity and identification with the male interviewer. Furthermore, men may have been reluctant to report fully to the female interviewer some areas that were considered negative and embarrassing for them such as sexual inadequacy postdivorce.

On the other hand, some men desired a woman to agree with their points of view. Others desired a woman to listen and to suggest various methods of coping with particular situations. Frequently, men desired validation from a woman that he had been a good husband—not perfect, but a good husband. Thus, the men often were confused as to what Black wives wanted and expected in marriage. To the female interviewer, they openly asked, "What do Black wives want from Black husbands? I've tried to give her everything she wanted." However, when both genders conducted the interviews, the respondents were more likely to report experiences of being physical and psychologically abusive husbands. It appeared that the presence of both a male and a female interviewer decreased feelings of vulnerability.

The history of our life experiences, professional training, and ideological stances affected our perceptions of divorce and interpretation of the data. Lack of consensus on data interpretation reflects the diversity of Black life experiences based on gender, which continuously revealed varied interpretations as new data were incorporated into the writing. Demythologizing negative images of the Black male in the family was an ongoing process that was central, especially for the male interviewer, because ethnocentric concepts held by mainstream social scientists about Black men continue to persist. Moreover, negative images are held by those in positions of making policy and programmatic decisions. Consequently, a large portion of creative energies of Black social scientists often is channeled into reactionary activities (McAdoo, 1997).

Although it is necessary to challenge blatant conjectures about Black men, it is equally important to go beyond the negative stereotypical views of Black men and to continue to examine Black family functioning. The significance of such an examination is underscored by the proliferation of problems that Black males encounter. For example, there are more Black men in prison than in college, more than 35% of Black men in U.S. cities are drug or alcohol abusers, more than 50% of Black men under 21 years of age are unemployed, approximately 32% of employed Black men have incomes below the poverty level, and the homicide rate of Black men is six times than that of White men (Dickson, 1993). These statistics have already sent an alarm through the Black community nationwide. Although the crisis of the Black male is not the worst predicament they have faced and survived, the female researcher believed that it is crucial to acknowledge that external and internal factors have had a profound effect on Black men. We hope that the tension between debunking Black males' negative images and an effort to present the diversity of Black divorced men will generate more research endeavors examining the experiences of Black men.

THE MALE PERSPECTIVE

I am a Black divorced father. Therefore, this research became more than a scholarly project. However, I tried to stick as strictly as possible to a grounded theoretical approach throughout the investigation. I was amazed at the way in which the men responded to me. It was clear that, most of the time, there was a respect for the title I carried and for the interest that I had in including them as part of my academic endeavors. It was common to have a respondent tell me that it was gratifying to see that a Black man had made it as far as I have, and then both of us would go into a spontaneous dialogue about the struggles of getting to this middle class. In every interview, I walked out feeling that I had gained a little more insight into my own life as a Black man. The stories of racism on the job and feeling the constant frustration of social marginality really hit home as a Black professional.

Two years into the data collection, I went through a divorce myself. That is when I really joined the brotherhood and the data truly came to life for me. All of the years spent on this research came to an emotional head, and I got a firsthand look at the frightened change in identities these men felt. I no longer was an intact provider for my wife of 14 years and my 10-year-old daughter. The dramatic feelings of loss, anger, and distrust not only were part of the cadre of transcripts I had collected but also applied to my own circumstances. This research truly serves as a catharsis for all the Black divorced men who have had the strength to share their pain, frustration, and disappointments in this study.

THE FEMALE PERSPECTIVE

I am unmarried due to a great deal of frustration in relationships, and often I have heard friends say, "The problem of the 20th century is the Black women's lament." This often is translated to mean that the socialization of Black men is antithetical to the formation of enduring monogamous relationships. I have heard horror stories of Black men mistreating Black women whose only crime was simply loving and supporting them. Some of my pregnant research participants eventually voiced distrust of Black men, feared rejection, and questioned the institution of marriage. The following was a common expression: "I'm simply tired of Black men. I would rather spend my life alone than to tolerate the stress of a Black man in my life."

Therefore, I was unprepared for my response. Not only did the interviewing process have an effect on the respondents, it strongly affected me as well. Listening to the men's painful descriptions of their marriages and trying to probe for their understandings of what had happened led to a sensitivity and understanding of the plight of Black men in the United States. "As long as I'm a Black man, my life will never be easy or my job will never go smoothly." When I heard words such as these repeated time and again, I thought about how much of what the men were saying was part of their experiences of social marginality and racial discrimination. Their heartaches were in the realization and pain of knowing that they and their children live in a world that judges character by the color of their skin.

Some men also expressed distrust in the institution of marriage. For example, one man said that he did not believe in supporting a family because it was like being in slavery and he wanted to be free. Other men also reported that marriage was like a prison sentence in that women want to "own" their husbands. Some even reported extreme distrust in Black women, for example, "I've always had a woman on the side, just in case my wife left me." A few men seemed uncommitted to marriage not because they were womanizers but because they were filled with grief, sorrow, hurt, and bitterness. This was because there were no more psychological games they could play to make the experiences of shattered marriages more bearable. There were no more dreams of permanent marriages, no more assumptions about finding the perfect women, and no more patience to "do the right thing." As one respondent said over and over again, "I foster no illusions about finding my soulmate. I just hope to meet someone I can get along with before I die."

At night, many men coped with chest pains. As they regrouped, their minds raced over the past and back to the future. Trying to bring logic to despair, they often were haunted by this representative thought: "I didn't know the person I married. What is wrong with me? I must have some deep psychological problems." Whereas many Black women are "waiting to exhale," a number of Black divorced men are simply "waiting," locked in an emotional prison while coping with stressors of noncustodial parenting, dealing with rejection, and labeling themselves as emotional catastrophes. Thus, the events surrounding the marital separations and divorces seemed surreal while they waited to get through the present with the thought, "I'll take one day at a time."

Although divorce was common in the respondents' social circles, the men indicated that the psychological experiences remained unreal until "it happens to you." They lived precariously on the edge of financial disaster as layoffs or cutbacks in overtime influenced their lives. They numbed themselves to the painful feelings of discontent and tried hard to avoid the question: "Is this all there is to life?"

I also was struck, as a Black woman, by the men's high regard for Black women. Contrary to popular literature suggesting that Black men often engage in female bashing, the men often blamed themselves for marital failures. In fact, they were the harshest critics of Black men. Although they admitted that there were substantive problems concerning relationships between Black males and females, they often referred to Black women as the strong ones who suffer from the twin burden of being both Black and female. They did not perceive their enemy to be Black women; rather, the enemy was the oppressive forces in the larger society. In fact, they said that Black men must search their souls for workable solutions to interpersonal conflicts and pleaded for Black women not to give up on them.

I also was surprised by the number of times mothers were mentioned during the interviews. As one man said,

After I received the divorce decree, I went to see my mother in the hospital. She was so thin and frail. Two days later, she died. The burden I felt was that she would have wanted to see my marriage work. She had always been a fixture in my life. I cried, sobbing in bursts of tears. Whenever I had trouble, my mom had always been there. So, I coped with [my] mom's death at the same time [that] I dealt with a divorce. She died as much as from a broken heart seeing my marriage dissolve as from her failed health.

Paradoxically, men expressed a high esteem for Black women in an abstract sense, especially for their mothers, but they often admitted difficulty in building relationships with Black women. It also was interesting to hear them talk about confronting their own anger and irresponsibility to enhance future relationships.

CONCLUDING REMARKS

We were both surprised by the men's grief and hurt due to emotionally distant fathers. The view of themselves as having made it without fathers remained in the background and related to notions about the power of personal motivation to succeed despite inadequate fathering. However, during their divorces, the lack close father-son bonds surfaced. One respondent recalled, "When I finally realized the marriage was over, I wished I could talk to my father about this and thought about the times I wanted to talk to him, but I abandoned all hopes and tried to make sense of life myself." Therefore, predivorce, some men often invested substantial energy in repressing emotions about their own fathers. Postdivorce thoughts of fathers surfaced involuntarily, and when those thoughts surfaced, they often were upsetting. We also were struck by the number of men who married but had little understanding of the responsibilities of married life. Thus, for some men, marriage was a drastic lifestyle change that they reluctantly embraced. They no longer were free to run around with the "old crowd" or to party whenever the mood struck. For example, this was a representative remark: "I didn't know what I was getting into and what marriage was all about, and when I realized what it involved, it was too late." Men frequently were disappointed as it became clear that their beliefs about marriage were mirages. Before marriage, they thought of it as a place to be cared for, perhaps the only place where one might find a haven. Following a couple years of marriage, they often felt disappointed and frustrated. A few began to spend time stopping off for beers after work, idealizing the past, and/or dropping in at favorite hangouts after dinner—behaviors their wives resented and that often escalated into marital conflict. Consequently, it is important to gain more knowledge of Black men's mate selection process and marital expectations.

The relationship between Black marital stability and the larger social environment is exceedingly complex. For example, many men desired marriage and a stable family life but found it difficult to obtain these until social factors changed as well. While constantly trying to overcome pervasive stereotypes, they devoted tremendous energy to gaining respectability. It is more than a statistical accident that the segment of society most vulnerable to high drug use, poor health, premarital pregnancy, and crime also is more prone to divorce. If future Black marital stability exists, then current social and economic disenfranchisement and entrenched negative stereotypes of Black men should be eliminated.

However, it is clear that solutions such as premarital education, parenting classes, and residential relocation policies directed to minority and poverty communities are less effective in a society that is more attuned to promoting negative stereotypes and building more prisons than it is to strengthening Black families. Thus, social policies proliferate at developing programs in hopes of changing the manners, mores, and lifestyles of Blacks. It is reasoned that Blacks will then be able to move into the privileged sectors of society with ideal White family structures and lifestyles. Rarely are programs to change Whites' perceptions of Blacks designed, funded, or implemented.

When money and politics get in the way of strengthening families, the entire country should stand up and say "no!" With an epidemic of drugs and violence in many Black communities, it is important to review and reevaluate many areas of Black family life. We no longer can believe in the Black, all-loving extended family. We no longer can lay claim to being the only people who take care of family members when in need. Black communities are losing smart and talented youths who feel angry with and alienated from family life and the world while perceiving their life choices as limited. This is illustrated in the following poem by Toni Warren:

The Gentle Giant: My Black Brother's Lament

Meek in manner, robust, and genteel
A boy inside, how does he feel?
Depictions of kindness, displays of refiness
Alas there opposes the thorns and the roses
And yes he is humble and yet he is proud
He will definitely rumble—may even be quite loud
I've seen tears of sadness and tears of pain
His outlook is bland
Happiness appears to refrain
Though his smiles are gregarious, they're often times harried
I feel his suffering, I feel his sorrow
What burdens are carried
And what of his tomorrow
His voice sings of marital despair
His eyes dispel apathy, "I don't care!"
Denotes his legacy of marital breakup
His emotions for children run deep
His tears he cannot keep
As a babe he did sparkle
His innocence and misery permeate his youth
Succumb not to pity, overcome, and endure
At moments right witty
An intellect for sure
You will find him quite raw, and oddly so pure
He is just a gentle, hurt giant

Used by permission of the author.

Appendix

Respondents ($N = 50$)

Name	Occupation	Age (years)	Ex-Wife	Children	Years Married	Years Divorced
Allen	College professor	45	Jean	2 daughters Remarried woman with 6 children	12	4
Alvin	Auto mechanic	36	Maria	1 daughter	4	3
Anton	Employment counselor	39	Thelma	13-year-old son (Shawn)	16	4
Arthur	Horse trainer	55	Miriam	27-year-old from previous relationship Son from current marriage	19	5
Barry	Security guard	46	Jennifer	2 sons	10	10
Ben	Accountant	43	Etta	2 stepdaughters 15-year-old son from previous relationship	12	8
Bernie	Bus driver	26	Shelia	1 son from previous relationship 3-year-old son 6-year-old son 2-year-old daughter	7	3

(continued)

Name	Occupation	Age (years)	Ex-Wife	Children	Years Married	Years Divorced
Bert	—	52	Norma	4-year-old son (Tabian) 22-year-old daughter from previous relationship	15	3
Brent	Electrician	40	Marilyn	15-year-old daughter 14-year-old son 10-year-old stepdaughter	13	8
Bronson	Car salesman	43	Sara	2 sons from current marriage 12-year-old stepson 2 daughters from previous relationship	12	3
Carl	Factory worker	42	Rita	13-year-old daughter 12-year-old male twins	14	3
Clyde	Electrician	41	Betty	2 daughters	11	5
Curtis	Registered nurse	47	Julie	10-year-old stepdaughter 8-year-old stepson 5-year-old son	6	3
Derek	Horse trainer	51	Joan	9-year-old daughter 12-year-old son 29-year-old son from previous relationship 17-year-old stepdaughter	14	2
Douglas	News reporter	47	Sharon	6-year-old son 8-year-old daughter 11-year-old son 15-year-old stepson	12	7
Dwayne	Retail store manager	46	Claire	20-year-old daughter from previous relationship 15-year-old stepson 13-year-old son	17	4
Edsel	Business executive	49	April	11-year-old stepdaughter 16-year-old stepdaughter 10-year-old son	14	2

Name	Occupation	Age (years)	Ex-Wife	Children	Years Married	Years Divorced
Eric	High school teacher	40	Bonnie	5-year-old son 9-year-old son 10-year-old son	15	3
Ernell	Retired army sergeant	51	Dee	16-year-old son 17-year-old son	20	5
Gerald	—	39	Molly	10-year-old daughter 8-year-old daughter	10	4
Graham	Hotel clerk	40	Tina	12-year-old daughter	15	6
John	—	42	Ellen	9-year-old son 8-year-old daughter 6-year-old son	10	2
Kenneth	Police officer	37	Mary	16-year-old daughter 9-year-old son	18	3
James	—	35	Ellen	13-year-old stepdaughter 4-year-old son 9-year-old son	13	3
Jim	—	40	Coleen	5-year-old son 7-year-old son	8	2
Henry	City manager	42	Linda	10-year-old son 13-year-old daughter	12	1
Ivan	Police officer	28	Margaret	7-year-old daughter 3-year-old son 13-year-old son	7	2
Larry	City administrator	34	Pat	10-year-old stepson 9-year-old stepson	6	3
Lawrence	Probation officer	46	Frances	10-year-old daughter 18-year-old stepdaughter	12	1
Lennie	—	41	Cheryl	15-year-old son 17-year-old son	17	2

(continued)

Name	Occupation	Age (years)	Ex-Wife	Children	Years Married	Years Divorced
Leon	—	40	Carol	12-year-old stepdaughter 7-year-old daughter 20-year-old son from previous relationship	9	5
Luke	Building contractor	35	Dawn	2-year-old son 6-year-old son 4-year-old daughter	7	3
Matt	Emergency room technician	42	Hazel	14-year-old son (Marcus) 16-year-old son (Dameon)	16	2
Maurice	Car salesman	40	Elaine	17-year-old daughter 20-year-old stepdaughter	20	5
Peter	Factory worker	39	Jackie	16-year-old son 13-year-old daughter 8-year-old son	18	4
Philip	Real estate agent	47	Pam	5-year-old daughter 8-year-old daughter 10-year-old stepson 14-year-old daughter from previous relationship	5	3
Robert	Counselor in city government	48	Anne	17-year-old son 15-year-old daughter 19-year-old daughter from previous relationship	20	2
Roger	Factory worker	52	Doris	14-year-old son	10	3
Roscoe	Construction worker	38	Cynthia	6-year-old son 13-year-old stepdaughter 9-year-old son	7	7
Sam	Graphic artist	32	Velma	13-year-old daughter (Celeste) 2-year-old son 12-year-old daughter from previous relationship	13	4

Name	Occupation	Age (years)	Ex-Wife	Children	Years Married	Years Divorced
Solomon	Nurse practitioner	47	Kaye	12-year-old stepson 10-year-old daughter 17-year-old daughter from previous relationship	18	6
Stanley	Elementary school teacher	33	Paula	5-year-old son 2-year-old daughter	7	2
Taylor	Parole officer	25	Joanne	2-year-old son 4-year-old son	5	5
Todd	Auditor	38	Rachael	13-year-old daughter (Cheryl) 14-year-old son from previous relationship	17	5
Truman	Retail store manager	49	Barbara	25-year-old son from previous relationship 14-year-old daughter 16-year-old stepson	16	6
Vance	Respiratory technician	30	Ella	3-year-old son 4-year-old son	10	3
Vince	State government employee	25	Sandy	8-year-old daughter 7-year-old daughter	7	2
Vincent	Apartment complex manager	36	Sally	10-year-old son 13-year-old son 14-year-old stepdaughter	16	5
William	—	40	Dot	14-year-old son from previous relationship 16-year-old stepdaughter 6-year-old daughter	9	1
Willy	—	33	Donna	10-year-old son from previous relationship 7-year-old daughter 5-year-old daughter	7	2

References

Ahrons, C. R., & Wallish, L. (1987). Parenting in the binuclear family: Relationships between biological and stepparents. In K. Pasley & M. Ihinger-Tallman (Eds.), *Remarriage and stepparenting*. New York: Guilford.

Albrecht, S. L. (1980). Reactions and adjustments to divorce: Differences in the experiences of males and females. *Family Relations, 29*, 59-60.

Aldrige, D. P. (1989). (Ed.). *Black male-female relationships*. Dubuque, IA: Kendall/Hunt.

Allen, W. R. (1978). The search for applicable theories in Black family life. *Journal of Marriage and the Family, 40*, 117-129.

Allison, K. W., Crawford, I., Echemendia, R., Robinson, L., & Knepp, D. (1994). Human diversity and professional competence. *American Psychologist, 49*, 729-796.

Amato, P. R., & Booth, A. (1991). The consequences of divorce for attitudes toward divorce and gender roles. *Journal of Family Issues, 12*, 306-322.

Ambert, A. M. (1988). Relationships with former in-laws after divorce: A research note. *Journal of Marriage and the Family, 50*, 679-686.

Ambert, A. M. (1989). *Ex-spouses and new spouses: A study of relationships*. Greenwich, CT: JAI.

Anaspach, D. F. (1976). Kinship and divorce. *Journal of Marriage and the Family, 38*, 323-330.

Anderson, E. (1989). *Streetwise: Race, class and change in an urban community*. Chicago: University of Chicago Press.

Arendell, T. (1992). Social self as gendered: A masculinist discourse of divorce. *Symbolic Interaction, 5*, 151-181.

Arendell, T. (1995). *Fathers and divorce*. Thousand Oaks, CA: Sage.

Asher, S., & Bloom, B. (1983). Geographic mobility as a factor in adjustment to divorce. *Journal of Divorce, 6*, 69-84.

Berman, W. H. (1985). The role of attachment in the post-divorce experience. *Journal of Personality and Social Psychology, 54*, 496-503.

Bernal, E., & Castro, F. G. (1994). Are clinical psychologists prepared for service and research with ethnic minorities. *American Psychologist, 49,* 797-805.

Billingsley, A. (1968). *Black families in White America.* Englewood Cliffs, NJ: Prentice Hall.

Billingsley, A. (1988). The impact of technology on Afro-American families. *Family Relations, 37,* 420-425.

Billingsley, A. (1992). *Climbing Jacob's ladder: The enduring legacy of African-American families.* New York: Simon & Schuster.

Black, L. E., Eastwood, M. M., Sprenkle, D. H., & Smith, E. (1991). An exploratory analysis of Leavers versus Left as it relates to Levinger's social exchange theory of attractions, barriers, and alternative attractions. *Journal of Divorce and Remarriage, 15,* 127-140.

Blassingame, J. (1972). *The slave community: Plantation life in the Antebellum South.* New York: Oxford University Press.

Bloom, B. L., Asher, S. J., & White, S. W. (1978). Marital disruption as a stressor: A review and analysis. *Psychological Bulletin, 85,* 867-894.

Bloom, B. L., & Clement, C. (1984). Marital sex role orientation and adjustment to separation and divorce. *Journal of Divorce, 7,* 87-98.

Bloom, B. L., & Kindle, K. R. (1985). Demographic factors in continuing relationships between former spouses. *Family Relations, 34,* 375-381.

Bogden, R. (1972). *Participant observation in organizational settings.* Syracuse, NY: Syracuse University Press.

Bohannan, P. (1985). *All the happy families: Exploring the varieties of family life.* New York: McGraw-Hill.

Booth, A., Johnson, D. R., & White, L. K. (1984). Women, outside employment, and marital instability. *American Journal of Sociology, 90,* 567-583.

Bowlby. J. (1969). *Attachment and loss, Vol. 1: Attachment.* New York: Basic Books.

Bowlby, J. (1973). *Attachment and loss, Vol. 2: Separation, anxiety, and anger.* New York: Basic Books.

Bowser, B. (Ed.). (1991). *Black male adolescents: Parenting and education in community context.* Lanham, MD: University Press.

Broman, C. L. (1991). Gender, work-family roles, and psychological well-being of Blacks. *Journal of Marriage and the Family, 53,* 509-520.

Bronfenbrenner, U. (1979). *The ecology of human development: Experiments by nature and design.* Cambridge, MA: Harvard University Press.

Brown, D., & Gary, L. E. (1987). Stressful life events, social support networks, and physical and mental health of urban Black adults. *Journal of Human Stress, 13,* 165-174.

Brown, P., Perry, L., & Hamburg, E. (1977). Sex role attitudes and psychological outcomes for Black and White women experiencing marital dissolution. *Journal of Marriage and the Family, 39,* 549-561.

Buchler, C., & Langenbrunner, M. (1987). Divorce-related stressors: Occurrence, disruptiveness and area of life change. *Journal of Divorce, 2,* 21-36.

Burns, A. (1984). Perceived causes of marriage breakdown and conditions of life. *Journal of Marriage and the Family, 46,* 551-562.

Campbell, M. L., & Moen, P. H. (1992). Job-family role strain among employed single mothers of pre-schoolers. *Family Relations, 41,* 205-211.

Carter, H., & Glick, J. (1970). *Marriage and divorce: A social and economic study.* Cambridge, MA: Harvard University Press.

Cate, R. M., & Lloyd, S. A. (1992). *Courtship*. Newbury Park, CA: Sage.

Cazenave, N. (1984). Race, socioeconomic status, and age: The social context of American masculinity. *Sex Roles, 11,* 639-656.

Cazenave, N. A., & Smith, R. (1993). Gender differences in perception of Black male/female relationships and stereotypes. In H. E. Cheatham & J. B. Stewart (Eds.), *Black families: Interdisciplinary perspectives* (3rd ed., pp. 149-170). New Brunswick, NJ: Transaction.

Chambers, D. (1984). Rethinking the substantive rules for custody disputes in divorce. *Michigan Law Review, 88,* 477-569.

Chan, L., & Heaton, T. (1989). Demographic determinants of delayed divorce. *Journal of Divorce, 13,* 97-112.

Chapman, A. B. (1997). The Black search for love and devotion: Facing the future against all odds. In H. McAdoo (Ed.), *Black families* (3rd ed., pp. 273-283). Thousand Oaks, CA: Sage.

Chatters, L. M., Taylor, R. J., & Jackson, J. S. (1986). Aged Blacks' choices for an informal helper network. *Journal of Gerontology, 41,* 94-100.

Chatters, L. M., Taylor, R. J., & Neighbors, H. W. (1989). Size of informal helper network mobilized during a serious personal problem among Black Americans. *Journal of Marriage and the Family, 51,* 667-676.

Cherlin, A. J. (1992). *Marriage, divorce, remarriage* (rev. ed.). Cambridge, MA: Harvard University Press.

Cherlin, A., & Furstenberg, F. F., Jr. (1986). The new American grandparent: A place in the family—A life apart. New York: Basic Books.

Chester, R. (1971). Health and marriage breakdown: Experience of a sample of divorced women. *British Journal of Preventive and Social Medicine, 25,* 231-235.

Chiriboga, D. A., & Culter, L. (1977). Stress responses among divorcing men and women. *Journal of Divorce, 1,* 95-105.

Chodorow, N. (1978). *The reproduction of mothering: Psychoanalysis and the sociology of gender*. Berkeley: University of California Press.

Christian, B. (1985). *Black feminist criticism: Perspectives on Black women writers*. New York: Pergamon.

Cleek, M., & Pearson, T. (1985). Perceived causes of divorce: An analysis of inter-relationships. *Journal of Marriage and the Family, 47,* 179-183.

Collins, P. H. (1991). *Black feminist thought: Knowledge, consciousness, and the politics of empowerment*. New York: Routledge.

Coombs, L. C., & Zumeta, Z. (1970). Correlates of marital dissolution in a prospective fertility study: A research note. *Social Problems, 18,* 92-102.

Cowan, C. P., & Cowan, P. A. (1992). *When partners become parents: The big life change for couples*. New York: Basic Books.

Crohan, S. E. (1992). Marital happiness and spousal consensus on beliefs about marital conflict: A longitudinal investigation. *Journal of Social and Personal Relationships, 9,* 89-102.

Denzen, N. K. (1970). *The research act: A theoretical introduction to sociological methods*. Chicago: Aldine.

Dickson, L. (1993). The future of marriage and family in Black America. *Journal of Black Studies, 23,* 472-491.

Dressler, W. W. (1985). Extended family relationships, social support, and mental health in a southern Black community. *Journal of Health and Social Behavior, 26,* 39-48.

DuBois, W. E. B. (1899). *The Philadelphia Negro: A social study.* Philadelphia: University of Pennsylvania Press.

Dullea, G. (1987, March 18). Divorces spawn confusion over stepparents' rights. *Omaha World-Herald,* p. A1.

Ehrenreich, B. (1983). *The hearts of men: American dreams and the flight from commitment.* Garden City, NY: Anchor/Doubleday.

Ely, M., Anzul, M., Friedman, T., Garner, D., McCormack, A., & Steinmetz, A. (1991). *Doing qualitative research: Circles within circles.* New York: Falmer.

Farley, R., & Allen, W. R. (1987). *The color line and the quality of life in America.* New York: Russell Sage.

Ferree, M. M. (1991). The gender division of labor in two-earner marriages: Dimensions of variability and change. *Journal of Family Issues, 12,* 158-180.

Fine, M. (1992). Families in the United States: Their current status and future prospects. *Family Relations, 41,* 430-435.

Fineman, M. A. (1991). *The illusion of equality: The rhetoric and reality of divorce reform.* Chicago: University of Chicago Press.

Frazier, E. F. (1932). *The Negro family in Chicago.* Chicago: University of Chicago Press.

Frazier, E. F. (1966). *The Negro family in the United States.* Chicago: University of Chicago Press. (Originally published in 1939)

Fromm, E. (1956). *The art of loving.* New York: Harper & Row.

Fulton, J. A. (1979). Parental reports of children's post-divorce adjustment. *Journal of Family Issues, 35,* 126-140.

Furstenberg, F. F., Jr. (1987). The new extended family: The experience of parents and children after remarriage. In K. Pasley & M. Ihinger-Tallman (Eds.), *Remarriage and stepparenting* (pp. 42-61). New York: Guilford.

Furstenberg, F. F., Jr. (1988). *Unplanned parenthood: The social consequences of teenage childbearing.* New York: Free Press.

Furstenberg, F. F., Jr., & Cherlin, A. J. (1991). *Divided families: What happens when parents part.* Cambridge, MA: Harvard University Press.

Furstenberg, F. F., Jr., Morgan, P., & Allison, P. (1987). Parental participation and children's well-being after marital dissolution. *American Sociological Review, 52,* 695-701.

Furstenberg, F. F., Jr., & Nord, C. W. (1985). Parenting apart: Patterns of childrearing after marital disruption. *Journal of Marriage and the Family, 47,* 893-904.

Furstenberg, F. F., Jr. & Spanier, G. (1984). *Recycling the family: Remarriage after divorce.* Newbury Park, CA: Sage.

Gallagher, M. (1997, July 24). Marriage covenants: Louisiana finds balm for divorce epidemic. *Dallas Morning News,* p. A27.

Garfinkel, I. (1988). *Assuring child support: An extension of social security.* New York: Russell Sage.

Garfinkel, J., & McLanahan, S. (1990). The effect of child support provisions of the Family Support Act of 1988 on children's well-being. *Population Researh and Policy Review, 9,* 205-234.

Gelles, R. J. (1984). *The violent home.* Beverly Hills, CA: Sage.

Genovese, E. (1976). *Roll Jordon roll: The world the slaves made.* New York: Random House.

Gerbner, G. (1990). *Violence profile.* Philadelphia: Annenberg School of Communication.

Gerstel, N. (1988). Divorce and kin ties: The importance of gender. *Journal of Marriage and the Family, 50,* 209-219.

Gibbs, J. T. (1988). *Young, Black and male in America: An endangered species.* Westport, CT: Auburn House.

Gibbs, J. T. (1993). Developing intervention models for Black families: Linking theory and research. In H. E. Cheatham & J. B. Stewart (Eds.), *Black families: Interdisciplinary perspectives* (pp. 325-351). New Brunswick, NJ: Transaction.

Giles-Sims, J., & Crosbie-Burnett, M. (1989). Adolescent power in stepfather families: A test of normative resource theory. *Journal of Marriage and the Family, 52,* 1065-1078.

Glenn, N. D. (1987). Continuity versus change, sanguineous versus concern: Views of the American family in the late 1980s. *Journal of Family Issues, 8,* 348-354.

Glenn, N. D., & McLanahan, S. (1982). Children and marital happiness: A further specification of the relationship. *Journal of Marriage and the Family, 44,* 63-72.

Glick, P. C. (1997). Demographic pictures of African American families. In H. McAdoo (Ed.), *Black families* (3rd ed., pp. 118-138). Thousand Oaks, CA: Sage.

Goldberg, H. (1979). *The new male: From macho to sensitive but still all male.* New York: William Morrow.

Goldsmith, J. (1981). The relationship between former spouses: Descriptive findings. *Journal of Divorce, 4,* 1-20.

Goode, W. J. (1959). The theoretical importance of love. *American Sociological Review, 24,* 38-47.

Gottman, J. M. (1979). *Marital interaction: Experimental investigations.* New York: Academic Press.

Gottman, J. M., & Krotkoff, L. J. (1989). Marital interaction and satisfaction: A longitudinal view. *Journal of Consulting and Clinical Psychology, 57,* 47-52.

Gove, W. R., & Shin, H. (1989). The psychological well-being of divorced and widowed men and women: An empirical analysis. *Journal of Family Issues, 10,* 122-144.

Gray, G. M. (1978). The nature of the psychological impact of divorce upon the individual. *Journal of Divorce, 1,* 289-301.

Grief, G. (1985). *Single fathers.* Lexington, MA: D. C. Heath.

Grier, W. H., & Cobb, P. M. (1968). *Black rage.* New York: Basic Books.

Griswold, R. L. (1993). *Fatherhood in America: A history.* New York: Basic Books.

Gullattee, A. (1979). Spousal abuse. *Journal of the National Medical Association, 71,* 335-342.

Gutmann, D. (1987). *Reclaimed powers: Towards a new psychology of men and women in later Life.* New York: Basic Books.

Guttentag, M., & Secord, P. (1983). *Too many women: The sex ratio question.* Beverly Hills, CA: Sage.

Hacker, A. (1992). *Two nations: Black and White, separate, hostile, unequal.* New York: Scribner.

Harper, F. D. (Ed.). (1976). *Alcohol abuse and Black America.* Alexandria, VA: Douglass.

Heiss, J. (1972). On the transmission of marital instability in Black families. *American Sociological Review, 37,* 82-92.

Hernandez, D. J. (1988). Demographic trends and the living arrangement of children. In E. M. Hetherington & J. D. Arasteh (Eds.), *Impact of divorce, single-parenting and stepparenting on children* (pp. 3-22). Hillsdale, NJ: Lawrence Erbaum.

Hetherington, E. M. (1989). Coping with family transitions: Winners, losers, and survivors. *Child Development, 60,* 1-14.

Hetherington, E. M., Cox, M., & Cox, R. (1977, October). Divorced fathers. *Psychology Today,* pp. 42-46.

Hetherington, E. M., Stanley-Hogan, M., & Anderson, E. R. (1976). Marital transitions: A child's perspective. *American Psychologist, 44,* 303-312.

Hill, M. S. (1988). Marital stability and spouses' shared time: A multidisciplinary hypothesis. *Journal of Family Issues, 9,* 427-451.

Hill, R. B. (1972). *The strengths of Black families.* New York: Emerson-Hall.

Hill, R. B. (1975). *Black families in the 1974-75 Depression.* Washington, DC: National Urban League.

Hill, R. B. (1989). *Critical issues for Black families by the year 2000: The state of Black America.* New York: National Urban League.

Hill, R. B. (1993). Economic forces, structural discrimination, and Black family instability. In H. E. Cheatham & J. B. Stewart (Eds.), *Black families: Interdisciplinary perspectives* (pp. 87-105). New Brunswick, NJ: Transaction.

Hochschild, A. R. (1989). *The second shift: Working parents and the revolution at home.* New York: Viking/Penguin.

hooks, b. (1990). *Yearning: Race, gender, and cultural politics.* Boston: South End.

Houseknect, S. K. (1987). Voluntary childlessness. In M. B. Sussman & S. K. Steinmetz (Eds.), *Handbook of marriage and the family* (pp. 369-418). New York: Plenum.

Ihinger-Tallman, M., & Pasley, K. (1989). *Remarriage.* Newbury Park, CA: Sage.

Ingoldsby, B. B., & Smith, S. (Eds.). (1995). *Families in multicultural perspectives.* New York: Guilford.

Johnson, B. H. (1986). Single mothers following separation and divorce: Making it on your own. *Family Relations, 35,* 189-197.

Johnson, L. B. (1997). Three decades of Black family empirical research: Challenges for the 21st century. In H. McAdoo (Ed.), *Black families* (3rd ed., pp. 94-113). Thousand Oaks, CA: Sage.

Jones, J. (1985). *Labor of love, labor of sorrow: Black women, work, and the family from slavery to the present.* New York: Basic Books.

Jordon, W. D. (1977). *White over Black: American attitudes toward the Negro, 1550-1812* (2nd ed.). New York: Norton.

Kaffman, M., & Talmon, M. (1984). The crisis of divorce: An opportunity for constructive change. *International Journal of Family Therapy, 6,* 233-246.

Keith, P. M. (1986). Isolation of the unmarried in later life. *Family Relations, 35,* 389-395.

Keith, V. M., & Finlay, B. (1988). The impact of parental divorce on children's educational attainment marital timing and likelihood of divorce. *Journal of Marriage and the Family, 51,* 797-809.

Kemper, K. J., & Rivara, F. P. (1993). Parent in jail. *Pediatrics, 92,* 261-264.

Kisker, E. E., & Goldman, N. (1987). Perils of single life and benefits of marriage. *Social Biology, 343,* 135-152.

Kitson, G. C. (1982). Attachment to the spouse in divorce: A scale and its application. *Journal of Marriage and the Family, 44,* 379-393.

Kitson, G. C., with Holmes, W. (1992). *Potrait of divorce.* New York: Guilford.

Kitson, G. C., Babri, K. B., & Roach, M. J. (1985). Who divorces and why: A review. *Journal of Family Issues, 6,* 255-293.

Kitson, G. C., Holmes, W. M., & Sussman, M. B. (1983). Withdrawing divorce petitions: A predictive test of the exchange model of divorce. *Journal of Divorce, 7,* 51-66.

Kitson, G. C., & Morgan, L. A. (1990). The multiple consequences of divorce: A decade review. *Journal of Marriage and the Family, 52,* 913-924.

Kline, M., Tschann, J. M., Johnston, J. R., & Wallerstein, J. S. (1989). Children's adjustment in joint and sole physical custody families. *Developmental Psychology, 25,* 430-438.

Kruk, E. (1991). Discontinuity between pre- and post-divorce father-child relationships: New evidence regarding parental disengagement. *Journal of Divorce and Remarriage, 16,* 195-227.

Kunjufu, J. (1995). *Countering the conspiracy to destroy Black boys.* Chicago: African American Images.

Kurdek, L. A., & Blisk, D. (1983). Dimensions and correlates of mothers' divorce experiences. *Journal of Divorce, 6,* 1-24.

Ladner, J. (1972). *Tomorrow's tomorrow.* Garden City, NY: Doubleday.

Lamanna, M. A., & Riedmann, A. (1994). *Marriages and families: Making choices and facing change* (5th ed.). Belmont, CA: Wadsworth.

Langelier, R., & Duckert, P. (1980). Divorce counseling guidelines for the late divorced female. *Journal of Divorce, 3,* 403-411.

Larson, J. (1992, July). Understanding stepfamilies. *American Demographics,* pp. 36-40.

Lederer, W. J., & Jackson, D. D. (1968). *The mirages of marriages.* New York: Norton.

Leigh, W. A. (1993). Federal government policies and the housing quotient of Black American families. In H. E. Cheatham & J. B. Stewart (Eds.), *Black families: Interdisciplinary perspectives* (pp. 69-86). New Brunswick, NJ: Transaction.

Levinger, G. (1966). Sources of marital dissatisfaction among applicants for divorce. *American Journal of Orthopsychiatry, 36,* 803-807.

Litcher, D. T., LeClere, F. B., & McLaughlin, D. K. (1991). Local marriage market conditions and the marital behavior of Black and White women. *American Journal of Sociology, 96,* 843-867.

Majors, R., & Billson, J. M. (1992). *Cool pose: The dilemmas of Black manhood in America.* Lexington, MA: Lexington Books.

Marable, M. (1994). The Black male: Searching beyond stereotypes. In R. Staples (Ed.), *The Black family: Essays and studies* (5th ed., pp. 91-96). Belmont, CA: Wadsworth.

Mare, R. D. (1991). Five decades of educational assortive mating. *American Sociological Review, 56,* 15-32.

Marsiglio, W. (1991). Stepfathers with minor children living at home. *Journal of Family Issues, 13,* 195-214.

Marsiglio, W. (1993). Contemporary scholarship on fatherhood: Culture, identity, and conduct. *Journal of Family Issues, 14,* 484-509.

Marsiglio, W. (1995). (Ed.). *Fatherhood: Contemporary theory, research, and social policy.* Thousand Oaks, CA: Sage.

Martin, G. (1990). *Social policy in the welfare state.* Englewood Cliffs, NJ: Prentice Hall.

McAdoo, J. L. (1981). Black father and child interactions. In L. E. Gard (Ed.), *Black men* (pp. 115-130). Beverly Hills, CA: Sage.

McAdoo, J. L. (1997). The roles of African American fathers in the socialization of their children. In H. P. McAdoo (Ed.), *Black families* (3rd ed., pp. 183-197). Thousand Oaks, CA: Sage.

McLanahan, S. S., & Bumpass, L. (1988). Intergenerational consequences of family disruption. *American Journal of Sociology, 94,* 130-152.

Melive, K. (1983). *Marriage and family today* (3rd ed.). New York: Random House.

Mergenhagen, P. M., Lee, B. A., & Gove, W. R. (1985). Till death do us part: Recent changes in the relationship between marital status and mortality. *Sociology and Social Research, 70,* 53-56.

Miller, A. A. (1970). Reactions of friends to divorce. In P. Bohannan (Ed.), *Divorce and after* (pp. 56-77). Garden City, NJ: Doubleday.

Miller, L. F., & Moorman, J. E. (1989). *Studies in marriage and the family* (Current Population Reports, Series P-23, No. 162). Washington, DC: U.S. Bureau of the Census.

Millette, R. E. (1993). West Indian families in the United States. In H. E. Cheatham & J. B. Stewart (Eds.), *Black families: Interdisciplinary perspectives* (pp. 301-317). New Brunswick, NJ: Transaction.

Mott, F. L., & Moore, S. F. (1979). The causes of marital disruption among young American women: An interdisciplinary perspective. *Journal of Marriage and the Family, 41,* 335-356.

National Center for Health Statistics. (1995). *Health, United States, 1994.* Hyattsville, MD: Public Health Service.

National Center for Health Statistics. (1996). *Health, United States, 1995.* Hyattsville, MD: Public Health Service.

Nobles, W. W., & Goddard, W. (1986). Drugs in the African American community: A clear and present danger. In *The state of Black America* (pp. 165-180). New York: National Urban League.

Norton, A. J., & Glick, P. C. (1979). Marital instability in America: Past, present, and future. In G. Levinger & O. C. Moles (Eds.), *Divorce and separation: Context, cause, and consequences.* New York: Basic Books.

Patrician, M. (1984). Child custody terms: Potential contributors to custody dissatisfaction and conflict. *Mediation Quarterly, 1,* 41-57.

Pinkney, A. (1993). *Black Americans* (4th ed.). Englewood Cliffs, NJ: Prentice Hall.

Plass, P. S. (1993). African American family homicide: Patterns in partner, parent, and child victimization, 1985-1987. *Journal of Black Studies, 23,* 515-538.

Ponzetti, J. J., & Cate, R. M. (1986). The developmental course of conflict in the marital dissolution process. *Journal of Divorce, 10,* 1-15.

Pressor, H. B. (1987). Work shifts of full-time dual earner couples: Patterns and constructs by sex of spouse. *Demography, 24,* 99-112.

Rainwater, L., & Yancey, W. (1967). *The Moynihan Report and the politics of controversy.* Cambridge, MA: MIT Press.

Randolph, S. M. (1995). African American children in single-mother families. In B. J. Dickerson (Ed.), *African American single mothers* (pp. 117-145). Thousand Oaks, CA: Sage.

Raschke, H. J. (1977). The role of social participation in postseparation and postdivorce adjustment. *Journal of Divorce, 1,* 129-139.

Raschke, H. J. (1987). Divorce. In M. B. Sussman & S. K. Steinmetz (Eds.), *Handbook of marriage and the family* (pp. 597-624). New York: Plenum.

Raschke, H. J., & Barringer, K. D. (1977). Two studies in postdivorce adjustment among persons participating in Parents Without Partners organization. *Family Perspective, 11,* 23-34.

Reissman, C. K. (1990). *Divorce talk: Women and men make sense of personal relationships.* New Brunswick, NJ: Rutgers University Press.

Reissman, C. K., & Gerstel, N. (1985). Marital dissolution and health: Do males or females have greater risks? *Social Science and Medicine, 20,* 627-635.

Renne, K. S. (1971). Health and marital experience in an urban population. *Journal of Marriage and the Family, 33,* 338-350.

Rodgers-Rose, L. F. (Ed.). (1980). *The Black women.* Beverly Hills, CA: Sage.

Rosenblatt, P. C., Karis, T. A., & Powell, R. D. (1995). *Multiracial couples: Black and White voices.* Thousand Oaks, CA: Sage.

Rosengren, A., Wedel, H., & Wilhelmsen, L. (1989). Marital status and mortality in middle-aged Swedish men. *American Journal of Epidemiology, 129,* 54-64.

Rubin, L. (1976). *Worlds of pain: Life in the working-class family.* New York: Basic Books.

Rubin, R. H. (1978). Matriarchal themes in Black family literature: Implications for family life education. *The Family Coordinator, 11,* 33-41.

Scott, J. (1986). From teenage parenthood to polygamy: Case studies in Black polygamous family formation. *Western Journal of Black Studies, 10,* 172-179.

Seltzer, J. (1991). Legal custody arrangement and children's economic welfare. *Journal of Marriage and the Family, 53,* 79-101.

Seltzer, J., & Bianchi, S. M. (1988). Children's contact with absent parents. *Journal of Marriage and the Family, 50,* 663-677.

Skarsten, S. (1974). Family disruption in Canada. *The Family Coordinator, 23,* 19-25.

Snyder, D. K. (1979). Multidimensional assessment of marital separation. *Journal of Marriage and the Family, 41,* 813-823.

South, S. J., & Lloyd, K. M. (1992). Marriage opportunities and family formation: Further implications of imbalanced ratios. *Journal of Marriage and the Family, 54,* 440-451.

Spanier, G. B. (1989). Bequeathing family continuity. *Journal of Marriage and the Family, 51,* 3-13.

Spanier, G. B., & Casto, R. (1979). Adjustment to separation and divorce: An analysis of 50 case studies. *Journal of Divorce, 2,* 241-253.

Spanier, G. B., & Thompson, L. (1987). *Parting: The aftermath of separation and divorce* (rev. ed.). Newbury Park, CA: Sage.

Stampp, K. (1956). *The peculiar institution.* New York: Knopf.

Staples, R. (1978). Masculinity and race: The dual dilemma of Black men. *Journal of Social Issues, 34,* 183-196.

Staples, R. (1981). *The world of Black singles.* Westport, CT: Greenwood.

Staples, R. (1982). *Black masculinity: The Black male's role in American society.* San Francisco: Black Scholar Press.

Staples, R. (1985). Changes in Black family structure: The conflict between family ideology and structural conditions. *Journal of Marriage and the Family, 53,* 221-230.

Staples, R. (1986). The political economy of Black family life. *The Black Scholar, 17,* 2-11.

Staples, R. (1987). Black male genocide: A final solution to the race problem in America. *The Black Scholar, 18,* 2-11.

Staples, R. (1991). Changes in the Black family structure: The conflict between family ideology and structural conditions. In R. Staples (Ed.), *The Black family: Essays and studies* (4th ed.). Belmont, CA: Wadsworth.

Staples, R. (1994). Changes in Black family structure: The conflict between family ideology and structural conditions. In R. Staples (Ed.), *The Black family: Essays and studies* (pp. 11-19). Belmont, CA: Wadsworth.

Staples, R., & Johnson, L. B. (1993). *Black families at the crossroads: Challenges and prospects.* San Francisco: Jossey-Bass.

Stewart, J. B. (1990). Back to basics: The significance of DuBois' and Frazier's contributions for contemporary research on Black families. In H. E. Cheatham & J. B. Stewart (Eds.), *Black families: Interdisciplinary perspectives* (pp. 5-27). New Brunswick, NJ: Transaction.

Stewart, J. B. (1993). Back to basics: The significance of DuBois' and Frazier's contributions for contemporary research on Black families. In H. E. Cheatham & J. B. Stewart (Eds.), *Black families: Interdisciplinary perspectives* (pp. 5-27). New Brunswick, NJ: Transaction.

Strauss, A. (1987). *Qualitative analysis for social scientists.* Cambridge, UK: Cambridge University Press.

Sudarkasa, N. (1997). African American families and family values. In H. McAdoo (Ed.), *Black families* (3rd ed., pp. 9-40). Thousand Oaks, CA: Sage.

Surra, C. A. (1990). Research and theory on mate selection and premarital relationships in the 1980s. *Journal of Marriage and the Family, 52,* 844-865.

Sutton, P. M., & Sprenkle, D. H. (1985). Criteria for a constructive divorce: Theory and research to guide the practitioner. *Journal of Psychotherapy and the Family, 1,* 38-51.

Szasz, T. S. (1976). *Heresies.* Garden City, NY: Doubleday/Anchor.

Taylor, R. J., Chatters, L. M., Tucker, B. H., & Lewis, E. (1990). Developments in research on Black families: A decade in review. *Journal of Marriage and the Family, 52,* 993-1014.

Tedder, S. L., Scherman, A., & Sheridan, K. M. (1984). Impact of group support on adjustment to divorce by single custodial fathers. *American Mental Health Counselors Association Journal, 6,* 180-189.

Tenhouten, W. (1970). The Black family: Myth and reality. *Psychiatry, 33,* 145-173.

Thoits, P. A. (1986). Social support as coping assistance. *Journal of Counseling and Clinical Psychology, 54,* 416-423.

Thompson, L., & Walker, A. (1989). Gender in families. *Journal of Marriage and the Family, 51,* 845-871.

Thurnher, M., Fenn, C. B., Melichar, J., & Chiriboga, D. A. (1983). Sociodemogaphic perspectives on reasons for divorce. *Journal of Divorce, 6,* 25-35.

Tinney, J. (1981). The religious experience of Black men. In L. Gary (Ed.), *Black men* (pp. 275-276). Beverly Hills, CA: Sage.

Trent, K., & South, S. (1992). Sociodemographic status, parental background, childhood family structure, and attitudes toward family formation. *Journal of Marriage and the Family, 54,* 427-439.

Troll, L. E., Miller, S. J., & Atchley, R. C. (1979). *Families in later life.* Belmont, CA: Wadsworth.

Umberson, D. (1992). Relationships between adult children and their parents: Psychological consequences for both generations. *Journal of Marriage and the Family, 54,* 664-674.

Umberson, D., & Williams, C. (1993). Divorced fathers: Parental role strain and psychological distress. *Journal of Family Issues, 14,* 378-400.

U.S. Bureau of the Census. (1983). *America's Black population, 1970-1982: A statistical view* (Current Population Reports, Series P-20, No. 442). Washington, DC: Government Printing Office.

U.S. Bureau of the Census. (1992). *Money income of households, families, and persons in the United States, 1991* (Current Population Reports, Series P-20, No. 180). Washington, DC: Government Printing Office.

U.S. Bureau of the Census. (1995). *Studies in marriage and the family* (Current Population Reports, Series P-23, No. 162). Washington, DC: Government Printing Office.

U.S. Bureau of the Census. (1996). *Household and family characterstics* (Current Population Reports, Series P-20, No. 417). Washington, DC: Government Printing Office.

U.S. Bureau of the Census. (1997). *Selected characteristics by race* (Current Population Reports). Washington, DC: Government Printing Office.

U.S. Department of Health and Human Services. (1992). *Health status of minorities and low income groups* (3rd ed.). Washington, DC: Government Printing Office.

Vaughan, D. (1986). *Uncoupling: Turning points in intimate relationships*. New York: Oxford University Press.

Veevers, J. E. (1991). Traumas versus Strens: A paradigm of positive versus negative divorce outcomes. *Journal of Divorce, 6*, 99-125.

Vermer, E., Coleman, M., Ganong, L. H., & Cooper, H. (1989). Marital satisfaction in remarriage: A meta-analysis. *Journal of Marriage and the Family, 51*, 713-725.

Wallerstein, J. (1986). Women after divorce: A preliminary report from a ten-year follow-up. *American Journal of Orthopsychiatry, 56*, 65-77.

Wallerstein, J. S., & Kelly, J. B. (1979). Divorce counseling: A community service for families in the midst of divorce. *American Journal of Orthopsychiatry, 47*, 4-22.

Wallerstein, J. S., & Kelly, J. B. (1980). *Surviving the breakup: How children and parents cope with divorce*. New York: Basic Books.

Walster, E., Bersheid, E., & Walster, G. W. (1974). New directions in equity research. *Journal of Personality and Social Psychology, 25*, 151-176.

Weiss, R. S. (1975). *Marital separation*. New York: Basic Books.

Weiss, R. S. (1979). *Going it alone*. New York: Basic Books.

Weitzman, L. (1985). *The divorce revolution*. New York: Free Press.

White, D. G. (1985). *Ain't I a woman: Female slaves in the plantation South*. New York: Norton.

White, L. K., & Booth, A. (1985). The transition to parenthood and marital quality. *Journal of Family Issues, 5*, 435-449.

White, L. K., & Booth, A. (1991). Divorce over the life course: The role of marital happiness. *Journal of Family Issues, 12*, 5-21.

White, L. K., Booth, A., & Edwards, J. N. (1986). Children and marital happiness. *Journal of Family Issues, 7*, 131-146.

White, L. K., & Keith, B. (1990). The effect of shift work on the quality and stability of marital relations. *Journal of Marriage and the Family, 52*, 453-462.

White, S. W., & Bloom, B. L. (1981). Factors related to the adjustment of divorcing men. *Family Relations, 30*, 349-360.

Wilkinson, D. (1980). Minority women: Social-cultural issues. In A. Brodsky & R. Haremustin (Eds.), *Women and psychotherapy* (pp. 285-304). New York: Guilford.

Williams, M. W. (1983). Polygamy and the declining male to female ratio in Black communities: A social inquiry. In H. E. Cheatham & J. B. Stewart (Eds.), *Black families: Interdisciplinary perspectives* (pp. 171-193). New Brunswick, NJ: Transaction.

Wilkinson, D. (1977). The stigmatization process: The politicization of Black males' identity. In D. Wilkinson & R. Taylor (Eds.), *The Black male in America* (pp. 145-158). Chicago: Nelson-Hall.

Wilson, B. F., & Clarke, S. C. (1992). Remarriages: A demographic profile. *Journal of Family Issues, 13,* 123-141.

Wright, D. H., & Price, S. J. (1986). Court-ordered support payments: The effect of the former spouse relationship on compliance. *Journal of Marriage and the Family, 48,* 869-874.

Wright, R. (1940). *Native son.* New York: Harper.

Wymard, E. (1994). *Men on divorce: Conversations with ex-husbands.* Carson, CA: Hay House.

Zeiss, A. M., Zeiss, R. H., & Johnson, S. M. (1980). Sex differences in initiation and adjustment to divorce. *Journal of Divorce, 4,* 21-33.

Additional Reading

Aborampah, O. (1989). Black male-female relationships. *Journal of Black Studies, 19,* 320-342.

Adams, B. N. (1968). *Kinship in an urban setting.* Chicago: Markham.

Adams, B. N. (1985). The family: Problems and solutions: *Journal of Marriage and the Family, 47,* 525-529.

Albrecht, S. L., Bahr, H., & Goodman, K. (1983). *Divorce and remarriage: Problems, adaptations, and adjustments.* Westport, CT: Greenwood.

Amato, P. R. (1988). Parental divorce and attitudes toward marriage and family life. *Journal of Marriage and the Family, 50,* 453-461.

Amato, P. R., & Keith, B. (1991). Parental divorce and adult well-being: A meta-analysis. *Journal of Marriage and the Family, 53,* 43-58.

Austin, R. L. (1993). Family environment, educational aspiration, and performance in St. Vincent. In H. E. Cheatham & J. B. Stewart (Eds.), *Black families: Interdisciplinary perspectives* (3rd ed., pp. 265-286). New Brunswick, NJ: Transaction.

Bahr, H. M., & Chadwick, B. A. (1985). Religion and family in Middletown, U.S.A. *Journal of Marriage and the Family, 47,* 407-414.

Baker. M. (1984). His and her divorce research: New theoretical directions in Canadian and American research. *Journal of Comparative Family Studies, 15,* 17-28.

Ball, R. E., & Robbins, L. (1986). Marital status and life satisfaction among Black Americans. *Journal of Marriage and the Family, 48,* 389-391.

Beckett, J. O., & Smith, A. D. (1981). Work and family roles: Egalitarian marriage in Black and White families. *Social Service Review, 55,* 314-324.

Berardo, F. M. (1985). Age heterogamy in marriage. *Journal of Marriage and the Family, 47,* 553-566.

Berkman, L. P., & Syme, S. L. (1979). Social networks, host resistance, and mortality: A nine year follow-up study of Alameda County residents. *American Journal of Epidemiology, 109,* 186-204.

Binion, V. J. (1990). Psychological androgyny: A Black female perspective. *Sex Roles, 22,* 487-507.

Blackwell, J. E. (1975). *The Black community: Diversity and unity*. New York: Dodd, Mead.

Bloom, B. L., Hodges, F. W., & Caldwell, R. A. (1982). A preventive program for the newly separated: Initial evaluation. *American Journal of Community Psychology, 10*, 251-264.

Bowlby, J. (1977). The making and breaking of affectional bonds: Aetiology and psychopathology in the light of attachment theory. *British Journal of Psychiatry, 130*, 201-210.

Boyd, S. (1993). investigating gender bias in Canadian child custody law: Reflections on questions and methods. In J. Brockman & D. Chunn (Eds.), *Investigating gender bias: Laws, courts, and the legal profession* (pp. 169-190). Toronto: Thompson.

Boyd-Franklin, A. (1989). *Black families in therapy: A multi-system approach*. New York: Guilford.

Boye-Beaman, J., Leonard, K., & Senchak, M. (1993). Male premarital aggression and gender identity among Black and White newlywed couples. *Journal of Marriage and the Family, 55*, 303-313.

Broman, C. L. (1988). Household work and family life satisfaction of Blacks. *Journal of Marriage and the Family, 50*, 743-748.

Brooks, A. (1984, July 29). Stepparents and divorce: Keeping ties to children. *The New York Times*.

Brophy, J. (1985). Child care and the growth of power. In J. Brophy & C. Smart (Eds.), *Women in law: Explorations in law, family, and sexuality*. London: Routledge and Kegan Paul.

Brown, D., & Gary, L. E. (1988). Unemployment and psychological distress among Black American women. *Sociological Focus, 21*, 209-220.

Brown, D., & Walters, R. (1979). *Exploring the role of the Black church in the community*. Washington, DC: Howard University, Institute for Urban Affairs and Research.

Caldwell, R. A., & Bloom, B. L. (1982). Social support: Its structure and impact on marital disruption. *American Journal of Community Psychology, 10*, 647-667.

Cancian, F. (1987). *Love in America: Gender and self-development*. New York: Cambridge University Press.

Cassel, J. (1976). The contribution of the social environment to host resistance. *American Journal of Epidemiology, 104*, 107-123.

Chadiha. L. A. (1992). Black husbands' economic problems and resiliency during the transition to marriage. *Families in Society, 73*, 542-552.

Chapman, A. B. (1986). *Mansharing: Dilemma or choice?* New York: William Morrow.

Chatters, L. M., & Jackson, J. S. (1989). Quality of life and subjective well-being among Black adults. In R. L. Jones (Ed.), *Adult development and aging* (pp. 191-214). Berkeley, CA: Cobb & Henry.

Cheatham, H. E., & Stewart, J. B. (Eds.). (1993). *Black families: Interdisciplinary perspectives* (3rd ed.). New Brunswick, NJ: Transaction.

Clayton, R. R. (1979). *The family, marriage, and social change* (2nd ed.). Lexington, MA: D. C. Heath.

Cohen, T. F. (1987). Remaking men: Men's experiences becoming and being husbands and fathers and their implications for re-conceptualizing men's lives. *Journal of Family Issues, 8*, 57-77.

Coleman, M., & Ganong, L. H. (1990). Remarriage and stepfamily research in the 1980s: Increased interest in an old family form. *Journal of Marriage and the Family, 52,* 925- 940.

Coleman, M., Ganong, L. H., & Goodwin, C. (1994). The presentation of stepfamilies in marriage and family textbooks: A reexamination. *Family Relations, 43,* 289-297.

Cooney, T. M. (1988). Young adults and parental divorce: Exploring important issues. *Human Relations, 41,* 805-822.

Cooney, T. M., Smyer, M. A., Hagestad, G., & Klock, R. (1986). Parental divorce in young adulthood: Some preliminary findings. *American Journal of Orthopsychiatry, 56,* 470- 477.

Cooney, T., & Uhlenberg, P. (1990). The role of divorce in men's relations with their adult children after mid-life. *Journal of Marriage and the Family, 52,* 677-688.

Cose, E. (1993). *The rage of a privileged class.* New York: HarperCollins.

Creighton-Zollar, A., & Williams, J. S. (1992). The relative educational attainment and occupational prestige of Black spouses and life satisfaction. *Western Journal of Black Studies, 16,* 57-63.

Davis, L., & Strube, M. J. (1993). An assessment of romantic commitment among Black and White dating couples. *Journal of Applied Social Psychology, 23,* 212-225.

Dean, A., & Lin, N. (1977). The stress-buffering role of social supports: Problems and prospects for systematic investigation. *Journal of Nervous and Mental Disease, 35,* 403-417.

Dodson, J. E. (1997). Conceptualizations of African American families. In H. McAdoo (Ed.), *Black families* (3rd ed., pp. 67-82). Thousand Oaks, CA: Sage.

Donnelly, D., & Finkelhor, D. (1992). Does equality in custody arrangement improve the parent-child relationship? *Journal of Marriage and the Family, 54,* 837-845.

Dudley, J. R. (1991). Increasing our understanding of divorced fathers who have infrequent contact with their children. *Family Relations, 40,* 274-285.

Dunkel-Schetter, C., Folkman, S., & Lazarus, R. S. (1987). Correlates of social support receipt. *Journal of Personality and Social Psychology, 53,* 71-80.

Easterlin, R. (1987). *Birth and fortune: The impact of numbers on personal welfare* (2nd ed.). Chicago: University of Chicago Press.

Eggebeen, D. J., & Hawkins, A. J. (1990). Economic need and wives' employment. *Journal of Family Issues, 11,* 48-66.

Eggebeen, D. J., & Lichter, D. T. (1991). Race, family structure, and changing poverty among American children. *American Sociological Review, 56,* 801-817.

Emery, R. E. (1988). *Marriage, divorce, and children's adjustment.* Newbury Park, CA: Sage.

Eshleman, J. (1993, February). *Ethnic diversity in the creation of single parent families in the United States.* Paper presented at the Fourth Australian Family Research Conference, Sydney, Australia.

Farkas, G. (1976). Education, wage rates, and the division of labor between husband and wife. *Journal of Marriage and the Family, 38,* 473-484.

Fine, M. A., McKenry, P. C., & Chung, H. (1992). Post-divorce adjustment of Black and White single parents. *Journal of Divorce and Remarriage, 17,* 121-134.

Fossett, M., & Kiecolt, J. (1993). Mate availability and family structure among African Americans in U.S. metropolitan areas. *Journal of Marriage and the Family, 55,* 288-302.

Franklin, C. W. (1980). White racism as the cause of Black male-female conflict: A critique. *Western Journal of Black Studies, 4,* 42-49.

Franklin, C. W. (1984). *The changing definition of masculinity.* New York: Plenum.

Franklin, C. W. (1986). Conceptual and logical issues in theory and research related to Black masculinity. *Western Journal of Black Studies, 4,* 161-166.

Freed, D. J., & Walker, T. B. (1988). Family law in fifty states: An overview. *Family Law Quarterly, 21,* 417-573.

Furstenberg, F. F., Jr. (1992). Good dads/bad dads: Two faces of fatherhood. In A. S. Skolnick & J. H. Skolnick (Eds.), *Families in transition* (7th ed., pp. 342-652). New York: Harper.

Ganong, L., & Coleman, M. (1986). A comparison of clinical and empirical literature on children in step-families. *Journal of Marriage and the Family, 48,* 309-318.

Garfinkel, I., & Oellerich, D. (1989). Non-custodial fathers' ability to pay child support. *Demography, 26,* 219-233.

Gary, L. E. (Ed.). (1981). *Black men.* Beverly Hills, CA: Sage.

Gaston, J. C. (1986). The destruction of the young Black male: The impact of popular culture and organized sports. *Journal of Black Studies, 16,* 369-384.

Gelles, R. J., & Conte, J. R. (1990). Domestic violence and sexual abuse of children: A review of research in the eighties. *Journal of Marriage and the Family, 52,* 1045-1058.

Gelles, R. J., & Straus, M. A. (1988). *Intimate violence: The definitive study of the causes and consequences of abuse in the American family.* New York: Simon & Schuster.

Gerstel, N. (1989). Divorce and stigma. *Social Problems, 34,* 172-186.

Giles-Sims, J. (1984). The stepparent role: Expectations, behavior, sanctions. *Journal of Family Issues, 5,* 116-130.

Gove, W. R., Briggs, C. S., & Hughes, M. (1990). The effect of marriage on the well-being of adults. *Journal of Family Issues, 11,* 4-35.

Greene, R. W., & Feld, S. (1989). Social support coverage and well-being of elderly widows and unmarried woman. *Journal of Family Issues, 10,* 33-51.

Greenstein, N. T. (1990). Love and marriage in modern America: A functional analysis. *Sociological Quarterly, 6,* 361-377.

Grief, G. (1985). *Single fathers.* Lexington, MA: Lexington Books.

Gutman, H. G. (1976). *The Black family in slavery and freedom, 1750-1925.* New York: Pantheon.

Haas, L. (1993). Nurturing fathers and working mothers: Changing gender roles in Sweden. In J. C. Jood (Ed.), *Men, work, and family* (pp. 238-261). Newbury Park, CA: Sage.

Hampton, R. L. (1979). Husbands' characteristics and marital disruptions in Black families. *Sociological Quarterly, 20,* 255-266.

Hampton, R. L. (1980). Institutional decimation, marital exchange, and disruption in Black families. *Western Journal of Black Studies, 4,* 132-139.

Hampton, R. L., Gelles, R., & Harrop, J. W. (1989). Is violence in Black families increasing? A comparison of 1975 and 1985 national survey rates. *Journal of Marriage and the Family, 51,* 969-980.

Hare, N. (1984). *The endangered Black family: Coping with unisexualization and coming extinction of the Black race.* San Francisco: Black Think Tank.

Hare, N. (1991). Substance abuse in the Black American family. *Urban Research Review, 13,* 1-20.

Harrison, J. L. (1978). Warning: The male sex role may be dangerous to your health. *Journal of Social Issues, 34,* 65-86.

Hawkins, D. (Ed.). (1986). *Violence among Black Americans.* New York: University Press of America.

Hess, R. D., & Camara, K. A. (1979). Post-divorce relationships as mediating factors in the consequences of divorce for children. *Journal of Social Issues, 36,* 79-96.

Hess, R. D., & Camara, K. A. (1985). Long-term effects of divorce and remarriage on the adjustment of children. *Journal of American Academy of Child Psychiatry, 24,* 518-530.

Horton, H. D., & Burgess, N. J. (1992). Where are the Black men? Regional differences in the pool of marriageable Black males in the United States. *National Journal of Sociology, 6,* 3-19.

Horton, H. D., Thomas, M. E., & Herring, C. (1995) Rural-urban differences in Black family structure. *Journal of Family Issues, 16,* 298-313.

Hughes, D., Galinsky, E., & Morris, A. (1992). The effects of job characteristics on marital quality: Specifying linking mechanism. *Journal of Marriage and the Family, 54,* 31-54.

Hunt, J. G., & Hunt, L. L. (1977). Dilemmas and contradictions of status: The case of the dual-career family. *Social Problems, 24,* 407-416.

Hunter, A. G., & Davis, J. E. (1992). Constructing gender: An exploration of Afro-American men's conceptualization of manhood. *Gender & Society, 6,* 464-479.

Jewell, K. S. (1988). *Survival of the Black family: The institutional impact of U.S. social policy.* New York: Praeger.

Johnson, C. L. (1988). Socially controlled civility: The functioning of rituals in the divorce process. *American Behavioral Scientist, 31,* 685-701.

Jones, A. P., & Demaree, R. G. (1975). Family disruption, social indices, and problem behavior: A preliminary study. *Journal of Marriage and the Family, 37,* 497-502.

Keith, V. M., & Herring, C. (1991). Skin tone and stratification in the Black community. *American Journal of Sociology, 97,* 760-778.

Kessler, R. C., & Essex, M. (1982). Marital status and depression: The importance of coping resources. *Social Forces, 61,* 484-501.

Kitson, G. C., & Langlie, J. K. (1984). Couples who file for divorce but change their minds. *American Journal of Orthopsychiatry, 54,* 469-489.

Kitson, G., & Raschke, H. (1981). Divorce research: What we know; What we need to know. *Journal of Divorce, 4,* 1-38.

Kunjufu, J. (1981). Moms, dads, and boys: Race and sex differences in the socialization of male children. In W. R. Allen (Ed.), *Black men* (pp. 99-114). Beverly Hills, CA: Sage.

Kunjufu, J. (1984). *Developing positive self-images and discipline in Black children.* Chicago: African-American Images.

Landry, B. (1987). *The new Black middle class.* Berkeley: University of California Press.

Lee, G. R., Seccombe, K., & Shehan, C. L. (1991). Marital status and personal happiness: An analysis of trend data. *Journal of Marriage and the Family, 53,* 839-844.

Lerman, R. (1986). Who are the absent fathers? *Youth & Society, 18,* 3-27.

Lewis, D. (1975). The Black family: Socialization and sex roles. *Phylon, 36,* 221-237.

Littlejohn-Blake, S. M., & Darling, C. A. (1993). Understanding the strengths of African American families, *Journal of Black Studies, 23,* 436-471.

Lowenstein, A. (1986). Temporary single parenthood: The case of prisoners' families. *Family Relations, 35,* 79-85.

Martin, E., & Martin, J. (1978). *The Black extended family*. Chicago: University of Chicago Press.

Martin, P., & Luke, L. (1991). Divorce and the wheel theory of love. *Journal of Divorce and Remarriage, 15*, 3-22.

Marx, K. (1936). *Capital*. New York: Modern Library.

McAdoo, J. L. (1986). Black fathers' relationships with their children and the children's development of ethnic identity. In R. A. Lewis & R. E. Salt (Eds.), *Men in families* (pp. 169-180). Beverly Hills, CA: Sage.

McAdoo, J. L. (1993, January). The roles of African-American fathers: An ecological perspective. *Family in Society: The Journal of Contemporary Human Services*, pp. 28-35.

McCubbin, H., & Dahal, B. B. (1985). *Marriage and family: Individuals and life cycles*. New York: John Wiley.

Moore, V. L., & Schwebel, A. L. (1993). Factors contributing to divorce: A study of race differences. *Journal of Divorce and Remarriage, 20*, 123-135.

Mosley, J., & Thomson, E. (1995). Fathering behavior and child outcomes. In W. Marsiglio (Ed.), *Fatherhood: Contemporary theory, research, and social policy* (pp. 148-165). Thousand Oaks, CA: Sage.

Moynihan, D. P. (1965). *The Negro family: The case for national action*. Washington, DC: U.S. Department of Labor, Office and Policy Planning and Research.

Norton, A. J. (1983). Family life cycle: 1980. *Journal of Marriage and the Family, 45*, 267-275.

Okpala, A. (1993). Child care and female employment in urban Nigeria. In H. E. Cheatham & J. B. Stewart (Eds.), *Black families: Interdisciplinary perspectives* (pp. 287-317). New Brunswick, NJ: Transaction.

Oliver, W. (1984). Black males and the tough guy image: A dysfunctional compensatory adaptation. *Western Journal of Black Studies, 20*, 15-39.

Oliver, W. (1986). Sexual conquest and patterns of Black-on-Black violence: A structural-cultural perspective. *Violence and Victims, 4*, 457-473.

Pleck, J. (1981). *The myth of masculinity*. Cambridge, MA: MIT Press.

Popenoe, D. (1988). *Disturbing the nest: Family change and decline in modern societies*. New York: Aldine de Gruyter.

Poussaint, A. (1982, August). What every Black woman should know about Black men. *Ebony*, pp. 36-40.

Price, S. J., & McKenry, P. C. (1988). *Divorce*. Newbury Park, CA: Sage.

Price-Bonham, S., & Skeen, P. (1979). A comparison of Black and White fathers with implications for parents' education. *The Family Coordinator, 28*, 53-59.

Rutledge, E. M. (1990). Black parent-child relations: Some correlations. *Journal of Comparative Family Studies, 21*, 369-378.

Sampson, R. J. (1987). Black urban violence: The effect of male joblessness and family disruption. *American Journal of Sociology, 93*, 248-382.

Sampson, R. J., & Laub, J. H. (1994). Urban poverty and the family context of delinquency: A new look at structure and process in a single study. *Child Development, 65*, 523-540.

Seccombe, K. (1991). Assessing the costs and benefits of children: Gender comparisons among child-free husbands and wives. *Journal of Marriage and the Family, 53*, 191-202.

Secord, P. (1983). *Too many women*. Beverly Hills, CA: Sage.

Secord, P. F., & Ghee, K. (1986). Implications of the Black marriage market for marital conflict. *Journal of Family Issues, 7,* 21-30.

Slaughter, D. T., & Dilworth-Anderson, P. (1988). Care of Black children with sickle cell disease: Fathers' maternal support and esteem. *Family Relations, 37,* 1-7.

South, S. J. (1986). Sex ratios, economic power and women's roles: A theoretical extension and empirical test. *Journal of Marriage and the Family, 50,* 19-31.

South, S. J. (1993). Racial and ethnic differences in the desire to marry. *Journal of Marriage and the Family, 55,* 357-370.

Spurrow, K. H. (1991). Factors in mate selection for single Black professional women. *Free Inquiry in Creative Sociology, 19,* 103-109.

Stack, C. B. (1974). *All our kin.* New York: Harper & Row.

Staples, R. (1970). Educating the Black male at various class levels for marital roles. *The Family Coordinator, 19,* 164-167.

Staples, R. (1974). The Black family revisited: A review and a preview. *Journal of Social and Behavioral Sciences, 20,* 65-78.

Staples, R. (1978). Race, liberalism, conservatism, and premarital sexual permissiveness: A bi-racial comparison. *Journal of Marriage and the Family, 40,* 733-742.

Staples, R., & Mirande, A. (1980). Racial and cultural variations among American families: A decennial review of the literature on minority families. *Journal of Marriage and the Family, 42,* 887-903.

Stets, J. E. (1990). Verbal and physical aggression in marriage. *Journal of Marriage and the Family, 52,* 501-514.

Stets, J. E. (1991). Cohabiting and marital aggression: The role of social isolation. *Journal of Marriage and the Family, 53,* 669-680.

Stewart, J., & Scott, J. (1978). The institutional decimation of Black American males. *Western Journal of Black Studies, 2,* 82-93.

Stier, H., & Tienda, M. (1993). Are men marginal to the family? Insights from Chicago's inner city. In J. Hood (Ed.), *Men, work, and family* (pp. 23-44). Newbury Park, CA: Sage.

Swinton, D. (1987). Economic status of Blacks in 1986. In J. Dewart (Ed.), *The state of Black America* (pp. 221-232). New York: National Urban League.

Swinton, D. (1991). The economic status of African Americans: Permanent poverty and inequality. In J. Dewart (Ed.), *The state of Black America.* New York: National Urban League.

Taylor, R. J. (1986). Receipt of support from family among Black Americans: Demographic and familial differences. *Journal of Marriage and the Family, 48,* 67-77.

Taylor, R. J., & Chatters, L. M. (1986). Receipt of support from family among Black Americans: Demographic and familial differences. *Journal of Marriage and the Family, 48,* 67-77.

Taylor, R. J., Leashore, B., & Toliver, S. (1988). An assessment of the provider role as perceived by Black males. *Family Relations, 37,* 426-231.

Teachman, J. D. (1991). Who pays? Receipt of child support in the United States. *Journal of Marriage and the Family, 53,* 759-772.

Thomas, S. P. (1982). After divorce: Personality factors related to the process of adjustment. *Journal of Divorce, 5,* 19-36.

Thomas, V. G. (1990). Determinants of global life happiness and marital happiness in dual-career Black couples. *Family Relations, 39,* 174-178.

Tucker, M. B. (1982). Social support and coping applications for the study of female drug abuse. *Journal of Social Issues, 38,* 117-137.

Tucker, M. B., & Taylor, R. J. (1989). Demographic correlates of relationship status among Black Americans. *Journal of Marriage and the Family, 51,* 655-665.

U.S. Bureau of the Census. 1990. *Money income and poverty status in the United States: 1989* (Current Population Reports, Series P-60, No. 168). Washington, DC: Government Printing Office.

U.S. Bureau of the Census. 1995. *Population profile of the United States: 1991* (Current Population Reports, Special Studies, Series P-23, No. 173). Washington, DC: Government Printing Office.

U.S. Bureau of Labor Statistics. 1992. *Employment and earnings characteristics of families: First quarter 1992.* Washington, DC: U.S. Department of Labor.

Uzzell, O., & Wilkins-Peebles, W. (1989). A focus on relational factors and intervention strategies. *Western Journal of Black Studies, 13,* 10-16.

Van den Berghe, P. L. (1967). *Race and racism: A comparative perspective.* New York: John Wiley.

Waite, L. J., & Lillard, L. A. (1991). Children and marital disruption. *American Journal of Sociology, 96,* 930-953.

Wallerstein, J., & Blakeslee, S. (1989). *Second chances: Men, women, and children—A decade after divorce.* New York: Ticknor & Fields.

West, C. (1993). *Race matters.* Boston: Beacon.

White, K. L. (1990). Determinants of divorce: A review of research in the eighties. *Journal of Marriage and the Family, 52,* 904-912.

White, S. W., & Mika, K. (1983). Family divorce and separation: Theory and research. *Marriage and Family Review, 6,* 175-192.

Wilkinson, D. (1969). Status differences and the Black hate stare: A conversation of gestures. *Phylon, 30,* 191-196.

Wilkinson, D. (1971). Coming of age in a racist society: The Whitening of America. *Youth & Society, 3,* 100-118.

Willie, C. (1970). *The family life of Black people.* Columbus, OH: Merrill.

Wilson, M. N. (1989). Child development in the context of the Black extended family. *American Psychologist, 44,* 380-385.

Wilson, M. N., Tolson, T. F., Hinton, I. D., & Kiernan, M. (1990). Flexibility and sharing of childcare duties in Black families. *Sex Roles, 22,* 409-425.

Zill, N. (1988). Behavior, achievement, and health problems among children in step-families: Findings from a national survey of child health. In E. M. Hetherington & J. D., Arasteh (Eds.), *Impact of divorce, single parenting, and stepparenting on children* (pp. 325-268). Hillsdale, NJ: Lawrence Erlbaum.

Index

maternal potential and, 27-28
pregnancy, premarital and, 30-31
rescuer/rescued, 26-27
time, pressure of, 29-30
Religious practice, 87-88, 91-92, 133-135
Rescuing behaviors, 26-27
Research methods, 10-12
data analysis, 14
interviewing, 12, 14
participant observation, 14
questions, 15
respondent statistics, 229-233
sample characteristics, 12, 13 (table)

Separation, 49-50, 57, 58
Sex ratio, 37, 41-42, 80
Slavery, 9
Social discrediting. *See* Marginalization
Social Learning Theory, 175
Social support, 128-129, 131-133, 153,
201-202, 211-212
community programs, 216-217
drug rehabilitation/work programs,
216
mediation programs, 214
mutual support groups, 215
parenting education, 214-215
parents/educators, 217
prison/military families, 216
training of counselors, 215-216
workplace programs, 216
Social systems, 7, 10, 20, 57
Socioeconomic status, 35-36, 39-40,
55, 90

Stepfathers. *See* Fatherhood
Stereotypes, masculine, 3, 15, 26, 79,
181-182
Stressors:
child support, 94, 100-102, 110
economic, 93-94, 96-100, 110
psychosocial, 94-95, 102-106
See also Postdivorce
Substance abuse, 38-39, 45-46, 166-168,
182, 200-201
Support services. *See* Social support
Survival skills. *See* Coping strategies

Trust, 23-24, 79

Unemployment:
divorce and, 62-65
education and, 66
spousal, 68-71
See also Socioeconomic status

Value incompatibility, 87-90
Values/context, cultural, 36-37, 41, 44, 177
Violence:
abuse in fatherhood, 164-166
battered husbands, 85-86
black marital conflict, 86-87, 111
negotiation failure, 81-85
Visitation. *See* Custody

White norms, 6

About the Authors

Erma Jean Lawson is Assistant Professor in the Department of Sociology at the University of North Texas. She received her doctorate from the University of Kentucky in 1990. She has investigated the relationship between marital disruption and health outcomes in Zimbabwe, Africa. She has served as a consultant for breast cancer prevention programs in Kentucky and has served in the International Black Women's Congress. Her research areas include family and medical sociology.

Aaron Thompson is Associate Professor of Sociology and Coordinator for Academic Success at Eastern Kentucky University. He has published in the areas of educational attainment, African American fatherhood, divorce in the Black family, and Black and White differences in marital expectations. Much of his research and publications surrounds the life aspects of race, gender, and African American families.